CONSUMPTION AND EVERYDAY LIFE

MARK PATERSON

Routledge
Taylor & Francis Group

LONDON AND NEW YORK

First published 2006
by Routledge
2 Park Square, Milton Park, Abingdon, Oxon, OX14 4RN

Simultaneously published in the USA and Canada
by Routledge
270 Madison Avenue, New York, NY 10016

Reprinted 2007 (twice)

Routledge is an imprint of the Taylor & Francis Group, an informa business

Typeset in Garamond and Scala Sans by Taylor & Francis Books
Printed and bound in Great Britain by MPG Books Ltd, Bodmin

British Library Cataloguing in Publication Data
A catalogue record for this book is available from the British Library

Library of Congress Cataloging in Publication Data
Paterson, Mark.
  Consumption and everyday life / Mark Paterson.-- 1st ed.
     p. cm. -- (The new sociology series)
  Includes bibliographical references and index.
  ISBN 0-415-35507-9 (pbk.) -- ISBN 0-415-35506-0 (hard cover) 1.
Consumer behavior--Social aspects. 2. Consumption (Economics)--
Social aspects. I. Title. II. Series.
  HF5415.32.P375 2006
  306.3--dc22

                    2005022317

ISBN10: 0–415–35506–0   ISBN13: 978–0–415–35506–3 (hbk)
ISBN10: 0–415–35507–9   ISBN13: 978–0–415–35507–0 (pbk)

T&F informa
Taylor & Francis Group is the Academic Division of T&F Informa plc.

CONSUMPTION AND EVERYDAY LIFE

This book introduces key ideas and theorists of consumption in an accessible way. Drawing on theories of everyday life, this is an engaging and comprehensible introduction of key themes in consumption and consumer culture.

- the semiotics of branding and advertising
- the representation of 'nature' and the environment
- the relations between consumer and producer
- ethical consumption
- the tensions between local spaces of consumption and globalised markets
- the history of consumption
- shopping and identity

This book is essential reading for undergraduates on cultural studies, sociology and cultural geography courses.

Mark Paterson is a lecturer in philosophy and cultural studies at the University of the West of England, Bristol, and is interested in the senses, phenomenology and technology. He has also written about haptics, the technology of touch, which allows us to reach out and touch virtual objects. Along with contributions to edited collections such as *Emotional Geographies* (Ashgate, 2005), *The Smell Culture Reader* (Berg, 2006), and *The Book of Touch* (Berg, 2005), he is currently writing a book for Berg entitled *The Senses of Touch*.

THE NEW SOCIOLOGY

Series Editor: ANTHONY ELLIOTT, University of Kent, UK

The New Sociology is a book series designed to introduce students to new issues and themes in social sciences today. What makes the series distinctive, as compared to other competing introductory textbooks, is a strong emphasis not just on key concepts and ideas but on how these play out in everyday life – on how theories and concepts are lived at the level of selfhood and cultural identities, how they are embedded in interpersonal relationships, and how they are shaped by, and shape, broader social processes.

Forthcoming in the series:

Religion and Everyday Life
STEPHEN HUNT (2005)

Culture and Everyday Life
DAVID INGLIS (2005)

Community and Everyday Life
GRAHAM DAY (2005)

Self-Identity and Everyday Life
HARVIE FERGUSON (2005)

Consumption and Everyday Life
MARK PATERSON (2005)

Globalization and Everyday Life
LARRY RAY (2006)

The Body and Everyday Life
HELEN THOMAS (2006)

Nationalism and Everyday Life
JANE HINDLEY (2006)

Ethnicity and Everyday Life
CHRISTIAN KARNER (2006)

Risk, Vulnerability and Everyday Life
IAIN WILKINSON (2006)

For my parents, David and Jennifer

CONTENTS

SERIES EDITOR'S FOREWORD

"The New Sociology" is a Series that takes its cue from massive social transformations currently sweeping the globe. Globalization, new information technologies, the techno-industrialization of warfare and terrorism, the privatization of public resources, the dominance of consumerist values: these developments involve major change to the ways people live their personal and social lives today. Moreover, such developments impact considerably on the tasks of sociology, and the social sciences more generally. Yet, for the most part, the ways in which global institutional transformations are influencing the subject-matter and focus of sociology have been discussed only in the more advanced, specialized literature of the discipline. I was prompted to develop this Series, therefore, in order to introduce students – as well as general readers who are seeking to come to terms with the practical circumstances of their daily lives – to the various ways in which sociology reflects the transformed conditions and axes of our globalizing world.

Perhaps the central claim of the Series is that sociology is fundamentally linked to the practical and moral concerns of everyday life. The authors in this Series – examining topics all the way from the body to globalization, from self-identity to consumption – seek to demonstrate the complex, contradictory ways in which sociology is a necessary and very practical aspect of our personal and public lives. From one angle, this may seem uncontroversial. After all, many classical sociological analysts as well as those associated with the classics of social theory emphasized the practical basis of human knowledge, notably Emile Durkheim, Karl Marx, Max Weber, Sigmund Freud, and George Simmel, among many others. And yet there are major respects in which the professionalization of academic sociology during the latter period of the twentieth century led to a retreat from the everyday issues and moral basis of sociology itself. (For an excellent discussion of the changing relations between practical and professional sociologies see Charles Lemert, *Sociology After the Crisis*, Second Edition, Boulder: Paradigm, 2004.) As worrying as such a retreat from the practical and moral grounds of the discipline is, one of the main consequences of recent global transformations in the field of sociology has been a renewed emphasis on the mediation of everyday events and experiences by distant social forces, the intermeshing of the local and global in the production of social practices, and on ethics and moral responsibility at both the individual and collective levels. "The New Sociology" Series traces out these concerns across the terrain of various themes and thematics, situating everyday social practices in the broader context of life in a globalizing world.

In *Consumption and Everyday Life*, Mark Paterson documents with verve and precision the location of consumption in our late modern or postmodern worlds. He does this, firstly, by reviewing developments in sociological theories of consumption – in Marxism, post-structuralism, postmodernism and, broadly speaking, what is termed cultural theory. From Marx to Marcuse, and from Benjamin to Barthes, he traces the possibilities and pleasures of shopping, the rhetoric and routine associated with consumerism. And in this respect his analysis is refreshingly reflexive and open-ended: there is no doctrinal insistence on one particular method of study, or rating of one theory against another. Rather, Paterson is out to make theory 'work' in the interests of elucidating consumption. Consumption, as he shrewdly perceives it, is intricately entwined with culture, capitalism, codes and colonialism – and so social theories need to be deployed to comprehend, combat, modify or transform the consequences of practices of consumption.

Which brings me to the second optic through which Paterson analyses consumption: namely, the everyday. That consumerism has in some ways become deeply interwoven with the processes, pleasures and perils of global capitalism is obvious enough from the attention it receives today in popular culture and the mass media. Throughout the polished, expensive cities of the West, consumption has become a central preoccupation of contemporary women and men attempting to navigate the dizzying array of choice on offer in the marketplace of advanced capitalism. Our contemporary mantra: I shop, therefore I am! Yet this is not just a matter that can be reduced to either the positive or negative – for Paterson insists there are both gains and losses here. But by a certain way of reading the consequences of consumption in our everyday lives (partly through drawing upon the brilliant conceptual departures of Michel de Certeau), Paterson renews emphasis on the signifying system of shopping and shopping malls, commodities and the spaces of consumption. The result is an introduction to the sociology of consumption which is rich and insightful, combining acute political engagement with generously interdisciplinary perspectives.

ACKNOWLEDGEMENTS

I am hugely grateful to a number of people who sustained me throughout this enterprise. My thanks go to my colleagues here at the University of the West of England and elsewhere, who were generous with their time and read drafts of chapters. My colleagues Rehan Hyder, Kieran Kelly, and Richard Hornsey offered many useful comments concerning youth culture, globalisation, and the spaces of consumption, respectively, and Matt Whatford told me all about trainers. At Cardiff University, Emma Roe and Adrian Evans helped me rethink food, the body and the history of consumption. I would also like to thank the Love birds, Cecilia and Lauren, for their forbearance, humour and support.

INTRODUCTION

CONSUMPTION AS EVERYDAY ACT

> Everyday life is what we are given every day (or what is willed
> to us), what presses us, even oppresses us, because there
> does exist an oppression of the present ... Everyday life is
> what holds us intimately, from the inside.
>
> (de Certeau *et al.* 1998)

We are all consumers. Yet when social theorists look at consumption as
an object of study, there tend to be two responses. Until the 1950s, on
the whole consumption made sense only in relation to production, so
studying consumption assumed that consumers were also producers or,
at least, involved in the production of material goods. Marxists strongly
criticised consumer capitalism for fostering desires rather than needs,
and saw the way that consumers were driven increasingly towards false
needs, including more, better, cheaper material goods, devices and experiences. This, they thought, was much to the detriment of true feelings
of community and social relations, and meant that as consumers we
were continually being manipulated and misled by advertisers, marketing, and the authorities that allow such things to take place. The thesis
of liberal economist J.K. Galbraith's The Affluent Society, written in
1958, solidified the equation, arguing that the promotion of false needs
such as prestige goods is necessary to stimulate production, revitalise
the economy, but also to equate affluence or wealth in terms of material
goods. "The more wants that are satisfied, the more new ones are born"

(2000: 218), in other words. However, while critiques of consumer capitalism from a political-economic perspective retain their power, there is a strong turn within cultural studies and the social sciences towards examining consumption as something people simply do, without necessarily judging it inherently bad. Especially with newly experienced post-war affluence, young people in particular had more money to spend, and more things to buy with it. Marketing advanced in order to accelerate this process, and interesting and notable cultural phenomena started to become visible, such things as changes in gender relations, in perceived status, expressions of individual and group identities and subcultures; notions of belonging, of taste and style. Along with these sometimes highly visible phenomena, other less visible cultural effects arise out of consumption too. By examining consumption as one thing people 'do', therefore, we are also discovering a series of cultural effects, and these effects are the concern of the book.

This introduction briefly defines the figure of the 'consumer', and outlines the acts and processes of consumption that will be referred to throughout the book. Then the contested term 'everyday life' will be sketched, and its relevance to consumption stated. Something like a trajectory of the argument throughout the book will also be conveyed. By themselves, each chapter may be a useful summary of a key area in the study of consumption, but together they build a cohesive argument, an argument that acknowledges some of the pleasures, rites and responsibilities of consumption: an ethics, a politics and a poetics of consumption in everyday life.

FIGURING 'THE CONSUMER'

So, just who is this blank, ghost-like figure invoked by economic theorists, marketing and advertising people for so many years, the 'consumer'? And what are these acts or processes of 'consumption' that will be examined in such detail? Throughout the book I will make reference not just to the individual *acts* of consumption but also to the larger *processes* of which they are a part. By isolating discrete moments or acts of consumption in common situations such as at the shop counter or within a mall, we can look at some of the important determining factors that lead up to the act of consumer choice and purchase. Hence a single *act* of consumption is readily identifiable as a particular moment in which the consumer is participating in a series of *processes*, having taken account of branding, images, notions of self-worth, responded to themes and signs that trigger elements of the sensory consciousness and the nonconscious states, and exercised the temporary satisfaction of a desire or felt need, for example. Part of the first-person experience of consumption comprises a certain level of irrationality, of daydreaming or wanting and wishing. The undercurrent of irrationality takes different forms and is encountered in different chapters. For the notion of the consumer as *homo economicus*, the paradigmatic rational consumer who only buys what they need, is discarded very early in the book.

Pursuing the suggestion of a core of irrationality within consumer experiences, there are several figures that are invoked along the way. Mythical or metaphorical bodies, for example, help to make sense of some of the practices of production and consumption. At various points I refer to the cyborg body, who lies at the boundary between culture and nature; vampyric bodies, those workers whose lifeblood has been extracted through the drudgery of mechanised industrial labour in Marx; and zombies appear too, as examples of what happens when mind is separated from body, and as a metaphor for the 'mindless' consumer in popular culture, such as Romero's film *Dawn of the Dead* (1978). Deborah Lupton's (1996) work on food consumption invokes the figure of the anorexic body, and anorexia could work as a metaphor for consumption in general since it describes appetites processes of discipline and restraint, and fear of ingestion or literal consumption of food. The dynamic is still hedonistic, she argues, since denial of food leads to greater pleasure, as thinness is equated with sexual attractiveness. Perhaps a better figure is that of the bulimic, whose food consumption is based on absolute pleasure and excess, and subsequent guilt and purging, whereby the cycle starts again.

Both the anorexic and the bulimic highlight the visceral, irrational nature of (not) consuming food. There is a *hunger*, and hunger is undeniably representative of a human rapaciousness, a sustained experience of bodily need, "a visceral questing that operates at the level of food, sex and money", says Probyn (2000: 80). So we get to another figure, that of the cannibal. The cannibal is omnivorous and therefore potentially capable of eating everything (and everyone). As a figure it represents our fear of the same, the endless appetites of consumer society. Are we not afraid of our own appetites in this way, where our insatiable hunger might take us? Yet, in Joseph Conrad's 1902 novel *Heart of Darkness*, an alternative viewpoint arises. The white traders who share a boat going upriver with native inhabitants feel edgy knowing that these people are supposedly cannibals. Why don't they eat us? Are we unappetising? The narrator of the story, Marlowe, comes to realise the essential reason: these half-starved cannibals, having not eaten properly for months, have something that the white traders, the exploiters of people and natural resources in the name of Empire, simply do not have: restraint. Compared to the white traders' unlimited rapaciousness and irrational, unbounded greed, Marlowe the narrator begins to respect the cannibals who show relative civility and restraint. The worst white offender, Kurtz, descends from European civility to become "the irrational, 'cannibalistic' principle of colonial expansion, the corporeal symbol of an utterly amoral desire to incorporate all within the province of exploitation" (Phillips 1998, in Probyn 2000: 95). The cannibalistic consumer is therefore another figure to focus practices of consumption around, who wishes to incorporate (consume) all. The tension between restraint and excess is something that characterises consumption in general, and mirrors the dynamic between production and consumption in history. Colonial history and modern consumption is an intersection that happens at several points in the book, in terms of the history of the trade of exotic goods (Chapter 1), the display of commodities at the Great Exhibition of 1851 (Chapter 3), and the clash of first and third worlds as a result of the sweatshop production of branded goods (Chapter 8).

POINT OF SALE? THE SHAPE OF THE BOOK

This distinction between acts and processes of consumption runs throughout the book. To look at individual acts of consumption, that is, the present moment of the consumer, we uncover a theoretical backstory that opens up various territories concerning the history and current theorisations of consumption. An argument runs like a thread throughout the chapters, starting with the history of consumption and the notion of commodities and material goods, including the trade in exotic goods only made possible through colonialism (Chapter 1, 'You are what you buy'). As the chapters progress, we move farther away from the consumption of material goods, and more towards the symbolic, the simulated or the virtual. This culminates in the last chapter, which looks at brand image and logos (Chapter 8, 'Logo or no logo?'), but also situates this within a history of colonialism.

Along the way we enter debates concerning the performance of identity (Chapter 2, 'Consumption and identity'), the psychology of retail and embodied experience (Chapter 4, 'Bodyshopping'), and the spaces of consumption (Chapter 7, 'Mallrats and car boots'). Putting some of these factors together, the negotiation between the position that consumers are manipulated or controlled, however subtly or unsubtly, and the position that consumption can be a creative act is explored, with especial attention to youth consumption (Chapter 6, 'The knowing consumer?'). Not only do we look at consumption of material goods but also of signs and symbols, and we see the circulation of not only economic capital but also what Bourdieu described as 'cultural capital' (1984, 1986b). As we move farther from the material commodity and regard the consumption of experiences and of simulations, I argue this is the prevailing mode in which we consume nature (Chapter 5, 'Nature, Inc.'). But to place these acts and experiences within larger historical contexts is to see the larger picture of the global economy, the need to renew consumer capitalism and export it ever further afield, and to utilise pools of inexpensive labour, cheap materials and production wherever possible. Of course, the connections between global and local consumption are manifold, and at many points in the text these connections will be pursued (more expansively in Chapter 3). Readers are encouraged to bear these connections between global and local in mind throughout, and to actively imagine these connections from their own experiences of consumption, too.

THEORIES OF EVERYDAY LIFE

Consumption of whatever kind, and not simply in the affluent West, is an everyday activity. But the definition of 'everyday' here is simplistic, for we can use it to mean a common activity, one that happens with great frequency. Just like the definition of consumption, the definition of the everyday is reflexive and, on further examination, reveals a series of assumptions, problems, and further questions. The realm of everyday life is neither immediate nor uncontested. Indeed, while the familiarity of everyday consumption helps us ground theoretical debates around consumption in a way most of us can easily understand, such as our experiences of supermarkets and shopping malls, it should not blind us to the complexities and assumptions behind these acts of consumption, and so in part the theorists of the everyday (for example Lefebvre, de Certeau) offer much in terms of a critical and also emancipatory reading of what has hitherto been unproblematic – this thing we call 'everyday life'. So why make it into a problem?

One of the tensions in looking at consumption, examined further in Chapter 7, is that between the consumer as a 'savvy' individual or as a 'sucker', duped by media, government and corporations into being a passive consumer. The 'savvy' consumer is able to creatively read and interpret signs, and to mobilise these readings and interpretations in order to engage in dialogue with other individuals within a culture or subculture. For example, a particular brand of computer like an Apple signifies a certain amount of style, success and creativity. The machine and its logo are instantly recognisable to other people who own the same brand, and are therefore indicative of status or aspiration. It is therefore to do with identity. Similarly, as we will see in detail, there are also interesting cases where products are *not* used for their original purpose, and this shows a creative twist in the consumption of that product. An example is the use of home-made embroidered designs on jeans or the sewing of patches in them, turning what is a mass-manufactured and fairly uniform product into something signifying individuality, creativity or even rebellion (Fiske 1989a). This reveals the other side of the tension, as the customisation by creative consumers then becomes co-opted by the manufacturers, and soon pre-embroidered or patched jeans become available for sale, removing the edge of individuality and creativity as a result. The other side of the equation therefore is not consumers as 'savvy', but consumers as 'suckers', and this has been mentioned above as the interpretation of what consumers do as being prescribed, determined, bad: a common criticism of consumer capitalism by Marxists is that it fosters "false needs", that it stimulates strong desires for material goods that are not strictly necessary for biological existence or even to foster a sense of community. In this view, consumer capitalism breeds a type of consumer who is alienated, unreflexive, inward-looking and routinised, where there is no real separation between work and leisure, and where the most that can be obtained is a form of "pseudo-enjoyment" where we are constantly in thrall to a series of spectacles that are staged for us. So argued Guy Debord in 1967 (1995), and despite its persistent negativity what he and others wanted to encourage was the reconnection of two things that have become separated within capitalism: art and life. To bring creativity, spontaneity, freedom and beauty into our everyday lives would be a form of utopia in the now, and would be a corrective to the alienation that critics of capitalism, from Marx through Weber, Adorno, Marcuse and others, had identified.

Theorists of everyday life therefore offer us alternatives to this entrenched 'structure' versus 'agency' debate in consumption. Lefebvre, Bourdieu and especially de Certeau move us on from the taken-for-granted quality of everyday life that we might have assumed. As a starting point, Gardiner (2000: 19) states there is nothing 'natural' or 'inevitable' about everyday life. As we start to examine what is taken for granted, it reveals itself as complex and processual rather than simple and reified. It consists of a vast number of conscious and unconscious processes, everything from simple tasks like tying shoelaces, to opening doors, browsing clothes in a store, or more complex tasks like driving or flirting. As it relates to consumption, it is now obvious that a large number of both conscious and unconscious processes take place in what was previously considered a routine or banal activity, and these actions and processes reveal very complex dialogues and transactions to do with identity, status, aspirations, cultural capital, and position within a social group. In addition they potentially show reflexive consideration of ethical, creative, and environmental concerns, consumers themselves placing their conscious experiences of acts of consumption into larger processes of globalisation. As de Certeau (1984) observed, consumer capitalism can never contain nor suppress the spontaneous and imaginative energies of the people, and even in consuming there is a form of cultural production as a result, especially when there is some form of creative appropriation ('transcription'), buying and using an object for a purpose other than its intended one.

PARADOXES OF CONSUMPTION

> [T]he use or appropriation of an object is more often than not both a moment of consumption *and* production, of undoing *and* doing, of destruction *and* construction.
>
> (Lury 1996: 1)

Throughout the book there are several concurrent paradoxes that characterise our messy pathways and negotiations through everyday life. As previously mentioned, one of them is the distinction between the consumer as 'sucker' and as 'savvy'. Even the definition of consumption is a paradox, as Clarke *et al.* (2003: 1) note. The word 'consumption' derives from *consumere*, "to use up, to destroy", such as being consumed by fire, or the Victorian term for tuberculosis which devastates the lungs. But also the Latin *consumare*, as in "to consummate", means to bring to completion, as in to consummate a marriage, to have sex. In French, *consommer* still has both senses, and this is useful to bear in mind throughout the book. Consumption is therefore simultaneously destroying (using up) and creating (bringing to fulfilment).

Another paradox occurs in Steven Miles's book *Consumerism – As a Way of Life*, which he flags up as 'the consuming paradox':

> the fact that in terms of our individual experience consumerism appears to have a fascinating, arguably fulfilling, personal appeal and yet simultaneously plays some form of an ideological role in actually controlling the character of everyday life.

> (1998: 5)

Along with an undeniable sense of fulfilment and gratification from consuming, we are still aware of the way our tastes are engineered, how we are manipulated. Arguably, this is a recognisable mode of our everyday experience of consumption, and is explored further in Chapter 7, 'The knowing consumer?'.

A further paradoxical strand is highlighted by Fredric Jameson, who attempts to think about the cultural evolution of late capitalism dialectically, "as catastrophe and progress all together" (1995: 47). Following Marx's passage in the *Communist Manifesto*, thinking about capitalism dialectically is "grasping the demonstrably baleful features of capitalism along with its extraordinary and liberating dynamism within a single thought", he continues. If applied to consumer capitalism we arrive at a similar formulation: that consumer capitalism allows us great freedoms and the ability to articulate important cultural phenomena such as self-identity and social identity, our identity within a group. The energy and dynamism that global brands like Nike promote is almost infectious, promising us familiar feelings such as belonging, but also more abstract values like competitiveness, sportsmanship, speed, dynamism, energy (explored in Chapter 8, 'Logo or no logo?'). But to partake, we must literally *buy into* these, requiring a not inconsiderable measure of disposable wealth, and also the knowledge that our tastes, desires and aspirations are almost inescapably engineered by the mass media to some extent. Negotiating these multiple paradoxes is one of the features of consumption in everyday life, and they will be revisited at various stages throughout the book.

A common complaint about mass culture and mass consumption is that of homogenisation. McDonalds, Coca-Cola, Microsoft and other multinational corporations, it is held, have flattened local differences and imposed a monolithic, universal and homogeneous form of culture that is mostly American. Yet, in order for there to be novelty and new products to consume, cultural variation must exist, and local franchises of multinational corporations will adapt to their nation's tastes, as is discussed in Chapter 3. This is a tension between homogenisation and heterogenisation, about the commodification and therefore the flattening of difference versus the celebration and even fetishisation of difference in terms of consumer choice. When it comes to ethnicity, though, it becomes extremely contentious, and the paradox of consuming the 'Other' in order to remain the same is brought up by the writer bell hooks (1992). She also makes the connection between cannibalism and consumerism, as an eating of the (racial) other, and this is useful for Chapter 8's discussion of 'commodity racism' (from McClintock 1995, in answer to Marx's 'commodity fetishism'). This dialectic of homogeneity versus heterogeneity, of sameness and difference, of cannibalism and consumerism, does seem to characterise another strand within our everyday experiences of consumption, as we shall see.

1

YOU ARE WHAT YOU BUY: THEORIES OF THE CONSUMER

FROM THE ECONOMIC TO THE SYMBOLIC

This chapter serves as an introduction to some general theories of consumption and the consumer, and will examine the two elements of *consumer* and *commodity* starting within the larger context of economics, and then within social theory more generally. We start with a brief historical overview of the commodity and the consumer for Marx, Veblen and Simmel, with Marx's famous notion of 'commodity fetishism'. Marx observed that consumer capitalism depended a great deal on the importation of foreign and exotic commodities such as foods, tea and coffee, tobacco and spices, and so the role of Empire in the movement and marketing of these goods is a consideration, especially in promoting a taste for the exotic and different. From this more economic analysis of consumer capitalism we turn to the philosophy and cultural theory of the Frankfurt School, whose ideas about the 'mass culture industry' are pertinent. Following from this, and continuing the trajectory of this chapter from the economic to the symbolic aspects of consumption, an overview of Fredric Jameson and what, after Ernest Mandel, he terms "late capitalism": the furthering of the aesthetic, the perpetually novel, "depthlessness" (1995: 12). Looking at these theories of consumer capitalism we can then begin to situate acts of consumption within larger economic processes, and we will revisit these theories of consumption when considering detailed case studies in later chapters. Limiting ourselves to more foundational socio-economic theories of consumption in this chapter first, we must be mindful of the way that ideas of the consumer and the commodity in political economy tell very little of the whole story. In fact there has been a historically impoverished understanding of the consumer and consumption in general by economists. As Ben Fine argues, often economists equate consumption with individual purchases and have no real understanding of who the 'consumer' actually is. They become an aggregate, a hypothetical figure in the imaginations of economists, such as the archetypal 'housewife', invoked to explain sets of statistics rather than seeing the consumer as flexible and the bearer of meanings or values. The problem of understanding consumers in this way is down to the limitations of models of 'neoclassical' economics, argues Fine (1993: 133). Political economy and theories of mass culture also often tend to diminish the role of the consumer, seeing their acts of consumption as trivial within the largely deterministic system of global capital, advertising and media.

To start to tell the other side of the story, about what the consumer actually *does*, is to argue literally for the *significance* of consumption in everyday life, to move from economic to symbolic explanations of consumer behaviour. This is to meld the material and the symbolic, to analyse consumption as *material culture* (see also Lury 1996). By outlining some theories of the consumer in economics, this chapter therefore acknowledges the importance of the consumer and the commodity in global political economy. But by trying to tell stories of consumption in everyday life settings, we bring out other relations between the consumer, the commodity and its signs. We can then route this into more everyday considerations by asking: What do changes in commodity markets, the growth of global media and advertising, and the expansion of cross-cultural tourism actually *mean* to us as consumers? How does this affect us in everyday acts of consumption? These questions will be answered through detailed case studies in later chapters. This chapter sets up the territory by firstly considering the *consumer*, and secondly the *commodity*.

Consumer

On the one hand, there is the consumer's point of view. Here we relate acts of consumption in late capitalism to everyday life through the eyes of the consumer, looking at concrete experiences of consumption and asking what kinds of things are motivating our decisions to buy, such as the concept of lifestyle, advertising and notions of consumer choice. These motivations, especially the notion of consumer choice, are seen as sacrosanct, encouraged and reproduced by the mass media, and by considering this we are laying the ground for a more detailed questioning of consumption in everyday life.

Commodity

On the other hand, there is the commodity's point of view, as it were. By tracing the material, social and cultural formations around the commodities that we buy, we can begin to outline some of the linkages between consumer culture and environmental and world development problems, and begin to trace the chains of cause and effect that link particular kinds of consumption to specific places, resources, people, and interests. This is a 'horizontal' notion of consumption (Fine 1993), concerned with the place of the commodity in its surrounding culture and therefore its symbolic value. Contrast this with the usual 'vertical' notion of consumption, which follows a particular commodity from production to its end use. While introduced here, the horizontal activity of tracing the social and cultural factors around commodities will be pursued in more detail through case studies and in later chapters, where the consumption of signs as well as commodities becomes more pertinent in thinking about identity, subcultures and so on.

Looking at both the consumer and the object in this way can highlight the important distinction between *consumption* and *consumerism*.[1] Consumption is not simply a series of individual acts of purchasing, as if purchasing a product were an end in itself. 'Consumerism', at least in the UK, is a mostly pejorative term, indicating the unreflective practices of people who apparently mindlessly buy into gadgets, technologies, brands and labels as a way of life. By looking at the consumer's multifaceted relation with the commodity, including, but not limited to, the economic, we can start to embark on the larger project of this book: examining the manifold meanings and cultural and social significances of consumption in everyday life. In addition, we start to move the framework of analysis from a 'vertical' (and predominantly economic) to a 'horizontal' (and primarily symbolic) account of consumption, seeing the commodity within the context of the factors that produced it, such as the chains of production, supply and retailing that enable us to act as consumers. Before examining some of the important features of consumption and everyday life in the modern world, it would be useful to look briefly at how consumption has been theorised historically. In particular, three theorists of economy and society remain crucial to current understandings of consumption, and their ideas will be revisited in later chapters.

A BRIEF HISTORY OF CONSUMPTION: MARX, VEBLEN, SIMMEL

Histories of consumption often include the figures of Marx, Veblen and Simmel, partly because there was little serious academic study of consumption before them, and partly because there is a large gap between Simmel at the very beginning of the twentieth century and the explosion of interest in consumption towards the end of that century, which continues today. No account of modern consumption is complete unless we look at the historical context, the move from purely socio-economic explanations of commodity exchange to consumption as expressions of desire and the production of signs. If we start with Marx and economic theory, however, we should bear in mind the myth of the prelapsarian society, for this lies in the background and, until relatively recently, seems to shape orthodox attitudes to consumption.

Consumption in itself is nothing new, but the date of the birth of consumer society is the subject of contention. Bermingham (1995) and McCracken (1988) suggest the sixteenth century or the early seventeenth century, as the court of Queen Elizabeth impressed upon her subjects the need to be fashionable, displaying new clothes and items in order to show one's status as a nobleman. Also at this time we can think of the expansion of trade networks around the globe and the cultivation of tastes for commodities such as tobacco and spices. Whenever a true 'consumer society' emerged in the modern sense, there are two general points to note. Firstly, the rise of a consumer society takes place in all phases of capitalism, even the earliest. There must be consumers in a marketplace to sell goods to, and therefore tastes are cultivated or shaped, from the gentry downwards. This is as true in the era of Sir Francis Drake's discovery of tobacco, or the later British Empire, as it is in the most recent wave of globalised capital and the rise of markets after the Second World War. Secondly, whenever 'modern' consumption actually occurred, whether in the sixteenth, seventeenth, eighteenth or nineteenth centuries, it is often founded on the myth of a prelapsarian society. That is, we assume that the birth of consumer society destroyed relations between the worker and the things he produced, and eroded the 'natural' relationships of families who lived a harmonious existence.

In short, the rise of consumer society is often seen in negative terms as unnatural and disharmonious, causing the breakdown of healthy relations and injecting alienation between producer and product. Marx himself is partly responsible for this view, having a romanticised view of the pre-capitalist, pre-industrial historical era of feudal society in the middle ages. In feudal society social relations are primary, even if they are based on dependency, and unlike industrialised society there is no separation of worker from work produced, hence no alienation. A craftsman owns his labour and therefore the means of production. But a factory worker's labour is for hire, so he no longer owns the means of production, the factory owner does. This alienates the worker from the work he produces. Marx considered transactions in feudal society to involve the particularity of labour rather than the abstract universal equivalent, that is the money form, necessary for commodity production. He therefore concludes:

> Whatever we may think ... of the different roles in which men confront each other in such a society, the social relations between individuals in the performance of their labour appear at all events as their own personal relations, and are not disguised as social relations between things, between the products of labour.
>
> (1990: 170)

The implication of course is that there is a purer form of sociality and relations with objects without alienation that existed prior to industrial capitalism, a notion maintained by historians such as Hobsbawm (1980), who sees a progressive mercantile culture in the United Kingdom before the industrial revolution around 1780.

Marx's understanding of consumption

Karl Marx (1818–1883) considered consumption more in terms of eating, drinking and procreation than in our more modern sense of accommodating new cultural forms and symbolic acts. For Marx, the consumption of commodities was understood more in terms of a development of 'commodity production', and therefore ties consumption explicitly into a dialectical relation with production. While consumption was not understood in the modern sense, he did notice the ever-spiralling growth of new commodities being sold and consumed. Since Marxist understandings and interpretations of capitalism and consumption have changed since his death we can assume, as Bocock does, that "there is now a new and distinct form of capitalism in the world, based on the ever increasing production of new commodities for consumption" (1993: 35). This new type of capitalism, so-called 'consumer capitalism', explicitly relies on increasingly sophisticated forms of consumption, and less emphasis is placed on production. While he wrote little in terms of what we understand now as consumption, Marx wrote extensively about the use-value and exchange-value of commodities in *Capital* (1867), where use-value is the worth of the commodity in terms of the actual cost of materials and production, and exchange-value is the price such an object may attain in the market-place – how much someone is willing to pay. The cost of raw materials and manufacture (use-value) is often marginal compared to the cost of the object to buy (exchange-value). The raw materials and cost of labour and assembly of a car, for example, probably lies in the tens of dollars, whereas it sells for thousands of dollars in car showrooms. The use-value and exchange-value are distinct because, in Marx's analysis, the commodity derives a socially ascribed market value irrespective of its worth as raw materials, and is therefore desired by consumers.

In selling a commodity, the difference between the use-value and the exchange-value is absorbed as pure profit along the retail chain, and Marx terms this the "surplus value". Thus, the monetary difference between the true cost of manufacture of a commodity and the price it attains in the marketplace relies on the exploitation of labour. In the case of a car, for a profit to be made the surplus value means that the cost of labour is not valued at its true cost, and the labourer who assembles the car is paid less than the true worth of the labour in order that the company makes money. This notion of surplus value involves the *alienation* of the worker from the product. Alienation between worker and the work he produces is a consistent theme in the history of consumption, and is treated throughout Marx's works, including *Capital* and *Economic and Philosophical Manuscripts of 1844* (1959).

This basic division into use-value and exchange-value is part of a 'vertical' analysis, that is, following a single commodity from inception through its life cycle, ending up being purchased, used and thrown away. It is different from the 'horizontal' analysis that looks at the context of the variety of factors which allowed it to be produced in the first place, such as "production, distribution, retailing, consumption and the material culture surrounding it" (Fine 1993: 142). Fine's advocation of a vertical analysis would be useful if we were to trace some of the commodity and supply chains for everyday objects, especially, such as tea or coffee.

Commodity fetishism

Talking about the *commodity*, Marx defined it as "an external object, a thing which through its qualities satisfies human needs of whatever kind" (1990: 125), which is then exchanged for something else. But this definition obscures some of the complexities of so straightforward an idea. "A commodity appears at first sight an extremely obvious, trivial thing. But its analysis brings out that it is a very strange thing, abounding in metaphysical subtleties and theological niceties" (1990: 163). To examine this further, he borrows the concept of *fetishism* from anthropology, which refers to some pre-modern beliefs that inanimate things have magical or godly powers. Together, the notion of the commodity and the magical powers that seem to inhere he calls 'commodity fetishism'. Referring back to the discussion about use-value and exchange-value above, as long as it is tied to its use-value the commodity remains simple. For example, in the transformation of a piece of wood into a table through human labour, its use-value is clear and, as product, the table remains tied to its material use. However, as soon as the table "emerges as a commodity, it changes into a thing which transcends sensuousness" (1990: 163). That is, the connection to the actual hands and experiences of the labourer is removed as soon as the table is connected to money, becomes exchange-value. In a capitalist society people therefore begin to treat commodities as if value inhered in the objects themselves, rather than in the amount of real labour expended to produce the object. "The mysterious character of the com-modity-form consists therefore simply in the fact that the commodity reflects the social characteristics of men's own labour as objective charac-teristics of the products of labour themselves, as the socio-natural proper-ties of these things", as Marx explains (1990: 164–165). A relation between *people* (the labourer and the capitalist) instead assumes "the fan-tastic form of a relation between *things*" (1990: 165, my emphasis).

In this, the real producers of commodities mostly remain invisible, and this furthers the thing-like relation between the producer and the product. We only approach their products "through the relations which the act of exchange establishes between the products" (1990: 165). That is, the 'reality' of an object derives from its exchange-value, and this value is based on labour power. In exchange-value there is an *equivalence* in terms of labour power, where every object can be traded for another. Let's say a pair of Diesel jeans can be traded for a bottle of Glenmorangie whisky; in this case there is an equivalence in labour power, they require equal amounts of time and energy to produce, so there is an equivalence in exchange-value. Since we only ever relate to those products through the exchange of money, we forget the underly-ing factor which alters the value of the commodity, the actual labour of the producer. It is "precisely this finished form of the world of com-modities – the money form – which conceals the social character of pri-vate labour and the social relations between the individual workers, by making those relations appear as relations between material objects, instead of revealing them plainly" (1990: 168–169). The social relation between *people* becomes the social relation between *things*. Gold and then paper money become "the direct incarnation of all human labour" (1990: 187), much as in pre-modern societies the totem becomes the direct incarnation of godhead. As the labour behind commodities is concealed and they become identified with abstract money-value, this entails the alienation of the worker from the work produced, even from other workers. "Men are henceforth related to each other in their social process of production in a purely atomistic way; they become alienated because their own relations of production assume a material shape which is independent of their control and their conscious individual action" (1990: 187). Market forces appear to exist independently of any individ-ual person, despite the fact that ultimately value accrues to an object only because of human labour. As Corrigan (1998: 35) points out, Marx describes the sphere of exchange and relations between producers, but there is no concern with what happens subsequently in consumption.

Moving on from Marx, Max Weber (1864–1920) developed insights concerning consumption and cultural values. In Protestantism and Calvinism he noticed the will to work, hence an emphasis on production, but not the will to consume, and he dubbed this the "work ethic" (1971). Briefly, his observation was that the religious values of Protestantism entailed a motivation to build up and invest in an enterprise, hence to be hard-working and productive, but crucially not to *consume* those products in luxurious living. This has the effect of delayed gratification, and therefore of deferred consumption. The virtues of thrift, hard work, and productivity are valued above decoration and spending on frivolous objects. This can be seen especially in contrast with Catholic cultures that stress extended family life, communal eating, and a more relaxed attitude to work and play.

Veblen and social emulation

Marx's analysis of a generalised, commodity-producing society showed that consumption is not simply a function of larger, determining economic relations, which is something that neoclassical models assume. Quantitative differences in ability to consume, based on income distributions that are associated with different class positions, have no immediate implications for differentiation in consumption itself. In other words, despite our social position and income levels, by and large we often desire and aspire to the same things. This idea, of 'social emulation', is not new, and assumes that those in lower socio-economic positions wish to eat and dress in a way that emulates the trendsetters, those rich and idle enough to be carried away by fashions and fancies. For example, champagne was historically such an expensive drink that only the very conspicuously wealthy could afford it; now, drinking champagne is more common amongst a range of different social groups at one time or another, more often amongst the upper middle classes than the lower middle classes. In this case, emulation as a model works, as there are a number of different luxury products that are increasingly available to, and purchased by, lower socio-economic groups. In the case of both emulation and champagne, there is another factor. As the lower socio-economic classes start to consume products once the strict reserve of the landed aristocracy, the truly elite now become increasingly discerning, looking to other fashions and products in order to justify their distinction, their good taste. This emulation and search for the truly distinctive to enhance separation from the majority of consumers was observed by Veblen in the early twentieth century, and is observable today in the world of hip-hop, where particular and distinctive brand names of champagne like Cristal (between US$150 and US$600 per bottle in 2004) are drunk conspicuously by black musicians like 50 Cent, brands that were once the strict reserve of the gentry. Let us now contextualise these ideas historically.

Thorstein Veblen (1857–1929) wrote about emulation through consumption practices in his classic book of 1924 *The Theory of the Leisure Class* (1994). In it he looks at the then newly wealthy bourgeois leisure class in New England. These *nouveaux riches* mostly gained their great wealth from manufacturing and industry, and Veblen noted how, through their consumption patterns such as styles of dress and food, they emulated upper-class life in Europe. Veblen noted there were two ways that their wealth could be displayed, to provide them with an elite social status. What he called "pecuniary standing" could be indicated by "conspicuous consumption", the purchase and display of expensive and tasteful commodities, and "conspicuous leisure", the ability to distance oneself from the dirty, sordid details of production through living a life of leisure, learning and travel. It was not just about "consuming freely of the right kinds of goods" but also that one "consume them in a seemly manner" (Veblen, in Corrigan 1998: 24). In a city of strangers, however, it is easier to show your status through conspicuous consumption, especially through fashionable clothes, than through conspicuous leisure.

Of course, being newly rich through industry has a different connotation than being rich through your family owning land for generations. Thus the *nouveaux riches* are often looked down upon by the older, landed aristocracies, who feel they have cultivated tastes. This idea of 'social emulation' is seen as key in the dramatic birth of consumption, as to emulate the consumption practices of a higher social order, with their fascination for perpetual novelty, requires large amounts of money. While Veblen concentrated on the new leisure class in the United States, the same principle of social emulation has been applied to the working classes and their consumption habits. It is one explanation for the continual drive towards increasing consumption in general and therefore the rapid growth of consumer society, and also an explanation for the shift in tastes that occurs at the top of the consumption hierarchy, who seek to show increasing refinement and discerning tastes in new areas, such as fashion, in order to distinguish themselves from the imitators, the *arrivistes*, who have newly acquired money but no taste. This idea is pursued more recently by Bourdieu (1984), whose theory of 'distinction' is discussed in the following chapter.

Within this model of social emulation, the drive to increasing competitive consumption is a marker of social status throughout the hierarchy, and we notice an upward move in terms of the choice and consumption of goods, and a downward move in terms of who dictates what is truly tasteful rather than vulgar. The upward movement is indicated by the fact that, in aspiring towards the higher end of the consumption hierarchy, according to Storey, people "pursued 'luxuries' in place of 'decencies', and 'decencies' in place of 'necessities'" (1999: 5). This upward trend tends to increase the standard of living, although sometimes 'necessities' like meat were substituted by sugary tea and jam, because the once-exotic commodity sugar started to become more commonplace, an inexpensive energy food for the industrial workforce (e.g. Mintz 1986). Generally, however, the emulation model is reliant on increased expenditure in order to maintain the aspirant's social position. The downward trend is the so-called 'trickledown' effect, where the (landed, aristocratic) rich are seen as the ultimate source of demand for consumer goods, and are the arbiters and manufacturers of good taste. What they dictate as tasteful and fashionable, often a seriously wasteful display of wealth, then trickles down the social hierarchy, meaning that lower social orders will seek the same items and attempt to consume similarly – first, the *nouveau riche*, then the upper middle class, and so on.

Simmel and urban consumption

Georg Simmel (1858–1918) looked at the massively changing and vibrant modern metropolis of Berlin at the turn of the twentieth century. He observed the new migrants entering the city, many of Polish descent, and in his 1903 essay 'The metropolis and mental life' (1997) he presciently observes that the modern city is "not a spatial entity with sociological consequences, but a sociological entity that is formed spatially" (in Bocock

1993: 16). That is, the city is not some pre-formed space into which we humans simply spill, but is made through and maintained by our social interactions and practices, including consumption. We might say that the city is more a state of mind than a physical place, a sentiment echoed by Lewis Mumford in *The City in History* (1961). In such a dynamic and ongoing conception of the city, with new immigrants and altered ways of life, Simmel noticed that we go through a psychological process of screening out complex stimuli as a response to the huge array of signs, posters, colours, smells, sounds and people in the city (see Harvey 1989). As a result we develop a blasé attitude towards others in the city, not noticing or acknowledging them the way we would in a smaller town or village. Within this larger, anonymous urban environment, one way we reassert our individuality and sense of identity is through patterns of consumption.

Thus it is easy to see the connection between newly urban forms of life and more modern patterns of consumption, since consumption from Veblen has been about articulating a sense of identity, adorning one's body with clothes and decorations, and eating and drinking in a way interpretable by others. Veblen had noted in the new leisure class, just as in the landed aristocracy, that typically it was women who organised social life, and were a means for men to display wealth through "vicarious consumption" – through commodities such as expensive clothes or jewellery, or through experiences such as travel to Europe, taking language lessons or horse riding. In the city, the display of wealth through adornments and entertainments leads to an increased awareness of style, and it is perhaps this word 'style' more than 'taste' that relates to our current practices of consumption in the city. For both Veblen and Simmel, the new bourgeois were attempting to legitimate their separation from the working class by displaying their wealth, and so make the social hierarchy appear natural. Putting distance between the display of wealth (consumption) and the source of such wealth (industrial production) effected this. The prestige of the display of wealth in their social life, that is, Veblen's notion of "conspicuous consumption", increased their authority over those further down in the social and economic hierarchy. And, as in Veblen's social emulation model, not only did conspicuous consumption preserve status and legitimate position within a hierarchy, it offered the display of material wealth as a model for others to aspire to. As Veblen put it, "the leisure class scheme of life ... extends its coercive influence" throughout society as a whole (1994: 83–84).

One neat way we can see consumption work as a marker of status within a hierarchy that subsequently encourages social emulation throughout, is through the history of one particular commodity: bread. From medieval times, white bread carried

> high prestige ... the further down the social scale, the darker the bread. The upper classes regarded black and brown breads with aversion – it was even claimed their stomachs could not digest them – while the lower orders aspired to white or whiter bread.
>
> (Mennell, in Storey 1999: 41)

In past decades, of course, the reverse trend operates whereby browner bread is identified with health as opposed to wealth. Nevertheless, the rippling effect of social emulation stands out in this example. Simmel himself wrote about the metropolis and the world of fashion in a way that extends Veblen's simple trickledown model of social emulation. Veblen had observed that dress was an expression of wealth, that "our apparel is always in evidence and affords an indication of our pecuniary standing to all observers at the first glance" (1994: 167). Corrigan (1998: 164) notes that Gabriel Tarde's *The Laws of Imitation* of 1900 made a similar point, that social beings are imitative and therefore society itself is imitation, and this is exemplified in fashion. But Simmel talked not only of imitation but also of differentiation in his 1904 essay 'Fashion' (1957), or in his terms "generalisation" and "specialisation". The "imitator" is freed from choice and creativity, for their fashion allows them instantly to be a member of a social group. But the "teleological individual" is not an imitator but someone specialised, different, "is ever experimenting, always restlessly striving, and [reliant] on his own personal convictions" (Simmel, in Corrigan 1998: 170). Simmel's writings on fashion show this tension between consumption as a marker of wealth and status within the norms of a society, and consumption as an exhibition of individuality. He saw fashion as developing primarily in the city, "because it intensifies a multiplicity of social relations, increases the rate of social mobility and permits individuals from lower strata to become conscious of the styles and fashions of upper classes" (Ashley and Orenstein 1990: 314). There is a dialectical process involved in the development of tastes in fashion, then, where the norm is a pattern of taste expressed through the purchase and display of certain styles of clothing. In fashion, as in other areas of taste, there is a continual cycle of establishing the norm, challenging it, and thereby deriving a newly altered norm which hastily abandons previously established norms. This dialectical process is accelerated by the urban environment, where cycles of purchase and display are more rapid. Simmel concludes: "Fashion ... is a product of class distinction" since as soon as lower social groups come to imitate the consumption practices and fashions of the higher social group, the latter strive for newer and more expensive fashions, in order to maintain their elite social status (1957: 544). Through mechanisms of inclusion and exclusion, fashion as consumption activity maintains and furthers the social distinctions and differences upon which it depends. The importance of distinction, the historical development of notions of taste to differentiate oneself from other social groups through economic and cultural capital, is examined more recently by Bourdieu (1984).

In short, fashion is an example of an antagonistic process, thought Simmel, which paradoxically allows personal values to be expressed at the same time as norms are followed. This coexistence of social norms and individual values in the context of tastes in fashion is echoed in other patterns of consumption, as we shall see especially in the following chapter. One of Simmel's general remarks on fashion will be useful in considering consumption and its relation to group and individual identity in the following chapter, especially Hebdige's influential concept of 'subculture': "fashion ... signifies union with those in the same class, the uniformity of a circle enclosed by it, and ... the exclusion of all other groups" (1957: 544). Underlying such antagonisms is the sometimes creative tension between the individual and their fear of incursion or intrusion by a collectivity, the throbbing organismic social entity of the city. "The deepest problems of modern life derive from the claim of the individual to preserve the autonomy and individuality of his existence in the face of overwhelming social forces, of external culture, and of the technique of life", as Farganis puts it (1993: 136).

THE ROMANTIC ETHIC AND THE MODERN CONSUMER

We have started to relate observable factors within economic theory and the practices of consumption, where consuming indicates social position and therefore becomes a bearer of meaning. If previously we have highlighted the separation between the rational economic and the symbolic aspects of consumption, Veblen's emulation model starts to stress the symbolic side. The trend towards the symbolic continues. There is another factor in the genesis of modern consumption that still heavily informs actual consumption practices today, shifting the emphasis from economic factors and the model of social emulation to the notion of the 'individual' within society, and the cultivation of the Romantic ideal of the individual in the late eighteenth century. We can place this in the context of a shift from elite consumption to mass consumption, arising out of the economic prosperity of England in the eighteenth century. Fashionable goods were opened up to all but the poorest as a result, and the well-known industrial revolution on the supply side was matched by a consumer revolution on the demand side. An indication of this emerging consumer revolution is given by Corrigan, who argues that attempts to mould taste were made in early advertising and marketing, such as those by Josiah Wedgwood, the famous ceramics producer, who tried to direct upper-class tastes knowing full well that the lower classes would follow. The observation that this constituted a new "consumption ethic" or way of thinking about consumption is made by Colin Campbell (1987). Campbell sees the continuity between the type of 'disenchantment' described by Max Weber (1970), being the separation of humans and emotions from the natural world, and the sense of loss of communion with nature that the Romantic movement felt. In fact, the title of Campbell's work, *The Romantic Ethic and the Spirit of Modern Consumerism*, obviously consciously echoes Weber's famous *The Protestant Ethic and the Spirit of Capitalism*. The Romantic element in the formation of consumerism is evidenced by the emphasis on sentiment and sensation in Rousseau, as is the beginning of the cult of the individual. An emphasis on the change of the person, the ideal of the individual, is a shift in thinking from more collective and socially cohesive patterns of behaviour. Along with the ideal of the individual arises an unashamed commitment to pleasure, and the perpetuation of the need to satisfy such cravings for pleasure:

> Romanticism provided that philosophy of 'recreation' necessary for a dynamic consumerism: a philosophy which legitimates the search for pleasure as a good in itself … [thus it] served to provide ethical support for that restless and continuous pattern of consumption which so distinguishes the behaviour of modern man.
>
> (Campbell 1987: 201)

It was the Romantic poet Coleridge for example who coined the term "self-consciousness", as if the phenomenon had not been experienced before, based on the existence of a reflective individual (although see Glennie and Thrift 1996). The argument that a new consumption ethic occurs comes from this development and acknowledgement of hedonism and the way that pleasure could be derived not just from sensations, which may be easily bought and sold, but also from emotions. As we will see in more recent theorisation of consumption, anticipation, desire and insatiability are not just recent psychoanalytic ways to think about consumption, but are consistent with Romantic ideas about daydreaming and phantasmagoria, and these themes of dreaming and phantasmagoria in the shopping arcades of Paris are dealt with explicitly by Walter Benjamin in his famous *Arcades Project* of 1935, and we shall revisit this territory in more detail in Chapter 7. Let us note briefly here the potential impact of daydreaming and desire on consumption as being cultivated from the Romantic period, and the shift from *having* to *wanting* as the focus of pleasure-seeking. Thus window-shopping, daydreaming and desiring objects becomes a culturally permitted form of consumption. The child-like fascination with perpetual novelty, the insatiability of desire, and hence imaginary anticipation as opposed to actual gratification are all consistent with this consumption ethic, and as applicable to shopping malls today as to the arcades of nineteenth-century Paris. The relevance to consumption of the ideal of the individual and the imagination since the Romantic era is underlined by Campbell when he remarks that it is important "to conceive of the cultural products as providing the *material* for day-dreams rather than as *being* day-dreams" (1987: 93, my emphasis).

THE FRANKFURT SCHOOL AND THE 'MASS CULTURE INDUSTRY'

The term 'culture industry' was coined in 1947 by Theodor Adorno and Max Horkheimer in their book *Dialectic of Enlightenment* (1973). It was used to describe what they saw happening especially in their newly adopted home, America, to describe the processes and products of mass culture. What they describe as 'mass culture' is the mass-marketed cultural products such as pop music, the films of Hollywood, and Disney and its theme parks (see also Adorno 2001, especially pp. 61–97). The Institute for Social Research was established at the University of

Frankfurt in 1923, but with the rise of Hitler's National Socialism some key members fled to New York in 1933, and became known as the 'Frankfurt School'. As high-minded émigrés they were extremely critical of populist forms of entertainment, so-called 'low-brow' culture. Their immediate target was not the superficiality or depthlessness of modern popular culture, but "instrumental reason", an extension into the modern age of Enlightenment rationality, the treatment of people in all aspects of their work and leisure in a systematic, ordered, reasoned, controlled way. This, thought Adorno and Horkheimer, was a natural progression in capitalism, which increasingly allocates thing-like properties to people as well as objects, to substitute the universal (abstract, exchangeable, calculable properties) for the particular (the actual properties of the person or object). Similarly they found a tendency in mass culture to homogeneity and predictability, where cultural products are marketed and sold in standardised forms to an undemanding public. The expansion of mass production, they held, led to the commodification of culture, and just as in any factory, from cigarettes to cars to culture, this leads to standardisation. With this homogeneity, predictability and standardisation, the culture industries mass-produce cultural products, and these are passively consumed by consumers. In this materialistic culture, commodities lack authenticity and meet 'false' needs – needs that are created, maintained and furthered by the mass culture industry. The message here is clear, as Mackay summarises: "this perspective attributed to consumers a profoundly passive role, portraying them as manipulated, mindless dupes, rather than as active and creative beings" (1997: 3). This tension between the consumer on the one hand as passive 'dupe' and on the other as active, creative agent is examined in more detail in Chapter 6, when this tension between the consumer as 'sucker' and the consumer as 'savvy' is explored.

More recent theory considers the consumer to be active, creative, and capable of appropriating the products of the culture industry and using them for different purposes than those intended by the manufacturers. Theorists such as Fiske (1989a; 1989b) and de Certeau (1984) for example pursue the active and creative aspect, assigning to the consumer a profoundly creative role. But before hastily dismissing the perspective of the Frankfurt School as outdated or anachronistic, trying to understand the expressive power and critical force of these critics is useful in considering the creative tension between these perspectives of the consumer as passive dupe or as creative agent. The charges of homogeneity, pre-dictability and standardisation of cultural products such as theme parks, Hollywood movies or popular music ring equally true in the early twenty-first century as they did at the end of the twentieth, or the mid-twentieth century, when the Frankfurt School were writing. One of the most powerful recent sociological critiques of consumer society, Ritzer's theory of 'McDonaldization' (1993, 1996), directly descends from the observations of the Frankfurt School, explored in great detail in Chapter 3. In addition, while they were often harsh in their judgements of popular culture, the illusory promise of satisfaction within the culture indus-try is noted by Adorno and Horkheimer, writing about the pseudo-pleasure rather than real pleasure on offer to the consumer: "all it actually confirms is that real point will never be reached, that the diner must be satisfied with the menu" (1973: 139). The anticipatory and ephemeral quality of consumer desire has been noted already in this chapter, and will be revisited via Freud, phantasmagoria, daydreaming and wishing in Chapters 4 and 7, on the body and spaces of consump-tion, respectively.

Another prominent intellectual within the school was Herbert Marcuse who, in an influential and polemical book *One Dimensional Man*, claimed that through the workings of the culture industry, capi-talism promoted an "ideology of consumerism". We have already encountered the way that affluence and conspicuous consumption for Veblen's *nouveaux riches* meant they pursued 'luxuries' in place of 'decen-cies', and 'decencies' in place of 'necessities', contributing towards an increasing display of affluence through the consumption of commodi-ties. Of course, this remains supremely relevant in our contemporary cli-mate of mobile phones and prestige cars. Marcuse noted how the ideology of consumerism entailed the creation and promotion of "false needs", that is, the fostering of the need for things not strictly necessary for survival. Further, by literally buying into this promotion of false needs, it works as a mechanism of social control (1968: 26–27). Not only is this a powerful attack on consumer capitalism, but our accep-tance of this ideology of consumerism makes us complicit with the sys-tem of the promotion of false needs through the culture industry. It leads to a depoliticised conformity, effectively limiting our goals and actions only to those realisable within the framework of capitalism, and rendering our political choices fairly meaningless. Marcuse's observation

of the creation of false needs as a mechanism of social control and alienation is important, but there are two other pertinent factors in his social
critique.

First, Marcuse's linking of consumer choice and politics is prescient,
as on the one hand we have the effective dampening of political action
by the shifting of our concerns onto false needs, new technologies and
commodities that can be bought, sold and aspired to. On the other
hand, there is recent discussion of the way that citizenship is performed
through consumption (e.g. Hall 1989; Miller 1993), and how people
find that identity constructed through consumption is more empower-
ing than through traditional means. While there may be positive
aspects to this, the reduction of the sphere of political action and social
communication into the consumption and display of commodities, from
Marcuse's post-Marxist point of view, would only further the ideology of
consumerism as a mechanism of social control. We have seen the corresponding movement in the rhetoric of politicians in the US and the UK
recently, confirming the sanctity of 'choice', a value paramount for consumers purchasing commodities, in the restructuring of public services
and policy decisions to the voting public.

Second, Marcuse's observation of the work/leisure distinction as
mutually reinforcing has become one of the central tenets of Ritzer's
McDonaldization thesis, and is the subject of much interest in sociologies and geographies of leisure. Marcuse essentially argued that, in the
same way that industrial capitalism has organised, observed and documented our work time, the culture industry similarly organises our
leisure time. One brief example will suffice. The queuing and spatial
manipulation of visitors at theme parks is often carefully disguised to
make the 'work' of queuing and waiting for the 'leisure' and thrill of
the ride converge, through such devices as the cartoon-costumed staff,
other displays to watch, and the careful hiding of the number of sta-
tionary, waiting people (time goes much slower if you see other bored
people in a non-moving queue; Underhill 2003: 191–194). Thus, often
using similar tricks and devices as those in the industrial and retail
organisation of time, our leisure time is similarly organised, and this is
an indication of the collapse of work and leisure as distinct categories
in post-industrial, consumer, or 'late' capitalism. As Gardiner documents in a book about everyday life, the French social theorists Guy
Debord and Henri Lefebvre both considered 'leisure' to be a site of

manipulated pseudo-enjoyment (Gardiner 2000: 14). In *Minima Moralia* (1974), Adorno was also concerned with the "withering away of experience" through just such a false divide between work and leisure, with the promise of pseudo-enjoyment from the culture industry, and with preserving the richness and particularity of experience from the homogenising effects of the commodity-form, especially those commodified experiences offered by the mass culture industry.

Before moving on to discuss the consumer in late capitalism, after our observations of the relevance of the Frankfurt School's critique to recent ideas in social theory, it is important to point out some shortcomings. The Frankfurt School's approach is a non-economistic extension of Marxism, whereby the social and cultural factors of consumption are examined as opposed to regarding it purely as an economic process. Despite providing analyses of the cultures and ideologies of consumption, there is no real critical engagement with acts of consumption themselves, and there is no room for the meaning or meaningfulness of consumption. They simply do not allow the possibility that consumption is a necessary human activity, since most needs are falsely implanted and we are indoctrinated through the mass culture industry. Under their lens, consumption is an unnecessary evil that only sustains the state apparatus and disempowers us. Their viewpoint suffers from being elitist and condemnatory of everyday practices, and allows little space for any notion of consumption as a symbolic activity in which meaning may be created and exchanged. To even sit down with a cup of coffee and discuss their post-Marxist ideas, we would be having to consume, and the everydayness or banality of such actions are not within their scope. To relegate large amounts of human everyday activity into meaningless banality is instead to be concerned with the larger theoretical picture, and the force of their criticisms of the ideology of consumerism is somewhat diluted when their cultural elitism is taken into account. As Storey formulates it, their model was that of "consumption as manipulation" (1999: 19), where the consumer mindlessly consumed whatever was presented to them through the mass culture industry. There is little space for resistance or independence from such an enveloping blanket of mass culture.

In Adorno's case, as Bernstein explains, mass culture is "more diverse, dynamic and conflictual than [his] theory allows" (2001: 20). Positing a theory of mass culture as Adorno did tends to unify and pacify a culture industry that mediates social change and conflict. Finally, the Frankfurt

School are still concerned with economic base and cultural superstructure, and even if their analysis is not limited to purely economic processes, their interpretation of cultural activities is severely hampered by this Marxist division. Stressing the *economic* aspects of consumption over the *symbolic* in this way narrows the range of cultural activities they consider meaningful, and we need to extend this analysis of consumption by accommodating the important and meaningful symbolic aspects, which concern us from this point onwards.

CULTURE AND THE CONSUMER IN 'LATE' CAPITALISM

> Popular culture is not consumption, it is culture – the active process of generating and circulating meanings and pleasures within a social system: culture, however industrialized, can never be adequately described in terms of the buying and selling of commodities.
>
> (Fiske 1989a: 23)

Moving away from the model of consumer as manipulated, it would be timely to re-establish what consumption actually is, and reconnect it with the purposive manufacturing and exchange of symbolic activity within culture. The majority of this chapter has been a historical consideration of consumption up to the Second World War. The remainder of this chapter is concerned with looking at consumption after this, a transition to mass consumption, and the way this impacted on an emerging popular culture. The post-war economic boom, with its new consumers and commodities for them to buy, signalled a shift both in patterns of consumption and in academic thinking about consumption. Continuing the trajectory of thinking consumption from the realms of the economic to the symbolic, the processes of culture that the quote from Fiske describes are based on the circulation of meanings and signs within a commonly held system. In a late capitalist consumer society, these meanings and signs are inextricable from, but not simply reducible to, the consumption and display of commodities; and the habitual, everyday use we make of them in constructing and maintaining aspects of our identity.

So-called 'mass consumption' started in post-war America and came to Britain, then Europe, as both mass production and consumption increased, meaning that the lower socio-economic strata could become consumers too. As Bocock describes, the 'new consumers' of the post-war era, but especially in the 1970s–1980s, organised themselves into groups often based on patterns of consumption. Especially after the 1950s it was the young that were identified as the new, major market, which accelerated the growth of marketing and brands, targeting consumers less on the basis of occupation or fixed social status than on self-ascribed notions of identity within social groups (1993: 21ff., 100). Such groups as the Teddy boys of the 1950s and the Mods and Rockers of the 1960s were notoriously defined by their clothes, their vehicles and their haircuts – all markers of status that occur through the performance of consumption. Of course, identity and branding have become massively important issues in consumption, and this is the concern of Chapters 2 and 8, respectively. The shift from fixed status groups to more mobile identities, constructed through dynamic patterns of consumption, is also well documented. The Mods of the 1960s, for example, found their identity within a group through buying a scooter, fixing mirrors to it, wearing smart Italian suits. If, for reasons such as marriage, mortgage or children, such a person can no longer take their place in the social group, then the consumption pattern alters too, substituting nappies for natty suits, or a new washing machine for the gleaming Piaggio scooter. The social identity and therefore the pattern of consumption was simple. Since those times, we now have a range of identities and affinities to social groups within our lifetimes, and we have a more sophisticated notion of "lifestyles", as Featherstone (1991a: 83) terms it, that are pursued, maintained and altered throughout our lifetimes. Crucially, altering lifestyles entails altering patterns of consumption.

One thing that connects up historical work on economic consumption and more recent academic debates about consumption is Fredric Jameson's idea of postmodernism as a cultural phenomenon emerging from late capitalism. One of the questions then becomes: how do we shift our thinking from *historical* debates concerning the economics of consumption to *present cultural activities* in this era of late capitalism, invoking post-war theories of the sign within consumer culture, especially as influenced by Roland Barthes. Jameson's massively influential 1991 book *Postmodernism, or The Cultural Logic of Late Capitalism* takes Ernst Mandel's definition of "late capitalism" as the historical stage that succeeds the stages of market capitalism and monopoly (or imperial) capitalism. Marx was writing at the stage of market capitalism, where production was inflexible, commodity-based, and mostly domestic. Monopoly or imperial capitalism acknowledged the globalisation of trade, but perhaps this is better described as 'internationalisation' since it was based on privileged trade relations between colonies and colonial powers. So the subsequent stage, that of 'late', 'multinational' or 'consumer' capitalism, derives from the broad shift from production in industrial capitalism to consumption in postindustrial capitalism. Jameson considers this stage to be the "purest" form of capitalism, with an associated rapid expansion in commodification (1995: 36). But there are particular features of the cultural forms that arise in late capitalism which radically alter our perceptions and experiences of culture itself. Postmodernism is therefore a self-conscious shift, and is "unthinkable" without the notion of "some fundamental mutation of the sphere of culture in the world of late capitalism"; he also notes the "prodigious expansion of the realm of the 'cultural'" (1995: 47–48). Unlike the previous era of modernism, exemplified in our discussion of the Frankfurt School, there was a clear separation between 'high' and 'low' forms of art. In postmodernism, the separation becomes less distinct and while commodification expands into ever-new areas, the notion of 'culture' widens to incorporate new areas. Jameson describes this as the collapse of all distance, including critical distance, in the spaces of postmodernism (1995: 48). In this expanded notion of culture, consumption can be seen as *the* characteristic socio-cultural activity of postmodern or 'late' capitalism.

It was just such a notion of expanded culture that allowed Roland Barthes to perform a semiological analysis of some of the myths and objects of mass culture. This was the subject of his 1957 book *Mythologies*. His project as a critic of mass culture, unlike the Frankfurt School's harsh elitist dismissal, was to make explicit the "falsely obvious" through examination of the mass media such as advertising, to examine the mythologies underlying mass culture (1973: 11). By looking at such myths as the allure of Marilyn Monroe, or the shape of a Citroën car, he saw how modern myths within mass culture were manufactured. Barthes looked at the secondary signification of such cultural items, that is, looked at their connotations as opposed to the primary significations of the images and the advertisements themselves, to try and understand how 'myths' are produced for mass consumption. Myth becomes a way to make sense of our world, and as consumers of images and advertising we have developed ways of reading and understanding such myths, and are therefore complicit. The secondary significations, the connotations of the objects, do not arise from nowhere but from our existing "cultural repertoire", as Storey (1999: 28) puts it. The sexual allure of a blonde actress draws directly from the mythology of Marilyn Monroe, for example, which itself reaches back into other aspects of our cultural experience such as the notion of the *femme fatale*. But why talk of 'myth', exactly? A crucial property of myths is that they have no historical character, they lose the memory that they were once manufactured. Myths seem timeless, and things pass from history into the realm of nature by way of myth; mythologies put into circulation ideas that are 'cultural', that is, arise from culture, and make them understood as 'natural', as belonging to nature and always having been there. Without history things lose their depth, and this depthlessness is the concern of Jameson, as we have seen, and Baudrillard:

> In passing from history to nature, myth acts economically: it abolishes the complexity of human acts ... it organises a world which is without contradictions because it is without depth, a world wide open and wallowing in the evident, it establishes a blissful clarity: things appear to mean something by themselves.
>
> (Barthes 1973: 156)

Barthes also talked of the *polysemic* nature of signs, that is, the way signs may point to multiple things simultaneously. While we bring our ever-expanding cultural repertoire to advertisements, for example, we understand that some signs denote ideas or qualities directly, such as a flag that represents a country. But we are aware often of other connotations: the flag also symbolises the political ideology of the nation-state and/or imperialism, for example, and may signify pride or dismay accordingly. These connotations could not exist if we had no cultural repertoire, any experience of other signs and myths. The image or the advertisement not only draws from our cultural repertoire but also expands it, creating increasingly sophisticated mythologies in the process. This idea of the polysemic nature of signs, exemplified in Barthes's *Mythologies* and an analysis of the magazine *Paris Match* in an essay of

1955, is crucial in our readings of the manifold mediations of popular culture.

CONCLUSION: TOWARDS THE SYMBOLIC

Recapitulating what consumption is at this stage is helpful, as it widens the usual definition from an isolated act of purchasing to the larger cultural processes we have started discussing, and shifts the emphasis from consumption as a discreet set of economic decisions to that of an ongoing dialogue with others in a cultural context. Rapaport (1997) once described "culture as conversation", and consumption can be seen as another way of expressing oneself. For example, the anthropologists Douglas and Isherwood see consumption in this light, as a form of expression, "making visible and stable the categories of culture" (in Storey 1999: 42). This is to apportion to consumption more than mere imitation, or inclusion and exclusion from a group. Commodities become a symbolic means to communicate with others, to engage in that conversation of culture.

I wish to end this chapter by returning to an earlier theme, that of Marx's observations concerning consumption. In a frank and prescient passage in the *Communist Manifesto* of 1848, Marx considers the development of capitalism both positively and negatively, an important step in thinking about the development of capitalism as a dialectical process. This is to simultaneously acknowledge the demonstrably malevolent features of capitalism alongside its undeniably liberating dynamism. Might we not claim this for consumption and consumer culture in the same way? Both the development of capitalism and that of consumption can be thought "as catastrophe and progress all together", in Jameson's words (1995: 47). There is much to be said about the proliferation of dynamism and creativity throughout consumption in later chapters, and while it is important to understand culture and its performances in an expanded and non-elitist way, it is equally important to bear in mind the negative elements of a consumer culture that values inclusion, but inclusion at a cost – to the poor, to the environment, to social values of community and family, and much else besides. Thinking of the Frankfurt School and the creation of "false needs", of Jameson's "depthlessness", we are in danger of relinquishing important political ground at the level of individual and state. The fact is, there is never 'enough' attained. We cannot speak of a singular act of consumption without locating it in larger processes, but we also think of consumption as endlessly delayed or deferred gratification, a continuous process. McCracken (1988) talks of "displaced meaning" where objects represent bridges to meanings that cannot be attained easily in the here and now. Instead, they may be displaced onto a golden past, or even a bright hope for the future. Whichever, goods are thought of as bridges to displaced meanings – bridging that gap between present lived reality and the set of ideals one keeps in mind. The watch that makes us feel like James Bond, even though our wardrobe is more Bob Dylan. This need to aspire to a different social group through the purchase and display of commodities is immediately recognisable, and leads McCracken to describe such goods as bridges to displaced meaning, and this, he says, is the engine of consumption. Whether this is indicative of bleak emptiness, or allows the romantic individual to come through in us, will be the concern of the next chapter.

NOTE

1 Miller (1993) notes that 'consumerism' in the US is a consumer rights movement.

2

CONSUMPTION AND IDENTITY
MANUFACTURING CHOICE

INTRODUCTION

> Properly manipulated [...] American housewives can be given
> the sense of identity, purpose, creativity, the self-realization,
> even the sexual joy they lack – by the buying of things.
>> (Advertising executive, in Friedan 1965: 181)

> Man is initially posited as a private property owner whose
> exclusive ownership permits him both to preserve his person-
> ality and to distinguish himself from other men, as well as
> relate to them ... private property is man's personal, distin-
> guishing and hence essential existence.
>> (Marx, in Bourdieu 1986a: 280)

In this chapter we explore the perception of choice as we experience it in
everyday acts of consumption. Starting from this seemingly simple task,
we are simultaneously asking about the role of consumer choice in the
production of identities. More specifically, seeing as all of us are embodied
consumers who originate from, or have histories that encompass, different
locales of this planet, it necessarily entails the production of gendered and
ethnic identities. Again, we identify a long reach of interconnection
between everyday acts of consumption and larger processes of identity formation, between concrete choice and abstract identity. These connections,

for the purposes of this chapter, can be approached in two ways. Firstly, by examining the notion of *choice* and its centrality in our everyday experiences of consumption. Secondly, by considering the role of *identity* in acts of consumption, as either the expression of one's 'authentic' identity or, conversely, as the manipulation of consumer desire and aspiration, as in the last chapter's reflections on the generation of "false needs" by the mass culture industry. At the nexus of choice and identity, a brand's importance lies in its historical context as much as its current, taking the previous chapter's discussion of Veblen's theory of "conspicuous consumption" as a starting point. These two themes, of choice and identity, will be pursued throughout the chapter, and will break down like this:

Choice

The ability to choose from a range of products is predicated on the *distinction* between products, and what is unique within a product must be made to stand out. By choosing certain products over others we are exercising our judgement of *taste*, through which we articulate our sense of class, background, and cultural identity. Hence the connection between taste, identity, and everyday acts of consumption. The choice of particular products over others, the judgement of taste, is therefore derived from our family background and the way we have been socialised. Thus 'lifestyle', the exercise of judgements of taste and our choice of products, is a mechanism for expressing identity. Lifestyle has a decisive link with consumption as, at least in part, we define who we are through what we buy.

Cultural identity

Advertising has been described as the poetry of capitalism. If advertising constructs products in the minds of consumers, it requires the complicity of the mass media. It subsequently becomes translated into consumer choices at the level of everyday life. In this pluralisation of choice, what happens to the politics of cultural identity? Is culture always subordinated to economic ends? There are enormous implications in terms of race and cultural appropriation, and the gendered roles that consumption reinforces and maintains. We begin to answer these questions of cultural identity in this chapter by relating Bourdieu's notions of taste, lifestyle and habitus to youth consumption. Post-war British youth, for example, rejected the values of their parents and formed their identities and the expression of their own, distinct cultures through the public display of affluence and hedonism. Not simply a rejection of the dowdiness and austerity of their parents' generation, this association of conspicuous consumption with youthful vitality and individual expression solidifies for us the relation between consumption and identity. The book will pursue this later with reference to the relationships between consumption, authenticity, and racial and gendered representation. This is especially the case with brands, as will be seen in Chapter 8. What we hold to be truly 'authentic' is crucial in terms of our ownership and display of certain commodities, and to a large extent moulds how we are seen, and how we wish to be seen. Thus throughout this chapter I will be following Barker's distinction between *self-identity* and *social identity*. "The conceptions we hold of ourselves we may call self-identity," he explains, "while the expectations and opinions of others form our social identity" (2000: 165). At the heart of this chapter, then, is the exploration of how the purchase and display of certain commodities impacts on how we see ourselves, and how others see us.

Connecting up these notions of consumer choice, brand and cultural identity it will be useful initially to look at the work of Pierre Bourdieu, whose book *Distinction* (1986a) provides a sociological analysis of the

---

Fight Club: What kind of things define me as a person?

In the film *Fight Club* (USA, 1999, dir. David Fincher), the protagonist Tyler Durden is looking through an IKEA catalogue, ordering over the phone, and wondering: "What kind of plates define me as a person?"

The whole film has an acute anticonsumerist ethic, a roaring need to reconnect with the 'authentic'. With a wry tone the narrator announces: "We are products of lifestyle obsession. Murder, crime, poverty do not concern me. What concerns me are celebrity magazines, television with five hundred channels and a designer name on my underwear."

way that social groups form and maintain their identities by a process of distinguishing themselves from others, this process of distinction being performed through acts of consumption. Bourdieu's notion of distinction therefore bridges the last chapter's historical consideration of consumption as deeply structured with more current ideas of the brand, choice and cultural identity. Proceeding from Bourdieu's influential but largely class-based analysis, we will then consider more fluid, individual and expressive roles of consumption that take more account of the role of personal choice, rather than class-based expectations, in the formation of individual identities. Seeing consumption as more creative, as a way of performing particular cultural and ethnic identities in multifarious ways, is to argue against Bourdieu and for a more playful appropriation of commodities for our own ends. This chapter also starts to introduce the theme of the aestheticisation of everyday life, which will become increasingly prominent in later chapters.

Positional consumption

Before discussing Bourdieu in some depth, two aspects of the historical approach in the previous chapter will help establish a context. We can use Celia Lury's phrase "positional consumption" (1996: 46) to summarise this. Commodities are purchased and used as markers of social position by consumers who are defining their relative position in regard to other consumers. Veblen's theory of the new 'leisure class', discussed in the previous chapter, held this view. Veblen's observations of these *nouveaux riches* revealed their patterns of consumption to be based on marking a social position, as well as innovating in terms of fashion or style, and it was these aesthetic innovations, that is, stylistic considerations and fashion statements, that instantly marked out the really wealthy from the nearly wealthy; the old money from the *nouveaux riches*; or those who had positions of cultural influence, who could dictate taste and fashion, from slavish followers. As discussed in the previous chapter, Veblen assumed a model of social emulation, in which the dictators of fashion and innovation were emulated by those lower down the scale. Another articulation of this marking out a position is that of Simmel.

When Georg Simmel was describing the transformation of social life then occurring in the increasingly large and bustling metropolis of the early twentieth century, he noted that we develop a "blasé outlook" (1997: 72) not present in smaller towns or within village life. In his classic essay of 1903, 'The metropolis and mental life', he hypothesises that we become psychologically attuned or adapted to the increased speed, rhythm and intensity of the urban environment. As such, he argues, this process of the intensification of consciousness extends into consumption:

> This is why the metropolis is the seat of commerce and it is in it that the purchasability of things appears in quite a different aspect than in simpler economies. It is also the seat of the blasé attitude. In it is brought to a peak, in a certain way, that achievement of the concentration of purchasable things which stimulates the individual to the highest degree of nervous energy.
>
> (1997: 73)

Simmel is making important connections here between the urban environment, our psychic life, and the process of consumption and identity formation. The increased tempo and the over-stimulation of colours and sounds of the metropolis alters the way we perceive things – in more recent parlance, it alters our perceptual ecology (e.g. Gibson 1966; Ingold 2000) – and, instead of responding emotionally or politely to everyone walking past us, we take notice of things only insofar as they stand out, obtrude, are marked as different. Hence the stimulation by consumer goods ("purchasable things") in gaudy shop window displays. And in order to stand out, says Simmel, the way people dress and behave must be marked as different, too, and this is a particularly urban phenomenon. Styles of dress and behaviour are exaggerated, eccentricities are in abundance, as our meetings and encounters with others in the urban environment are so fleeting and fast. The display of eccentricities and extravagances through clothing and behaviour is "a form of 'being different' – of making oneself noticeable" (1997: 77). Relating this to our psychic life, the motivation for marking oneself out as 'different' arises not only as a result of the increased tempo and speed of perception in the urban environment, but as a way of asserting individuality, of maintaining self-esteem. This is especially so in the face of an increasingly indifferent and impersonal city, where the individual must struggle to assert themselves. As against the "impersonal cultural elements and existing goods and values" that constrain the individual's sense of unique identity and personality, "extremities and peculiarities and individualizations must be produced and they must be over-exaggerated merely to be brought into the awareness of the individual himself" (1997: 78). We get the sense here that, like the processes of natural selection, the metropolis encourages and amplifies the rapid development of markers of difference, to reassert individuality in the face of an impersonal environment, and to become noticed. This is an important theme in the formation of cultural identity through consumption, the subject of a later section.

In the same way, we can see 'lifestyle' as a set of positional markers that define a social group and that mark difference from other groups, with different lifestyles, through the use and display of consumer goods (e.g. foods, clothes, carpets, scooters) and cultural goods (e.g. music, art, film). As we started to argue in the previous chapter, this is a move from the economic and strictly material to the symbolic, or as Baudrillard (1988) puts it, from the logic of production to the logic of signification, from use-value or material utility to sign-values. This is a relatively recent move, as Hirsch (1977) has noted. Historically, only elites could (literally) afford to exhibit positional consumption, so the democratisation of positional consumption occurs especially after the Second World War. The uneasy transition from wartime austerity to the post-scarcity economics of mass consumption necessarily produces ripples through the cultural fabric of developed Western economies.[1]

Subsequently, in a post-war boom economy of mass-produced and standardised goods, consumption becomes competitive. As was noted in Chapter 1, what were previously classified as 'wants' suddenly become 'needs', and this was facilitated by the shift in the organisation of capitalism from Fordism to post-Fordism. In the escalation of wants into needs, the separation of luxuries from necessities must be maintained, and this can only happen in stable societies. As Mary Douglas notes, any consumer society is competitive and the way we signal to others is through how we consume – and this relies on the maintenance of some distinction between luxury and necessity:

> The truth is that consumerism is a highly competitive way of living, in which everything must be dragged in to the purpose of pleasing a client or ally. Competitive consumerism needs luxuries all the time for

a rational deployment of resources. Competition needs to tear down community boundaries, to expand the range of its dealings. There is no surprise that it scoffs at the restraints on spending as well as the disciplines of the body which keep consumption within bounds.

(Douglas 2003: 149)

Douglas's anthropological perspective is resolutely recognisable here, and future chapters will look at the notions of restraint and excess, of the discipline and transgression of the body in consumption. The distribution of luxuries and necessities, effected through the "rational deployment of resources" within a society, is significant for us in terms of both social emulation and positional consumption. That is, through our display and conspicuous consumption of particular luxury goods we indicate our identities and aspirations. After the Second World War, the brand functioned increasingly as a marker of taste, of social identity and aspiration. The importance of the brand for global capitalism will be discussed in detail in Chapter 8, but in terms of the nexus between choice, identity and, increasingly, ethnicity, the section 'Identity through consumption' (below) will explore further theories and examples.

Moving from a logic of production to a logic of signification might entail, however, that signs flatten out, are splayed or displayed before us. The endless production and consumption of signs would seem to promote the "depthlessness" that Jameson (1995) proclaims. MTV, youth television and its new rhetorics of the image seem to flicker and entrance like the magic lanterns of the nineteenth century, as depthless images whirl past at breakneck speed. Baudrillard's hyperbole goes further, later, declaring there is a potentially infinite play of signs, and as members of society we become merely carriers of those signs. This is one symptom of what he calls the "implosion of the social" (1994a, especially pp. 100–102). As you may be able to surmise, Baudrillard's writing on consumption is equally flawed and fascinating. Some of this will be appraised later, especially in Chapter 9 which concerns the postmodern consumer. The point concerning the infinite play of signs is raised here, however, to warn of the potential danger of ignoring the concrete actualities underlying those acts of consuming and bearing signs. As embodied beings, brute economics hits us in our homes and places of repose, materially affecting our bodily processes through the foods we eat and the clothes we can barely afford to wear. Our income level, our gender and our ethnicity impose restraints and alter our potential to participate in this free play of signs. Before celebrating the implosion of the social, therefore, we need to grasp in what ways the work of consumption is performed by particular social groups, in what ways identity is formed and performed therein.

BOURDIEU: TASTE AND 'DISTINCTION'

The work of the distinguished French sociologist Pierre Bourdieu (1930–2002) would be an ideal bridge between historical theories of consumption and more recent discussions of a "new consumer sensibility" that is based on 'lifestyle' (e.g. Hebdige 1988; Featherstone 1991a). Bourdieu's strong influence on social theory in general, and the relevance of his work on consumption in particular, will be discussed in this chapter along two lines. Firstly, his ideas about distinction, with the theoretical and empirical investigation of how commodities become markers of taste or distinction between groups. Secondly, and corresponding to concerns of everyday life in this book, his notion of 'habitus' and how that helps shape and determine lifestyle and patterns of consumption.

Habitus and lifestyle

Bourdieu's *Distinction* (1986a) is a long, involved study that merges Marx's and Veblen's strong concern with social class. From Marx he draws on the structural distinction between classes, but from Veblen he draws on the desire to display distinction. However, Bourdieu makes these class distinctions more supple by distinguishing between two forms of capital, *economic capital* (pay, monetary value) and *cultural capital* (status, societal value). Certain professions, such as teachers or college lecturers, are accorded a higher status in society than their pay and consumption patterns would suggest. At least in France, teachers and lecturers enjoy a relatively high level of cultural capital, while receiving a lower level of economic capital. In Britain, plumbers are the reverse, enjoying a relatively high level of economic capital but not achieving the influence, respect or status that cultural capital entails. Bourdieu thinks that cultural capital, while often related to economic capital, is fostered within the *lifestyle* of a class ("class fraction").

Lifestyle, the choice of products and the desire for certain goods, is not simply a function of high or low income. It is generated from the *habitus*, the way that the perception of the social world is structured. Therefore, social distinction does not derive from social class directly, but is the result of socialisation into a way of life, the 'habitus'. Bourdieu here refers to a "systematicity" (1986a: 173), arguing that lifestyles are *systematic* products of habitus, that is, habitus is a system through which we surround ourselves with, and desire, certain objects according to our perceptions of the social world. The habitus is therefore manifested in an orientation to the present, through surrounding oneself with certain objects and not others. It is also manifested in the future, such as the way certain groups stress instant gratification over delayed gratification.

From the habitus of an individual, based on their socialisation into a group that has certain tastes and is manifested in a certain lifestyle, cultural objects are acquired or consumed. Things that indicate social position or status, which require being knowledgeable or a connoisseur, the acquisition of such cultural objects needs time. This pursuit of *distinction* is a "pure, pointless expenditure" says Bourdieu (1986a: 280)

Figure 2.1 One of the supreme pleasures of life? Picking olive oils.

SHOPPERS PICK OLIVES

OLIVE oil is outselling Britain's traditional cooking oils for the first time.

Analysts say foreign travel and a hunger for healthier options helped the Mediterranean favourite overtake the lower-priced vegetable and sunflower-based products.

The Italian-made Filippo Berio brand is now the country's best-selling cooking oil, with old favourite Crisp 'N Dry second. Six other brands in the top ten are all from the Mediterranean.

Source: *Daily Mail*, 2 August 2004, p. 11. 2004, Associated Newspapers Ltd.

which shores up cultural capital, enhancing social status and prestige, but taking time and taste, discernment.

Let us take the example of the consumption of olive oil (see the newspaper extracts). The cook Elizabeth David once described olive oil as "one of the supreme pleasures of life" (in Townsend 2000), and its popularity certainly seems to be symptomatic of a general trend to develop a more sophisticated, more Mediterranean, healthier lifestyle. But it is not necessarily a function of *class* whether you buy olive oil, or a particular brand, or whether you simply buy cheaper vegetable oil. It is a function of the *habitus*, the way of perceiving and negotiating the social world, so that our choice of olive oil over vegetable oil derives from being socialised into choosing the supposedly healthier option. This taste for a more expensive and supposedly healthier product is not simply related to level of income. Bourdieu argues that it is *taste* rather than high or low *income* which structures the practices associated with consuming such resources, and that, depending on one's position within a system based on identifying oneself with a social group and distinguishing oneself from others, this generates a set of 'choices' that constitute 'lifestyles' (1986a: 175). Choosing olive oil over vegetable oil is a choice that indicates an orientation to future health as opposed to instant gratification, is a matter of taste in that it is a luxury rather than a necessity, and so is a choice of the more 'knowing', healthy consumer. By putting olive oil in our shopping basket, we instantly join the more select, knowing body of consumers with a sensible and healthy

OLIVE OIL – IT'S A SLIPPERY ISSUE

DO WE REALLY NEED TO KEEP FIVE DIFFERENT TYPES IN THE CUPBOARD? ANNIE BELL REPORTS

Until recently, we're reminded, we had to rely on the chemist for ear-drops to drizzle over our bruschette. Now, according to the marketing message, our salvation lies in embracing the rich diversity of olive oil.

Bertolli now sells a range of no less than five olive oils, each for a different purpose, in the UK. Hang on, at the last count we only needed three. Now we're told: "No Italian kitchen has just one olive oil that is used for everything, three is the absolute minimum but for preference, five is the perfect number." This oily proclamation is echoed by the UK-based company Beluza, which is promoting three regional extra virgin olive oils. One is "ideal for fish, vegetables and carpaccio", another for "grilled vegetables or use in marinades", and yet another is good for "soups, casseroles and perfect for grilling and roasting meat".

Source: from the *Independent* (London), 28 April © 2001, p. 17. 2001, Newspaper Publishing PLC.

lifestyle, as opposed to those with a less healthy lifestyle. *We* sauté our potatoes in olive oil; *they* fry their chips in vegetable fat.

Once a luxury product in the UK, the consumption of olive oil on a large scale is a relatively recent phenomenon, and even more recent is the proliferation of different brands and types of olive oil that expand into niche luxury markets. Once a generic but luxury product, particular brands and types (virgin, extra virgin) say much about our social position and the place of being knowledgeable about foodstuffs, and indicate some more general tendencies in consumption. Such tendencies include, but are not limited to: our increasing awareness of foodstuffs' locales and places of origin, which goes hand in hand with the gastronomic component of tourism (gastro-tourism); the increased sophistication in terms of flavours, textures and taste that comes from familiarity and discernment at home and away, which takes time and money; and apportioning a relatively larger amount of income on luxury goods, especially luxury foodstuffs, in certain sections of society. One final general tendency, discussed further in the following section, is an increasingly sophisticated awareness by the consumer of brands and their role in the construction of specific or aspirational lifestyles, and thus in the formation of cultural identity.

Habitus, lifestyle, and the effects on the body

Bourdieu's observations on distinction, taste and lifestyle are not limited to class-based observations concerning consumption, as we have seen, but incorporate the larger perceptions of, and interactions within, the social world. Hence there are real, concrete effects on bodies that result from these perceptions and interactions, ways of being socialised. The pursuit of distinction, the development of taste, is not only conceptual but also corporeal. In describing the consumption of those cultural objects signifying a bourgeois lifestyle, for example, he points to something of the range of these other corporeal and stylistic effects:

> In the ordinary situations of bourgeois life, banalities about art, literature or cinema are inseparable from the steady tone, the slow, casual diction, the distant or self-assured smile, the measured gesture, the well-tailored suit and the bourgeois salon of the person who pronounces them.
>
> (1986a: 174)

Similarly, one's taste in food is reflected in, and literally incorporated into, each class or class fraction's idea of the body. Not only in terms of gait or posture (erect and proud versus sloping and slovenly), but in terms of body shape. This is in part the accumulated effects of foodstuffs of various kinds, alongside movement and posture, and so the culture of the body, its health, strength and beauty, is affected by these factors, and alters between class fractions with their different notions of habitus. "Taste, a class culture turned into nature, that is *embodied*, helps to shape the class body" (1996: 192, original emphasis). It is a materialisation of class taste, the literal incorporation of attitudes to caring for and treating the body, the attitude to healthy or unhealthy lifestyles, the accumulated acceptance of some bodily postures and movements over others.

To massively simplify, the class body will be shaped and act differently according to whether you eat Crisp'n'Dry or virgin olive oil.

Bourdieu's study has allowed us to consider some key concepts in consumption, providing a platform from which to investigate further the dynamics of identity and choice within larger structures of family background, socialisation and class. The implications of Bourdieu's notion of 'taste' and 'lifestyle' we can summarise as threefold. Firstly, by analysing taste as a pursuit of distinction from other social groups it suggests that the field of consumption is not as open to us as some would claim. Our taste in commodities is in large part structured by our need to distinguish ourselves from other consumers. Secondly, and related to this, our social class and groupings already structure how we consume and the knowledge we bring to it. The element of choice is then diminished to a function of our class background, and we are less likely to choose a commodity outside of the perceived range of products appropriate to our habitus. Referring back to the olive oil example, Volvo owners are more likely to buy branded olive oil than Crisp'n'Dry. Finally, and as a consequence of this, cultural hierarchies and subordination are perpetuated as a result.

The above limitations point to an overly structural analysis. Bourdieu's notion of 'taste' points towards those socially observable ways in which we do cultural work, by individuating ourselves within a chosen cultural group, and through differentiating ourselves from other such groups. Yet we have seen how the ability to articulate our notions of identity may be limited by factors such as social class. Unlike Veblen's new leisure class, post-war consumption has departed from a singular model of social aspiration. There are other, less structuralist articulations of consumption and identity that allow more playful, ironic or creative ways of actively choosing commodities, or choose to use them in different, sometimes unintended, ways. Featherstone's discussion of 'lifestyle' has pointed in this direction, and we will continue on this path.

'Lifestyles'

Following on from Bourdieu's observations about the role of lifestyle and taste in the formation of the body and its habits, shape and attitudes, we arrive at a more expanded notion of 'lifestyle', no longer based in class structures but more readily reflecting the shifts and transformations of identity and consumption occurring within the social sphere. Featherstone writes of this more marketing-led, familiar notion of 'lifestyle' that derives from post-war affluence and increased consumption amongst different age groups and across classes. This notion of lifestyle is not fixed to certain classes or fixed social groups, but is indicative of a more fluid notion of a style of life, the aestheticisation of everyday life through the consumption of certain commodities over others:

> The term 'life-style' is currently in vogue [...] within contemporary con-
> sumer culture it connotes individuality, self-expression, and a stylistic
> self-consciousness. One's body, clothes, speech, leisure pastimes, eat-
> ing and drinking preferences, home, car, choice of holidays, etc. are to
> be regarded as indicators of the individuality of taste and sense of style
> of the owner/consumer. In contrast to the designation of the 1950s as
> an era of grey conformism, a time of *mass* consumption, changes in
> production techniques, market segregation, and consumer demand
> for the wider range of products, are often regarded as making possible
> greater choice [...] We are moving towards a society *without fixed sta-
> tus groups* in which the adoption of styles of life (manifest in choice of
> clothes, leisure activities, consumer goods, bodily disposition) which
> are fixed to specific groups have been surpassed.
>
> (Featherstone 1991b: 83, my emphasis)

Here, then, is the nexus between lifestyle, choice and identity as per-formed through the consumption and display of particular purchasable goods. The acknowledgement that our identity owes less to structured class groups, as Bourdieu would have it, and more to our choices and patterns of consumption that are more fleeting, capricious, ephemeral, is significant. We consume less to mark out our fixed social position, therefore, and more to indicate our aspirations, our intentions, our social trajectories at that time. Lifestyles then are no longer "macro-social phe-nomena of marketing lore", or even class structure, but become "an expression of continuous social change and the development of unrei-fied, affective groupings" (Shields 1992: 14).

Nevertheless, the more flexible definition of lifestyles still places emphasis on two concepts that are contiguous with Bourdieu, taste and cultural capital. As will be pursued in more detail within the spatial context of the shopping mall (in Chapter 7, concerning the spaces of consumption), malls are hothouses of social groupings based less on fixed, shared background or class structure, and more on shifting, shared feelings, affinities or identifications. As Langman (1992: 58) shows, adolescents in particular find in malls a space free from the scrutiny of parents or teachers, and social groups cohere through a common definition of 'cultural capital', becoming temporal subcultures that are based on consumer tastes – the right kind of clothes, trainers, tattoos, sports equipment, and so on:

> In contemporary consumption sites it is hypothesized that new modes of subjectivity (at the level of the person), interpersonal relationships (at the level of the group) and models of social totality are being experimented with, 'browsed through' and 'tried on' in much the same way that one might shop for clothes.
>
> (Shields 1992: 15)

CONSUMPTION, AUTHENTICITY AND IDENTITY

One of the pervasive attitudes to consumption in academic circles is disdain, scepticism, the sense that – almost by definition – consumption is opposed to *authenticity*. The previous chapter highlighted the history of theorising consumption and marked out the Frankfurt School in particular as an influence that was highly sceptical of the generation of "false needs" by consumer capitalism. But the argument that buying consumer goods or services only further alienates the consumer from the rest of society only holds so much water. Danny Miller for example has labelled as myth the idea that consumption is opposed to authenticity, because "new, unprecedented forms of cultural difference" may be as significant or authentic as existing forms (1993: 25). Often, culture cannibalistically consumes and reinvents itself, such as in the Renaissance pastiche of classical styles in art and architecture. An essay by Trevor-Roper in *The Invention of Tradition* (1983) rather intriguingly examines how the Victorians reinvented older traditions and made them their own, thereby complicating the question of what is truly 'authentic'. The familiar call of cultural critics is that the exercise of irrational or fantastic desires through acts of consumption is unprecedented, as if there has been a decline from an earlier state of use-value or necessity. This is a staple element of Marxist cultural critique, discussed in the previous chapter as the myth of a prelapsarian society pre-existing the onset of capitalism. Miller, being an anthropologist, points out that rarely are objects valued for their functionality alone. In Melanesian society, for example, the decoration of pots suggests effort is expended in the crafting of an object that extends beyond mere use-value. Instead, he asserts that it is the *abstraction* of pure function, the idea that things can be separated into their use-value and exchange-value, that is unprecedented (1993: 26). In other words, for us to posit an idea of the use-value of an object, this is itself a Western economic abstraction from the manifold meanings and significances that a crafted item accrues within a material culture. Admittedly, the phenomenon of *over*-consumption, especially in more developed Western societies, the stimulus to consume above one's means, may be unmatched in other societies.

In a range of economies and societies, therefore, what is generally undeniable is the way that objects have a cultural significance along with their purposeful utility. Hence we refer to them as cultural objects. We can shift the focus of questions of authenticity then to the context of social groups, to the centrality of the formation of 'lifestyle' as opposed to 'class', as Bourdieu has done. To return to the theme of positional consumption at the beginning of this chapter, with the increasingly fluid formations of cultural identities in post-war society, individuals move from one subcultural group to another, and consumption – *the* characteristic socio-cultural activity of postmodern capitalism, according to Jameson (1995) – is the positional marker within that subcultural group. Contrasted to this are the mutually exclusive patterns of consumption and leisure practices that are separate and distinct, typical of modernity thinks Bocock (1993: 81). Thus, rather than thinking about consumption as a positional marker of relative wealth and display, that is, Veblen's idea of conspicuous consumption, we can think of consumption as a marker of status and position within a loosely formed social group. Consumption functions not as the enforcement of the separation of the means of production from the display of consumption, hence asserting one's status through affluence and expenditure *per se*. In this model it functions instead as the display of cultural objects that indicate one's social position or cultural style within a group, consumers defining their own position in regard to other consumers (see Lury 1996: 46).

To have *is* to be ...?

Of necessity, therefore, material possessions have come to signify identity so that, at least for modern Western societies, *to have* is *to be* (Lury
1996, after Dittmar 1992). Referring back to pre-industrial societies
and their circuits of reciprocity and exchange of material goods, the
anthropologists Mary Douglas and Baron Isherwood examine the importance of material goods (cultural objects) as meaningful markers of
social relations, considering the historical continuity between pre-industrial and industrial societies (1979). Summarising their work, Lury
remarks that: "It is in acquiring, using and exchanging things that individuals come to have social lives" (1996: 12). Elsewhere, Douglas has
written about the "semiotic richness" of objects, notwithstanding how
the artistry and eccentricity of commodities must fit within the framework of the community. Objects are coded, she says, and this affects all
consumption within that community:

> Everyday objects are minutely graded to their uses. Special objects are
> endowed with semiotic richness and their consumption is hedged
> with rules, so that they can mark the occasions that the community
> celebrates itself. The objects are coded, and to know the coding is to
> claim membership. This is the basis of the tyranny which embeds
> every consumption choice in a communication system.
>
> (Douglas 2003: 148)

The 'tyranny' that she speaks of is that of the surveillance of neighbours
who ensure that the coded objects are used appropriately within the
communication system.

 If the movement of goods in this way becomes part of a larger social
system of symbolic exchange, cultural objects imbue their owners with
particular characteristics by virtue of the relations of ownership, and
this is what enhances the desirability and therefore exchangeability of an
object. Social bonds between individuals in groups, and between groups
themselves, are cemented in this way. This core mechanism is central to
notions of the cultural value of the object, authenticity and cultural
identity, especially so in late capitalism. The additional factor here is an
increasingly reflexive awareness of social identity and self-identity. The
individual in late capitalism becomes the "possessive individual", where

relations to material property are based on individualised rather than collective conceptions of the acquisition and ownership of objects. As Dittmar explains,

> in Western materialistic societies ... an individual's identity is influenced by the symbolic meanings of his or her own material possessions, and the way in which he/she relates to those possessions. Material possessions also serve as expressions of group membership and as means of locating others in the social-material environment. Moreover, material possessions provide people with information about other peoples' identities.
>
> (1992: 205)

Lury goes on to argue that our increasingly reflexive relations to self-identity are accelerated by the development of so-called 'expert knowledges'. There are numerous examples: the increasing proliferation of fashion and lifestyle magazines, the popularity of makeovers and makeover television shows, whether for the home, the garden, the body or the face. Magazines that tell us how to dress to impress, that contain fashion tips and cosmetics advice, penetrate into many areas of readership, to teenager level (e.g. *Sugar* magazine's tagline: 'Britain's no. 1 teen mag') and below. The tendency for expert knowledges to encroach upon many material and social aspects of our lifestyles goes beyond mere buying advice. A recent trend has been for 'life coaches', the practice of employing experts to turn one's life around, to make us healthier, happier, fitter, more competitive (see e.g. Ballinger 2003). In almost Veblerian style, a practice employed by celebrities and the extremely wealthy is now available for the rest of us. Thus our lifestyle, an area of experience in which previously we were in command of our practices of consumption and display, itself becomes commodified, available for purchase.

The acceleration of the commodification of aspects of our experience continues. As we shall see in Chapter 4, 'Bodyshopping', consumption

ADVERTISEMENT FOR 'LIFE COACH':
"Are you ready for a healthier, happier, easier life?"
(reallifecoach.com)

engages not only with consumer goods or consumer services, but also with the buying and selling of actual experiences, and, as in the advertisement above, guidance for ways of life. This process is going increasingly from the tangible commodity or consumer object to the intangible services that companies provide, to the marketing and selling of actual embodied experiences such as travel and tourism, or the pristine freshness of an Indonesian river when using a particular facewash or shampoo.

Earlier this chapter we asked: What makes things stand out or obtrude, given the "blasé outlook" that Simmel had identified in the early twentieth-century metropolis? In the fast-paced, anonymous city, what makes our 'true' selves and our personalities come across to strangers, given a shortness of attention and accelerated perception? By making the uncontroversial suggestion that material possessions have a symbolic value within a culture, we have begun to see how our social status and identity within a group is formed through the consumption and display of certain objects that have cultural significance. Whether this indicates our status as ruler or as farmworker, the objects we have and display communicate to ourselves and others our status; that is, our sense of *self*-identity and *social* identity, following Barker (2000). From Adidas to Bhangra Beat and beyond, there are innumerable stories to tell about consumption and identity, since whether we live in pre-industrial or late capitalist societies, our identities are irrevocably intertwined with the exchange and display of commodities. But some groundwork has been done here that will form the basis of later explorations concerning identity, ethnicity and the hotly contested notion of 'authenticity'. We will then be in a position to proffer conclusions about the role of consumption in the formation and maintenance of cultural identities, and return to some questions raised in the previous chapter about the mass culture industry and its engineering of values and design, versus our creative appropriation of products as a form of resistance. So we will revisit this territory to make a bridge between the notion of *buying into* lifestyle and identity politics, and the notion of 'appropriation' in Chapter 6. In the next section, the first story concerning cultural identity and commodities is historical, reintroducing the mass consumer after the Second World War and charting the emergence of youth cultures and therefore of a distinct youth identity. This will be followed up in Chapter 8 ('Logo or no logo?'), where a detailed examination of the role of brands and branding in the formation of identity, along with our allegiances and appropriations of them, will build on observations in this chapter concerning the semiotic richness of commodities and our identifications with them.

A QUESTION OF IDENTITY?

This chapter started with how lifestyle and the variability of taste is a function of the habitus, the particular perceptions we are socialised into. We have seen how, for Bourdieu, the habitus informs our choice of certain products or brands over others, and leads us to pursue particular lifestyles as a result. We have also considered the way that material possessions become indicators of particular lifestyles, and how this communicates meaning and therefore social identity to others. Our position within a certain social group, and a group's position in relation to another group, is articulated through the consumption and display of certain key objects with symbolic value. Therefore a major way that both self-identity and social identity is established and maintained is through the consumption of particular goods and services, and this was particularly noticeable in newly emerging youth cultures after the Second World War (see Chapter 6). By looking at the history of consumption, as we have been doing in the past two chapters, we can identify a long historical arc that reaches back to pre-industrial societies, where gift exchange and unnecessary or even excessive expenditure was the assurance of social status and power within a social collective, as in Bataille's "accursed share" (especially 1991: 38). This historical arc continues with the maintenance of status and identity through other, more sophisticated but equally excessive forms of symbolic and commodity exchange.

But I wish to conclude with a major question concerning identity that will find resolution in later chapters, but which is nevertheless important to introduce here. For while the axiom 'to have is to be' would suggest that any notion of identity expressed through acts of consumption is necessarily shallow or unfixed, the opposite pole of fixity and authenticity is still meaningful. It will re-emerge as extremely significant in later considerations of branding and identity. The point here is that we bring forth another dialectic, since our notions of the attainment and maintenance of status, of position, of self- and social identity, are at once based on an assumption of *flux*, in that identity can be altered or changed as we wish, and *fixity*, in that there is a 'we' or an individual self that does the choosing or wishing. In our habitual, everyday consciousness this dialectic is unproblematic, since we will and act according to assumptions of a continuous sense of self that may be transformed or altered over time. But let's continue this logic further. Bourdieu's habitus was limiting, based on an imposition on our everyday actions and lifestyle choices of class structure. Douglas had shown the rigidity of the rules of commodity exchange in pre-industrial cultures, and the difficulty of transgressing appropriate boundaries. In an age of mass production and mass consumption, though, we are supposedly free to identify with smaller and less permanent subcultural groups, to shift our allegiances. By doing so we may escape pre-given and entrenched forms of identity and, in the words of Stuart Hall, the Enlightenment notion of the rational, "fully centred, unified individual" (1992: 275). Hall then goes on to postulate:

> The subject assumes different identities at different times, identities which are not unified around a coherent 'self'. Within us are contradictory identities, pulling in different directions, so that our identifications are continually being shifted about. If we feel that we have a unified identity from birth to death, it is only because we construct a comforting story or 'narrative of the self' about ourselves.
>
> (1992: 277)

Yet to what extent are we finding our 'true' selves, our 'real' identity, as opposed to pursuing temporary affinities with tribes or groups, when buying a skateboard or donning an Armani suit? By buying into distinct subcultures, are we not forming our own narratives of the self, effectively accomplished through the choice of a particular lifestyle and the exercise of taste in certain goods? This question is of enormous significance, not only in terms of the relation between consumption and identity but also in terms of authenticity, the feeling of a 'real' identity being especially pertinent in the case of ethnicity, origin, and the sense of belonging to deeply held cultural roots. As we shall be exploring in later chapters, new identities may be bought and worn as if trying outfits on at the mall, to be discarded later (Shields 1992: 15). But in such a case, you are *not* what you wear.

Having raised this deeper question concerning identity at this late stage, it is only fair to gesture towards ways of answering this. Being irrevocably intertwined with the practices of consumption, questions of identity will recur throughout later chapters in different ways. The particular issues of youth and identity will be treated in Chapter 6, 'The knowing consumer?', since nowhere is the consumer paradox of innovation and trend-setting more evident than in youth subcultures, yet these are the most co-opted and targeted by marketing and advertising. The shifting patterns of identity and neo-tribes within different spaces will be continued in Chapter 7, 'Mallrats and car boots', where identities and allegiances shift between home, school and shopping mall. The important relation between 'authenticity' and identity will be raised with particular respect to brands and logos, certain brands heavily involving the politics of ethnicity. This will be covered in Chapter 8, 'Logo or no logo?'.

The following chapter, however, deals not with identities as such but with 'McDisneyfications', the set of increasingly homogeneous logics of rationalisation that answer our needs for predictability in our experiences of consumption. Such diverse areas of consumption as fast-food restaurants, theme parks, DIY stores, shopping malls, supermarkets and the rest become spaces that are increasingly regulated and homogeneous, attempting to provide the consumer with a similar experience whether in Boston or Beijing.

NOTE

1 The language of 'West' and the 'Rest' is problematic, and I do not subscribe to the dichotomy of the 'Global North' and 'Global South' either, since Australasia also embodies democratic, Judaeo-Christian economic values and ideals. Hence I revert to the 'West' as a less inadequate term, which nevertheless indicates the legacy of Euro-American industrial capitalism and its expansion elsewhere.

3

McDISNEYFICATIONS

OR, HOW WE STOPPED HATING AMERICAN IMPERIALISM AND EMBRACED MASS CONSUMER CULTURE

INTRODUCTION: THE STARBUCKS EFFECT™

In an episode of *The Simpsons*, 10-year-old Bart goes to the Springfield Mall to get his ear pierced. His friend Millhouse had sparked this latest fashion trend, garnering the adoration of fellow pupils, and Bart cannot stand being upstaged. As he walks through the mall, he passes one Starbucks after another, including a store that is clearly being renovated with a sign posted in the window saying: 'Soon to open: Starbucks'. Finally reaching the piercing emporium, its owner asks Bart whether he is 18. Bart lies in the affirmative, and the owner then says: "Well, better make it quick, kiddo. In five minutes this place is becoming a Starbucks." In the next scene Bart walks out of the store, his ear sporting a shiny stud, a satisfied smile on his face, carrying a cup of Starbucks coffee. While a humorous example, anxieties about the spread of multinational corporations into local spaces, and a more general homogenisation of cultures through the spread of mainly American commodities and ways of consuming, are of great concern. As a way into these sprawling and complex issues and anxieties, and with a little irony, we can term this the 'Starbucks effect™'.

What has Starbucks done to feature like this? As consumers we are aware of the effects of multinational corporations and their globalised trade networks, and can see on our local high streets and in our out-of-town shopping centres and malls that the front line is everywhere. The history of consumption (surveyed in Chapter 1) has tended to see mass consumption as a response to 'false needs' created by the mass culture industry. With increasing amounts of trade, advertising and marketing at the global level, the effects on the local are often held to be negative, as homogenising, flattening out local differences and identities in favour of bold, new, brash, and predominantly American values and products. Hebdige (1988) for example looks at the early importation of McDonalds restaurants in Britain in the context of a longer historical fear of global homogenisation, of Americanization. However, other aspects of food, culture and displacement will be considered to puncture some of the myths of globalisation and simplistic understandings of 'McDonaldization' (Ritzer 1993, 1996, 1998).

For the purposes of this chapter I conflate two notions, McDonaldization and Disneyization, into one term, 'McDisneyfication', to describe and critique the effects of globalised production and everyday consumption of commodities and experiences. Therefore, a considerable proportion of the chapter will build towards this. The reader must be warned that a variety of similar-sounding terms are employed throughout, with some combination of 'Mc-' and 'Disney' being prevalent. However, these concepts are often distinct, sometimes allied and sometimes opposed, sometimes critical or pejorative and sometimes merely descriptive or observational. The first section, 'McTheory', will describe some continuities with previous theorisations of consumption, focusing in particular on the sociological legacy of Max Weber, whose infamous "iron cage" of rationalisation was clearly the inspiration for Ritzer's McDonaldization thesis. This section sets the groundwork for considering myths about globalisation being equated with homogenisation. In the following section we then engage directly with definitions and analysis of Ritzer's 'McDonaldization', assessing the strengths and limitations of a model that seems to capture the sociological imagination. Subsequently, we see how Ritzer and Liska extend this, and Bryman aids them significantly, into the notion of 'Disneyization'. We are then able to come up with a more developed account of something that combines the good business sense of modernist rationalism found in McDonaldization with the creation of themed experiences within new Disneyised spaces of consumption. So, rather than speak of 'McDisneyization', which Ritzer and Liska (1997) coin but do not significantly develop, instead I use the term 'McDisneyfication'. The term is employed as a logical development of McDonaldization, combining it with Disneyization, and noting its ability to be applied to a number of different contexts. This will be especially useful for the following chapter on the consumption of nature in theme parks, shopping malls and on safari.

To aid this project, in the final section we regard the dialectic of local and global production and consumption within our everyday experience in terms of 'Globa-cola' or 'Loca-cola?'. Whether we drink Coke, Pepsi or bottled water, it is extremely likely that the products we habitually imbibe and consume have rich histories that utilise ingredients from around the world and that touch on international networks of distribution and exchange. Considering this dialectic of local and global (or 'glocalisation'), we reach the heart of the debate raised in previous discussions of McDonaldization and Disneyization, about the homogenisation and heterogenisation of global culture. These discussions will aid the comprehension of other elements of consumption and everyday life elsewhere in the book, including the consumption of nature and experience in tourism (Chapter 5), the ubiquity of the globalised, homogeneous retail space of the mall (Chapter 7), and the ubiquity of the global brand and the logo (Chapter 8).

McTHEORY – RATIONALISATION, PRODUCTION AND CONSUMPTION

A difficulty with some modern, popular sociological theory is that the notion of an all-inclusive system of rationality and bureaucracy keeps recurring. But it was the German sociologist Max Weber (1864–1920) who first prophetically spoke of the "iron cage" of bureaucracy, and foresaw the extension of processes of rationalisation into ever-new areas of modern life. For Weber, the larger private corporations operate a type of bureaucracy "rivalled only by the state bureaucracy in promoting rational efficiency, continuity of operation, speed, precision, and calculation of results" (1970: 49). Both Weber and Simmel saw a major characteristic of modernity as this process of rationalisation, "formal and objectifying systems of administration, control and calculation, by quantification, methodicity and rules", explains Slater (1997: 117). Combined, these work as a coherent and pervasive form of rationalisation that we effortlessly recognise, applicable to areas in modern life as diverse as industrial production (the automotive industry), the provision of services (transport companies' timetabling and route-planning, immigration control), cultural production (fast-food culture, sportswear) and the provision of experiences (theme parks, videogames).

Fordism

With what Gramsci (1971) had termed "Fordism", in the era of Henry Ford's automobile, the industrial production of commodities was straightforward. The mainstay was mass production and standardisation, making the same standard product repeatedly in exactly the same way – the production line. From 1908–1927, over 15 million Model 'T' Fords were made. Workers were paid a respectable wage, so were able for the first time to purchase the commodities they manufactured. Standardisation meant that costs were kept down, and significantly the automobile was no longer a luxury item but within the reach of some industrial workers. Standardisation of the production process, and rationalisation of labour through the production line, meant every car within the Ford factory in Michigan was built to exactly the same specification, including even the colour. Henry Ford had joked, "People can have the Model T in any color – so long as it's black." Consumers were unsophisticated, assumed to need or desire the product. Technical innovations on the production line increased output, minimised expenditure on materials and labour, and therefore maximised profit. Any tailoring of output was not to accommodate consumer preferences or tastes, but simply to increase efficiency and maximise output. The famous example of innovation in efficiency is Taylor's measuring of human movements through time and motion studies, which tracked the movements of workers over time and tried to 'rationalise' them, reducing unnecessary movements and operations in order to maximise speed and efficiency. The result was an almost brutal machine logic applied to human labourers, thought Gramsci (1971: 306–307), to make the human worker more like a "human robot" (Ritzer 1996: 103; Latham 2002), an appendage to the industrial machine. Marx of course had realised the exploitation of human labour in industrial production in *Capital*. In Part II he also observed that as production becomes more automated, the role of the worker shifts, from labouring to actually produce commodities to over-seeing the production process.

Post-Fordism

Latterly, the transition from the Fordist model of standardised pro-duction to post-Fordism, or what Harvey (1989) prefers to call "flexi-ble accumulation", entails a shift to a more flexible method of accumulation of capital, one still concerned with production but which is now more reflexive and able to accommodate variations in the production process. The niche marketing of products, products tailored to the consumer's preferences, along with new logistical arrangements of 'just in time' delivery meant that it became possible to deviate from a standardised model or template, to produce varia-tions in colour, style, upholstery and so on. Instead of saturating the market with the same standardised product, diversification meant a variety of different products became available. In addition, built-in obsolescence, the notion that the product has a particular expected life-cycle, encourages a repeat purchase. In the case of Walkmans, cars and mobile phones, for example, we upgrade them regularly, meaning the market no longer reaches saturation point with a standardised product.

Along with the economic aspects of post-Fordism, shifts in the culture of consumption were evident. Work-based identities, as we saw in Chapter 2, became less important. Consumption was much more central to how we distinguish ourselves from others and our relationships. Significantly, products we buy are rarely produced by us but by third-world workers, so there is a shift in the geographies of capitalism. If production is increasingly sited elsewhere, tradi-tional manufacturing jobs are relocated to other parts of the world, mostly the developing world (see Harvey 1989; Massey 1984). For example, the well-documented Temporary Economic Zones in South East Asia (see Chapter 8 and e.g. Klein 2001; Hertz 2002) mushroom due to lax labour laws, and inward investment is encouraged by gen-erous tax breaks, low wages and cheap land rental. These are condi-tions that encourage unregulated child labour, an ethical issue in consumption that will be more fully addressed in the final chapter. The post-Fordist shift means that products are marketed not at class groups or work-based identities, but instead at types of people or 'lifestyles' (e.g. Featherstone 1991a).

This extremely brief survey of economic history cannot do justice to the complexity of the topics. However, running through the shift from Fordism to post-Fordism is a core of rationalisation, which Weber and Simmel had identified as an important characteristic of modernity, involving bureaucracy, administering and control. For Simmel, rationalisation results in part by the generalisation of exchange relations, where objects become substitutable and exchanged for others, and money facilitates this. This process should be familiar from the discussion of Marx's "commodity fetishism" in Chapter 1. With money and universal exchange, things in the world are treated as impersonal objects, quantified, calculable and exchangeable. This even applies to social relations, where indifference towards people results from this objectification of the world. The abstraction of money, which makes it universally exchangeable by reducing all qualities to some form of quantitative equivalence, makes it impersonal. It promotes a continuous quantitative calculation, thought Simmel:

> The life of many people is filled out with ... reducing of qualitative values to quantitative ones. This certainly contributes to the rational, calculating nature of modern times against the more impulsive, holistic, emotional character of earlier epochs.
>
> (in Slater 1997: 118)

This core of rationalism is especially applicable to Fordism's rationalisation of production, in terms of ever-increased efficiency, and therefore to McDonaldization. Yet Simmel's romanticised invocation of an earlier, simpler era before the harsh rationalisation of modernity, the "impulsive, holistic, emotional character", is applicable to current forms of consumption, especially by youth, and Disney theme parks exemplify this when appealing to youth or to adults' youthful imagination. Simmel's seemingly romantic or simplistic earlier age is applicable to postmodern consumer experience, including tourism, themed malls and theme parks. Against Fordism's rationalisation of *production*, then, is post-Fordism's rationalisation of *consumption*, the tailoring of production to accommodate consumer taste and lifestyle, to engineer the consumption of experiences through theming and spectacle.

Before waxing lyrical about postmodern consumption, we note that these rationalisations have heralded geographically significant shifts in labour and manufacturing in order to accommodate shifts in consumption and the development of taste; a reflexive or two-way process that has very real, material effects. Now I wish to map the shift from Fordism to post-Fordism onto the production of culture. In recent years a number of sociological theories have emerged that attempt to encapsulate increasingly globalised processes of production, and assess the impact on global and local culture. Thus we have not only 'McDonaldization' (Ritzer 1993, 1996, 1998) but also 'Disneyization' (Bryman 1999a, 2004), and 'Coca-Colonization' (Prendergrast 1993; Heath and Potter 2005). The remainder of the chapter will encounter each term in more detail, explaining the principles behind them, and considering the effects of such globalised corporate machinery, the production of mass culture, at a local level. Consequently, we will follow the thread of rationalisation, starting from the predominantly Fordist rationalisation of consumption that McDonaldization exemplifies, to the post-Fordist tailoring of the experience of consumption – and the consumption of experiences – that Disneyization seeks to explain.

McDONALDIZATION

Just like the Starbucks effect, which shows the effects of macro-level economic processes upon the urban geographies of our nearby towns and malls, the process of McDonaldization is a set of ideas and processes that detail what is happening to the service and leisure industries in particular, a template or model of business that McDonalds has found particularly successful at the global level, and imposes clone-like upon many countries in the world. Ritzer's observation of the processes of McDonaldization, originally published in 1993, is not a criticism of McDonalds as such, nor even the fast-food business in general, but an analysis of how fast-food organisational practices have permeated into myriad aspects of our social lives. In a nutshell, McDonaldization is "the process by which the principles of the fast-food restaurant are coming to dominate more and more sectors of American society as well as the rest of the world" (1993: 3). According to Ritzer, the fast-food model pushes consumers towards ever greater reliance on the fostering of quantity over quality, of attainment over efficiency, encourages the creation of predictability, and reduces much of our life experience to a coldly calculated 'value'. Reading further and taking in the diverse landscape of specific illustrations for these trends, we begin to see the 'McDonaldization' influence everywhere. Then we grasp why so many of us are bemoaning the demise of free time in our lives, and how we have become unwitting captives of the mindless inertia of "I want it fast, I want it now, I want what's next" mentalities.

All this is not new, as Ritzer himself acknowledges, and builds upon established sociological theory, as suggested in the previous section, 'McTheory': "all the basic dimensions of McDonaldization are part of what Weber called the rationalization process" (1996: xix). However, Ritzer argues this is not simply an updating of Weber's ideas within a modern idiom. Nor is it simply the extension of the frontiers of rationalisation, from state bureaucracy to private corporations, and thence into the realms of private life. Instead, he argues, McDonalds is *the* model for rationalisation, as not only is the magic McDonalds formula – ruthless efficiency, calculability, predictability and control – applicable to the corporation, but its template for success extends across the globe. The McDonaldization formula is truly globalised, the same recipe for success, the same ingredients of rationalisation enabling McDonalds to be a multinational corporation (MNC) or transnational corporation (TNC). Any business enterprise wishing to rapidly reach global proportions had better follow the template of McDonaldization. Likewise, any truly global corporation exhibits most, if not all, the tendencies of McDonaldization, whether it deals with fast food, cars, financial services or computer software.

The four features of McDonaldization

McDonaldization as a model sets customer expectations, argues Ritzer, and involves imposing four elements: efficiency, predictability, calculability and control (Ritzer 1993, 1996). The result is that products are standardised all over the world, so customers can walk into a McDonalds restaurant in Boston, Bahrain or Beijing and receive the same product, and effectively have the same experience. This globalised standardisation of commodities or experiences is a continuation of Fordist production, only with a late capitalist emphasis on the production of cultural capital – what you are buying in Beijing is not just a hamburger but a portion of America, the Good Life, of Freedom. Not only that, but even "the distinctively American way of eating" that fast-food culture entails, and American ways of consuming, such as credit cards (Ritzer 1998: 84, 117ff.).

There are several features of the process of McDonaldization that are important to examine. They are not unique to McDonalds or even the fast-food industry as a whole, but serve as the template for globalised, standardised provision of commodities, services or experiences. Table 3.1 provides a brief synopsis of each of these, compiled from several of Ritzer's publications, with examples.

'The irrationality of rationality'

There are many benefits to these processes of McDonaldization, of course, such as variety, 24/7 banking and shopping, and speedier and more efficient service. But there is a certain sense that these rational systems tend to turn in on themselves, to lead to irrational outcomes. Ritzer describes the adverse effects as the "irrationality of rationality" (1996: 13), and sees this as an equally important aspect of McDonaldization:

> Most specifically, irrationality means that rational systems are *unreasonable* systems. By that I mean that they deny the basic humanity, the human reason, of the people who work within or are served by them.
>
> (Ritzer 1994: 154)

For example, queues at fast-food restaurants and theme parks can be very long, and waiting to get to an amusement ride might take longer than the ride experience itself. Both fast-food emporia and theme parks must process large numbers of people at a time, and efficiency, calculability, predictability and control are necessary for this to occur. In such a regulated environment geared towards handling numerous people, why

Table 3.1: The four features of McDonaldization

		Examples
Efficiency	Efficiency is described as the "optimum method for getting from one point to another" (1996: 9). Each and every process of the business is organised to ensure that everything happens at the right time and the right place, with the least amount of cost or effort. The idea of efficiency is typically advertised as a benefit to the customer, especially in terms of convenience. Yet this efficiency is usually imposed upon the consumer by the institution, so that what might be efficient for the company is not necessarily efficient for the customer.	**Examples:** The drive-up window, salad bars, self-service petrol stations, cash machines (ATMs), voicemail, microwave dinners, and supermarkets (self-service compared with the personal contact of a grocer). Ritzer gives the example of salad bars, where you take a bowl and serve the salad yourself. Often the customer ends up doing the work previously performed for them, and the business soaks up the savings.
Calculability	Calculability is "an emphasis on the quantitative aspects of products sold (portion size, cost) and service offered (the time it takes to get the product)" (1993: 9). This is an emphasis on what can be ruthlessly calculated, counted, quantified. Size, quantity, value is stressed, whereas time should be minimised so that everything is provided as fast as possible. The erroneous assumption is that *more* always equals *better*. "Quantification refers to a tendency to emphasize quantity rather than quality. This leads to a sense that quality is equal to certain, usually (but not always) large quantities of things" (1994: 142).	**Examples:** 'Super size' portions, the '*Big Mac*', the '*Whopper*', '*Big Gulp*', food advertised by its weight, such as quarter-pounders. Along with greater quantity, greater speed means less time is taken: Lose weight *fast*', microwaving allows for less time spent in the kitchen, and even news reporting, where bitesize chunks of information substitute for in-depth coverage.
Predictability	A McDonaldized society "emphasizes such things as discipline, order, systemization, formalization, routine, consistency, and methodical operation" (1993: 79). In such a society, people prefer to know what to expect most of the time. It also makes the work routine for the employees of that company.	**Examples:** A Big Mac is *le Big Mac* is *eine Big Mac*, wherever you are and however you pronounce it. The movie industry builds upon this concept of predictability by releasing sequel after sequel. The spin-off TV series or

	Predictability makes the experience of the consumer consistent at every location of a McDonaldized company, so that the same experience we received last week in London will be repeated next week in Los Angeles. Shopping is predictable in the mall; the same stores, often the same layout, enclosed and protected from unpredictable weather.	videogame, or the success of authors like Stephen King, also represent the importance of predictability: once the characters and the idea are sold to the public, publishers and producers can be assured of a predictable profit. This is increasingly the case across different media simultaneously.
Control	Control is strongly related to increasing mechanisation, the substitution of nonhuman for human technology. To increase control, in other words, is to mechanise the process wherever possible. Thus control extends to both the employee and the consumer, as people are "the great source of uncertainty, unpredictability and inefficiency in any rationalizing system" (1993: 101). If the job of human operators can be mechanised, it will remove messy human error and increase the other factors (efficiency, calculability, predictability) in McDonaldization. Everything is pre-packaged, pre-measured and automatically controlled. The human employee just follows the instructions, oversees the process, pushing buttons now and then. In the fast-food restaurant, deep-fat fryers are timed and will lift the fries automatically at the end of the cycle, beeping to let employees know.	**Examples:** Just like fast-food employees, supermarket cashiers simply scan the barcode, and sometimes we have even weighed and labelled the produce for them. "The next step in this development is to have the customer do the scanning", argues Ritzer (1994: 150). And indeed, self-service scanners are beginning to replace cashiers. Whether self-scanning or running our goods past the cashier, we accept the infallibility of the computerised check-out – the barcode never lies, and like a relentless conveyor belt the cashiers need only oversee the process, pressing buttons and vocalising the pre-calculated total cost. At home, even our ovens and microwaves tell us when our food is done, or the meal comes complete in one convenient package.

Source: Author's own, with material adapted from Ritzer (1993, 1998).

the long queues? This is an irrational outcome of a rationalised environment, an outcome that occurs surprisingly frequently.

There are other unpredictable elements that emerge from a supremely rational and efficient set of processes. The food we eat, so-called 'industrial food' (see following chapter), is often less nourishing, loaded with additives, fats, salt and sugar. This is certainly not in our interests, either as consumers or as biologically functioning beings. Packaging used in the fast-food industry pollutes the environment, leading to long-term degradation of the natural world for present and future generations. The "need to grow uniform potatoes to create those predictable French fries" for example entails huge monocultural farms making extensive use of pesticides, which then contaminate the water supply (Ritzer 1996: 13). Another highly contentious example that many will recognise is automated customer service phonelines, and the proliferation of call centres to service them. Being told we are the fifth person in the queue by an impersonal announcement is little consolation when performing a simple transaction that can take all morning. *Our* time and inconvenience is money saved by the corporation. In no way is this good public relations or real customer service, and call-centre staff then have to calm customers down or defuse tensions as a result of long waiting and annoying muzak.

Taken to its logical conclusion, the principles of McDonaldization can be applied to the Holocaust, as Ritzer does tentatively in the second edition of his book (1996), and Beilharz (1999) examines further. It is the ultimate irrationality of rationality. Nevertheless, as Ritzer acknowledges, "the fast-food restaurant *cannot* be discussed in the same breath as the Holocaust" (1996: 24, original emphasis), as it risks trivialising the tragedy, so we will desist from making comparisons. After McDonaldization and its globalised culture, we will now attend to the related but separate theoretical template of Disneyization.

DISNEYIZATION

In the leisure industry, Disney's theme parks and stores purvey similar notions of a standardised experience, although more imaginative, and based less on the production and selling of commodities than the production of experiences within a consistently themed space. This focus on the standardisation of themed experiences rather than commodities is known as 'McDisneyization' (Ritzer and Liska 1997; Ritzer 1998) or 'Disneyization' (Bryman 1999a, 1999b, 2004). It is clear from Ritzer's discussion of 'McDisneyization' that theme parks and organised tourist attractions have much in common with McDonaldization. While McDisneyization is really a conflation of McDonaldization with Disney theme parks, with more emphasis on the 'Mc' side of McDisneyization, Bryman's Disneyization is something distinct. We will remember that McDonaldization is "the process by which the principles of the fast-food restaurant are coming to dominate more and more sectors of American society as well as the rest of the world", according to Ritzer (1993: 3). Similarly, what Bryman calls the 'Disneyization' of the world is "the process by which the principles of the Disney theme parks are coming to dominate more and more sectors of American society as well as the rest of the world" (1995: 25). It is worth mentioning here since it follows neatly from McDonaldization, although the notion of the Disneyization of zoos and the natural world will be considered in more detail in Chapter 5, 'Nature, Inc.'

Disney theme parks can be seen as exhibiting the characteristics of McDonaldization, that is efficiency, calculability, predictability and control. Theme parks are also subject to Ritzer's "irrationality of rationality", as the efficiency of processing large numbers of visitors involves long queues for the popular rides, something which equates with *in*efficiency for the visitor (Bryman 1999b: 110). There are other parallels that show theme parks as McDonaldized, including the fact that the first Disney theme park opened the same year as the first McDonalds restaurant, in 1955. However, Bryman argues that "there is more to the parks than the fact they are McDonaldized institutions" (1999a: 26), and hence the term "Disneyization" is coined. One major feature of Disney and therefore of Disneyization is the consistency of characters and themes, an all-enclosing series of themed experiences that rarely refer to an outside. Wasko writes about the "Disney Universe" in this way, that it "has created a self-contained universe which presents consistently recognizable values through recurring characters and familiar repetitive themes" (1996: 349). Especially in Disney's films, features of the Disney Universe include escape and fantasy, innocence, romance and happiness, sexual stereotypes, individualism and the reinvention of folk tales.

The four features of Disneyization

Just like the four features of McDonaldization that Ritzer identified, there are four key features of Disneyization for Bryman. These features or trends are: theming, dedifferentiation of consumption, merchandising and emotional labour. Each will be outlined below, but in considering them we should be aware that while the theoretical legacy of McDonaldization is in modernity and the sociology of Weber, Bryman claims that Disneyization is rooted more in consumer culture and postmodernity. While comfort, hygiene, safety, punctuality and the like are valued, consistent with McDonaldization, theme parks and other Disneyized sites of *spectacular consumption* (see Chapter 5 for more discussion of this), for example hands-on science museums or living historical villages, exhibit features of postmodernity, namely "the proliferation of signs, dedifferentiation of institutional spheres, depthlessness, cultivated nostalgia, and the problematization of authenticity and reality" (1999a: 43). These terms are pervasively present throughout this book, and have either been introduced in previous chapters (depthlessness), will be discussed shortly (dedifferentiation), or will be discussed in detail in Chapter 5, on tourism and the consumption of nature.

Theming

Theming is found in restaurants and restaurant chains such as Hardrock Café and Planet Hollywood, and specially themed hotels such as the Madonna Inn in California. Other easily recognised examples include sports bars, the proliferation of Irish pubs around the world, and even themed cruise liners, as Ritzer and Liska (1997) observe. While theming has been a staple of amusement parks since Disney's first theme park in 1955, this tendency is spreading. Shopping malls such as the West Edmonton Mall and the Roman-themed Forum Shops in Las Vegas (see Chapter 7) are consistently themed, and even airport lounges are exhibiting tendencies towards theming. Historically, this concentration on theming, Bryman suggests, is a result of Disney's impatience with regular amusement parks, which had plenty to entertain children but little for the adults who accompanied them. Theming, either through appeals to imagined progress (EPCOT, Space Mountain) or the celebration of nostalgia (around the Wild West, the dinosaur era, etc.), supposedly bridges this divide. Rather than the loose assemblage of entertainments that non-themed amusement parks could provide, theming was Walt Disney's great innovation, establishing coherence between the different activities or rides, making the experience more connected. The result is a sense of immersion, the lack of intrusion from the outside world through undisturbed consistency of features, themes and characters. What theme parks and themed environments provide is the transformation of attractions, shops or amusements into a singular themed environment, a consistency in imagined and fantastical geography.

Some have seen the establishment of theming within amusement parks prior to Disney. One precursor is at Coney Island, the slightly tawdry seaside resort full of amusements for New Yorkers, although theming was primitive, a mechanism for attracting customers (Bryman 1999a: 32). More significantly, there are continuities between Disney theme parks, Expositions and World's Fairs. These types of events were hugely popular. There were over 6 million visitors to the Great Exhibition in Crystal Palace in 1851, and 57 million visitors to the Paris Universal Exposition in 1900. As temporary events, their purpose was to exhibit values of progress, to advertise trade and the virtues of empire and industry to the general public. Displays of people, food and artefacts from colonies and dominions around the world were arranged in themed areas as a form of globalised commodity display. As McClintock describes, the Great Exhibition was, like modern food courts, a space in which many colonies displayed their commodities and their culture, and was a venue where "the mass consumption of the commodity spectacle was born" (1995: 209). New technologies were proudly paraded before an awed public, such as the first escalator at the Paris Exposition. Yet American innovation was still unmistakably evident at the event, leading the influential English newspaper editor W.T. Stead to describe the Exposition tellingly as "the Americanization of the world" (1901).

Dedifferentiation

'Dedifferentiation' is simply the elision or collapsing of distinct areas of consumption. It is "the general trend whereby the forms of consumption associated with different institutional spheres become interlocked with each other and increasingly difficult to distinguish" (Bryman 1999a: 33). A well-noted general area of dedifferentiation is that between shopping and theme parks. Increasingly, theme parks are based on consumption of food and merchandise at many different points throughout the park, even at the exit of particularly popular rides (1999b: 104). Correspondingly, shopping malls are increasingly becoming themed and incorporate elements of theme parks, for example the well-documented 'Fantasyland' which includes differently themed areas within the West Edmonton Mall. Convergence of consumption types from traditionally separated strands is a tendency that not only maximises revenue from each site, but can work synergistically. "Thus, we see in the Disney parks a tendency for shopping, eating, hotel accommodation and theme park visiting to become inextricably woven" (Bryman 1999a: 34). Staying at the comparatively overpriced Disney hotels, for example, not only maximises the revenue stream by having Disney accommodation within a Disney park, but completes the sense of immersion, and maintains the consistency of Disney themes. Hotel guests are also guaranteed a place in the queue for the rides, and restaurant reservations can be made, allowing visitors to be a step ahead of the hordes of tourists (a by-product of the irrationality of rationality of McDonaldization). Staying in Disney hotels is therefore another example of dedifferentiation, maintaining the consistency of theme but including other benefits. It is more of the Disney Universe: more of it, and more immersive.

Merchandising

This should be a self-evident strand of Disneyization. If Disney did not invent the concept of merchandising, he was the first to understand its true profitability, and one year after Mickey Mouse appeared in 1928, the Disney studio was split into four, one part being devoted purely to merchandising and licensing (Bryman 1999a: 36). The theme parks themselves provide more than ample opportunities to purchase Disney merchandise, significantly contributing towards profits. In addition, the theme parks provide their own specific merchandise, with the name of the specific park branded onto them, simultaneously fulfilling the need for souvenirs and memorabilia that any tourist pursuit demands, while also offering official Disney-branded product. In the case of T-shirts, the wearer of the branded souvenir is also a walking advertisement for the company. At the launch of new feature films, the associated merchandise also works as part of the endlessly self-referential form of advertising, including tie-ins with McDonalds.

The influence of Disney-style merchandising tie-ins has spread to many different sectors. University logos on casual-wear, especially in the US, and the merchandise of football teams in the UK, are particularly successful. In the latter case, the sales of Manchester United merchandise largely helped to triple its turnover over five years (Kuper 1996: 2, in Bryman 1999a: 39). In fact, it has been so successful in marketing team strips (the current shirts of the season) that accusations of unfair practices have been levelled at the team (e.g. Barrow 2002: 15). In such an extremely profitable area, and with the low cost of manufacture from Asian factories, prices can be fixed artificially high by outlets, and the changeover of the season's colours becomes more rapid since it stimulates further purchasing.

Emotional labour

Employees of Disney theme parks interact with visitors in an obviously staged, inauthentic way. The interaction between service employees and customers is, in other words, scripted. Not only insincere or inauthentic, scripted interactions are part of what Ritzer acknowledges is the deskilling of service-sector employees (1998: 64). Saying "Have a nice day" at the end of each transaction is only the beginning. The more scripted the interactions are, the more self-control is necessary, and expression of suitable emotions for each stage of the transaction becomes more demanding. This is what Bryman terms "emotional labour" (1999a: 39). Being consistently cheerful or polite in transactions requires a level of performance and consistency that is difficult to maintain, but for the 'cast members' (employees) of Disney theme parks, some of whom must be 'in character' (quite literally in a furry mouse suit) all day, such emotional labour reaches new heights. Control of these employees through scripted interactions is a key element of Disney theme parks, and helps maintain the approachability and friendliness that visitors value (Bryman 1995). These features are dependable in the Disney environment, where scripted interactions and a consistently upbeat attitude have been emulated within other employment sectors.

The instilling of self-control is partly as a result of the corporation being in control of the interactions between employees and customers. Drawing on research on insurance salespersons and airline flight attendants, Ritzer hints at some of the mechanisms by which interaction with clients is controlled, but also how the organisation wishes to control how the employees see and feel about themselves (1998: 64). The way that practices of self-control are extended through the training and management approach of the organisation or company is reminiscent of Foucault's extensive discussion of the power of the State inscribed over the individual body in *Discipline and Punish* (1977).

Putting these four elements together, Bryman's purpose has been to establish the process of Disneyization as distinct from McDonaldization. It should be clear that certain institutions may simultaneously exhibit features of both McDonaldization and Disneyization, either, or none, much like a Venn diagram. Not all McDonaldized organisations are Disneyized, and not all Disneyized institutions are McDonaldized, as they are distinct and are derived from different theoretical traditions. If McDonaldization reminds us of the Fordist principles of production that remain at large in the service sector and the culture industry, Disneyization allows us to add some filters of postmodernity, of post-Fordist principles more attuned to the consumer and their experience. How themes are maintained through the consistency of signs and experiences, the implosion of consumption and leisure, the everyday performance of self and the scripting of encounters are important elements of any Disneyized organisation. We will pick up these themes and develop them further in the following chapter, as discussions of tourism and "post-tourism" (e.g. MacCannell 1976; Feifer 1985) are deeply concerned with the consumption of nature, heritage and authenticity.

AND NOW ... *DISNEYFICATION?*

Interviewed concerning the opening of Euro Disney in Paris, a French politician protested that it will "bombard France with uprooted creations that are to culture what fast food is to gastronomy" (in Ritzer

1996: 14). A better encapsulation of the deleterious effects of American economic and cultural imperialism, conflating two particularly visible areas within modern life, would be difficult to find. While the two processes of Ritzer's McDonaldization (1996, 1998) and Bryman's Disneyization (1999a, 1999b, 2004) have different sociological foci, they are complementary, both being expressions of the fear of creeping homogenisation of global culture. If the first is concerned with the pursuit of rationalisation into ever more areas of modern life, the second is concerned with the maintenance of signs, images and an immersive simulation in which global culture is portrayed as a theme park, and presented to us in a carefully managed, consistently themed, seamless form.

In a biography of Walt Disney, what Schickel calls "Disneyfication" (1986: 225) refers to the way that rich cultural phenomena and folk tales are put through a Disney machine, resulting in simplistic understandings and overly sentimental portrayals. The lyrical invention and complex beauty of the ancient Greek epic poems of Homer are reduced to a standardised 'product' like *Hercules* (1997), for example. And the same recognisable process is consistently applied to other historical epochs and ancient traditions such as First Nation tribes and in fact focusing on an indigenous female tribe member in *Pocahontas* (1995), thereby associating a people – and the female protagonist – with the forces of Nature as opposed to Culture and its trappings. This simplistic understanding of Nature does not aim to invigorate debates in First Nation issues, nor does it serve to address issues of land and community or environmental degradation (the dichotomy of Nature/Culture is discussed at length in the following chapter). Common to whatever subject matter of Disney films, then, is the portrayal of irreducibly complex history, of the interplay of social, historical and political phenomena, as a form of mass culture, as pure entertainment. This is the process of 'Disneyfication' that Schickel coins,

> that shameless process by which everything the Studio later touched, no matter how unique the vision of the original from which the Studio worked, was reduced to the limited terms Disney and his people could understand. Magic, mystery, individuality … were consistently destroyed when a literary work passed through this machine that had been taught there was only one correct way to draw.
>
> (1986: 225)

Exchanging the last word 'draw' with 'portray' better captures the way that cartoons, and increasingly other Disneyfied media such as theme park rides and videogames, involve the transformation of culturally complex history and tradition into mass-produced cultural product. The concept of Disneyfication is sympathetic to the critique of the mass culture industry, for example the Frankfurt School, but also reflexively applicable to social theory and its popularisation – for example, the theories of 'McDonaldization' and 'Disneyization' themselves.

GLOBA-COLA OR LOCA-COLA? GLOBALISED CONSUMPTION, LOCALISED CULTURES

An inevitable consequence of debates raised in the previous discussions of McDisneyfications (McDonaldization, Disneyization and the rest) is the globalisation of consumption. Despite their theoretical shortcomings, their recognisability as organisational templates at a global level means there is a double movement: of the imposition of a multinational, globalised form upon local cultures on the one hand, and the influence of local cultures in their appropriation of the form, their use and modification of it on the other. Globalisation is a vast set of economic, political and social issues, so this section will limit discussion to the impact of globalised corporations on local cultures, and one term for understanding these global-local effects and modifications is 'glocalisation', an ugly word popularised by Robertson (especially 1995: 28). In this section we look at everyday examples such as Coca-Cola, bananas and Irish pubs to ask whether these globalised forms equate with homogenisation, with "Americanization" (after Stead 1901 and Ritzer 1998), or with the "sterile cultural monism" of "McWorld" (Barber 2003: xiii; see also Vidal 1997). To what extent does local culture influence these forms, make them more supple and heterogeneous? Just how bidirectional are these global-local interactions?

This debate between globalisation and localisation will be pitched at the level of culture and consumption, between 'Globa-cola' and 'Loca-cola'. The debate between homogenisation and heterogenisation is separate yet related, so will be covered later in the section. The phrases 'Globa-cola' and 'Loca-cola', however, neatly bring forward the issues at stake, of globalised frameworks of business, economics and organisation and localised negotiations at the level of everyday consumption within a local culture. Importantly, they are *not* equated with 'globalisation' and 'localisation', although we have encountered too many '-isations' already. The differences are outlined in a series of definitions below, and should make this clearer. Afterwards there is more extensive discussion of the effects of globalisation on local cultures.

Globa-cola

To say that consumption is globalised is a cliché, and an everyday anthropology of international supermarket chains such as Wal-Mart attests to this. One day you go into British supermarket chain Asda to buy bananas, the bananas are from the Dominican Republic and the profit goes to a British board of directors. Then, almost overnight, the supermarket is taken over by Wal-Mart, the bananas are from Puerto Rico, and the profits go to the US retail giant. What happened? Just like Bart Simpson and the Starbucks effect, a large part of our consumption practices involves global chains of stores and restaurants. This should not be mistaken for the upbeat, stylistic sheen that globalisation promises. Although a Big Mac in Beijing might evoke the imagined, unattainable glamour of the West for a local resident, in Western cities like Boston or Bristol they are eaten by a range of people, including those on lower incomes. Considering globalised consumption practices like this helps firm the ground for other chapters, by asking how urban retail spaces like the shopping mall have exactly the same stores whichever urban centre they are situated in, whether Dubai, Moscow, Boston or London; the ubiquity of the globalised, homogeneous retail space of the mall (Chapter 7), and the ubiquity of the global brand and logo (Chapter 8).

Globalisation

The tendency for businesses, technologies and political philosophies (e.g. democracy) to spread across the world. The global economy is trumpeted as a totally interconnected marketplace, irrespective of local time zones or national borders. This is a world of "time-space compression", the annihilation of space by time (Harvey 1989: 232ff.), meaning that geographical distances collapse and communications become almost instantaneous. A business transaction or media event can be conducted over vast distances with minimal time lag through the internet, for example, collapsing both space and time. Therefore, the proliferation of McDonalds restaurants around the world is an example of globalisation, although adapting their menus to local cultures is an example of 'glocalisation' (see below). The world as a massively interconnected marketplace, where transactions are instantaneous and space-time is compressed, is seductive. Inevitably, though, there are political issues. While some argue that true globalisation will result in a level playing field, with all nations able to trade equally, critics believe that it only increases the opportunities for wealthier nations to take advantage of poorer ones. As Zygmunt Bauman articulates this, *"rather than homogenizing the human condition, the technological annulment of temporal/spatial distances tends to polarize it"* (1998: 18, original emphasis). Another fear is that of homogenisation, that a homogenised world culture will eradicate regional diversity and local cultures in favour of a single, homogeneous, global culture.

Loca-cola

Localised consumption might involve farmers' markets and other localised spaces of interaction and consumption. Or it may involve buying locally or globally produced, branded and non-branded goods in a local setting such as a grocer's, rather than a supermarket. These are forms of defiantly localised consumption. Fruit and vegetables bought at the local grocer's are not usually locally produced, however, and are mostly imported. A local grocer may not have the range and variety of exotic produce that larger supermarkets have, partly as they have less purchase power. Produce from the grocer's may only be from hundreds of miles away, as opposed to the thousands of miles that exotic commodities have to travel to supermarkets. In addition we can consider the effects of globalisation upon localised consumption and regional identities. In most towns there remain individual non-franchised, non-chain shops, and often these remain popular. Local coffee shops and cafés may be chosen in conscious defiance of chains like Starbucks or Caffè Nero, or simply as a result of convenience or habit (for discussion of Starbucks' aggressive practice of 'store clustering', see Chapter 8; and Klein 2001:

135ff.). Regional chains of stores or supermarkets still remain, of course, but their accumulation and growth is fed by increasingly globalised trade networks through the importation of produce.

Localisation

By contrast with local consumption, localisation works within the framework of globalisation, adapting a product or service to a particular culture or language, to provide a more local look or feel to products available around the world. There should be mechanisms in place to make this process easier, for example when choosing computer software the range of languages on offer should be specific to certain regions, and the sale of commercial DVDs also attests to this. Manuals for electronic goods are often produced with a template whereby local translations can be inserted. This process is also termed 'internationalisation'. When a globalised product or service becomes localised, in addition to language translation other details such as time zones, currencies, national holidays and other geographic sensibilities must be considered. A successfully localised product or service will appear as if developed and produced locally. One example of this is financial services, which almost fetishise locale in advertising campaigns. In 2002 the recently merged banking multinational HSBC proclaimed themselves "The world's local bank" (hsbc.com, 2005), and a series of advertisements attempted to depict a sensitivity to geographical locales, showing specific meanings of objects and gestures in different countries around the world. This has ironically been a global advertising campaign. Another example of attempts at localisation is the farming-out of call centres to less developed countries, especially India. For large corporations it is simply cheaper to reroute the calls to India, as local wages are far lower and English is spoken extensively. In a much publicised move, British companies have provided their Indian employees with daily updates of events in soap operas and weather conditions, so that in conversation the service seems local (e.g. Khan 2003: 19).

Glocalisation

'Glocalisation' is obviously a term that combines 'globalisation' with 'localisation', and is used to emphasise the fact that the globalisation of a product or service is more likely to succeed if an attempt at adaptation to the local culture is made. The term therefore includes the meaning of localisation, above, but also includes the influence of the local culture on the globalised product. Hence it recognises that this is a two-way process. If global pressures temper local conditions, the opposite may also be true, as local conditions may alter the policy or stance of the global corporation. 'Glocalisation' has been popularised by the sociologist Roland Robertson, who describes it as "the simultaneity – the co-presence – of both universalizing and particularizing tendencies" (1997). Globally, and indeed in this chapter, we are never far from a McDonalds restaurant. Certain meals will be available, and exactly the same, in every country, whereas an attempt to appeal to local palates is often made (Featherstone 1991a; Ritzer 1998: 85; Bell 2002). Glocalisation is therefore the complex, reciprocal relationship between global pressures and local conditions.

Globa-cola: the McDonaldization of culture?

Referring back to Ritzer's McDonaldization, its efficiency, calculability, predictability and control are suited to any form of standardised production, from burger bars to boy bands, from coffee houses to cars. To satisfy the consumer's need for the perpetually novel, for cycles of fashion and popular culture to constantly spin, new areas of culture must become assimilated and absorbed to keep producing more cultural product. In this section we move on from McDonaldization and Disneyization as templates or models to address a separate yet related question: that of the supposed homogenisation of culture that results from the global export of McDonaldized or Disneyized practices. Fast-food culture, MTV, credit cards and the increasing uptake of the internet are shaping the products and services on offer, making them available to more people in more places, and are even influencing the ways people consume them. McDonaldization does not equate directly with Americanization or homogenisation, since diversity and a range of localised products can be made available. In the case of McDonalds restaurants, not only do they adapt themselves to local markets, selling vegetable burgers in Holland and McHuevos in Paraguay, but locals adapt these restaurants to their cultures. Local cultures may offer more appropriate or culturally specific alternatives to these global chains, such as Nirula's across India, or the Pans & Co. chain in Spain. Or McDonalds may adopt a different meaning within the local culture, such as a place for an impressive date, or a family treat that requires months of saving, as Ritzer acknowledges (1998: 85). Reminding ourselves just what proportion of an average month's wages a Big Mac costs in Beijing would certainly accentuate this observation.

Reminiscent of the stark critiques of the mass culture industry that the Frankfurt School specialised in (see Chapter 1), German sociologist Richard Münch sees the culture industry as globalised, and therefore unable to communicate real difference:

> Culture no longer passes on a way of thinking; rather it becomes the service station of an expanding spectrum of needs, which can be produced for the purpose of assuring the sales of cultural products through extensive marketing. Creativity does not get lost; rather it is constantly used more inclusively and quickly by a growing cultural industry. As a result of this, the moments of creative authenticity become shorter and shorter, are therefore exhausted faster and faster, and correspondingly the faster they have to be replaced by something new.
>
> (1999: 145)

Critics from the Frankfurt School looked to Hollywood as an example of the mass culture industry, consuming dreamy distraction from the realities of everyday life. The way that even French shop girls adapted the styles and comportment of American movie stars in their everyday interactions implies that, from around the 1920s onwards, Hollywood films became a form of enculturation, influencing the way people talked, looked and acted (e.g. Kellner 2000). This was to acknowledge the culture industry as already globalised. Yet, cycles of innovation proceed ever faster, and what marketing has called 'synergy' entails that the movie is released with the toys, themed McDonalds meals, and the licensed videogame. Global cultural production therefore relies on a high degree of standardisation, yet also a high degree of innovation that is cyclical, that requires continual renewal. When consumed, these products offer correspondingly shorter experiences of satiation, pushing forward the cycles of innovation. Münch regards this as the "interplay of technical rationalization and the dynamic of the cycles of pop culture", where the cycles of genuine cultural innovation cannot keep up with the cycles of popular culture; the end result is "cultural standstill with incredible movement" (1999: 138–139). Perhaps this is the legacy of applying McDonaldized principles of organisation, along with Disneyized forms of commercial consumer experiences, to culture.

Loca-cola: heterogeneity, appropriation, difference

Yet even Münch recognises that genuine cultural innovation does have a place within this globalised, standardised system. The sheer variety of authentic cultures and folk traditions means that, while often marginalised or kept on the periphery of mainstream culture, there is always a source of innovation that becomes assimilated into and influences the mainstream. Whether it is the sudden global popularity of Michael Flatley's *Riverdance* and Irish dancing in the early 1990s, or of salsa, J-Lo and Latino culture more recently, this is an example of "taking a local culture to market" in order to keep it alive (Münch 1999: 142). Of course, the flipside is that if a local culture does not capture the public imagination, fails to make incursions to the centre (mainstream culture) from the periphery (local, authentic, or 'folk'), then it may whither and die unnoticed. One thing that is obviously different from the Frankfurt School critique is the way that the standard of culture was often based around bourgeois, acceptable middle-class values of taste. Prior to the twentieth century, the model of cultural innovation was a standoff between the Bohemian avant-garde and more traditional bourgeois values. This is the model that the Frankfurt School assumed up until the first half of the twentieth century, where a sequence of revolution and restoration of culture occurs in the art world. More recently, however, there is an interplay of experimental culture and entertainment culture, a mutual inspiration that is particularly evident in terms of digital design and innovative musical forms. On the other hand, what was once avant-garde and shocking (*musique concrete*, impressionism) becomes kitsch, especially if used in advertisements for insurance.

But 'Loca-cola' is about the everyday experience of consumption at the local level, and is a negotiation between local factors and availabilities, and globalised forms of business and organisation. To revisit

Featherstone's celebration of 'lifestyle' (see Chapter 2), it could be argued that 'lifestyle' is like a hangar, supporting a number of aspirational consumption choices based around certain key global products (eating Big Macs, wearing Gap and Nike), yet which limit our agency in the process, making us passive or receptive consumers of globalisation rather than active or creative negotiators. In *A Primer for Daily Life*, Susan Willis connects up the everyday experience of shopping for bananas in a local supermarket, comparing their adhesive labels with their evocations of exoticism and distant possibilities. These labels conceal the real relations of labour, working conditions, exploitation and, in the case of Guatemala, governmental overthrow (1991: 51ff.). In other words, at the local level of consumption, vast differences at the level of production are reduced to differences between tiny adhesive labels on bananas.

A common argument, claims Miller, and one that relates consumption to identity, is that in this materialistic world of global brands and globalised capital we orient ourselves less to people, and more towards objects. Instead of objects symbolising people, then, "we have now become merely 'lifestyles' – that is, the passive carriers of meanings which are created for us in capitalist business" (1997a: 22). In this argument, a logical extension of the construction of identities within the mass culture system, this formation of lifestyle and the process of globalised consumption is simply

> a continuation of the forces of capitalism and bureaucracy which destroy local difference in the name of global homogeneity, or, more recently, foster a diversity which sells goods but has no depth or contribution to make to cultural development.
>
> (1997a: 22)

But, as he argues elsewhere (e.g. 1987, 1997b), the relation between people and things – in other words, material culture – is more complex and social, and local identities can be formed within the larger mechanisms of globalised branding, as he shows in the case of the consumption of Coca-Cola in Trinidad. Drawing on his extensive fieldwork as an anthropologist there, he observes that the processes of growing up with, and becoming socialised with, such a product have unpredictable effects. One of these is that rum and Coke is identified as a specifically

Trinidadian drink, due to the fact that rum is local and plentiful. Rum – with Coke – is far more popular than beer or other alcohol on the island. Another is that virtually all the ingredients to the Coke sold there come locally from the island, and are processed there. Coke is, at least by association, central to being Trinidadian. This contests the common observation that Coca-Cola has become "a kind of clichéd shorthand for global homogenization" (1997a: 33), and hence 'Coca-Colonization'. Instead of being a superficial emblem of uncaring multinational companies, then, such global brands "may evolve complex and highly local connotations" (1997a: 35). Miller contradicts the commonly held assumption of the passivity of a local culture in the face of global business, and in his observations of Trinidad at least, shows how this reasserts a localised identity into a globalised brand. As should be clear by now, the specifically local and creative consumption of global products helps to build a sense of regional identity, and so this 'Locacola' is synonymous with neither 'localisation' nor 'glocalisation'.

THE NEW MEANS OF CONSUMPTION

Briefly wrapping up, let us return to the Starbucks effect. After an initial observation from *The Simpsons* concerning the effects of globalised business practices on local environments, we then explored some ways that globalised models of McDonaldization and Disneyization have deleterious effects on culture. Nevertheless, we have suggested that creative consumption, whether of Big Macs, theme parks, or rum and Coke, allows different articulations of locality, regional or national identity, and therefore reasserts local time and local space into what is often fetishised as time-space compression. We have also suggested the theoretical limits of the various McDisneyfications of social theory, that is, the attempt to reduce what are irreducibly complex sets of global-local interactions of commodities and culture into bitesize McNuggets of McTheory.

A comprehensive survey of theories of globalisation, glocalisation and their effects on culture has not been the purpose of this chapter. But we can roughly characterise the arc or trajectory as having followed a thread of rationalisation, from the beginning of the chapter, from global production through to local consumption. By starting with McDonaldization, the notion of globalised production of standardised commodities (burgers), we then proceeded to consider consumer experiences within Disneyization (themes, fantasy), and thence to the reassertion of local identity in the consumption of global products (Trinidadian rum and Coke). We have therefore disputed the common assumption that globalisation equates with homogenisation, although it is sometimes the case. Instead, in a twist to this argument, Ritzer expands upon his McDonaldization thesis to describe the Americanization of culture as a result of the way globalised consumption must take place. For anyone to be able to consume in this global, interconnected marketplace, we need access to credit cards, the internet, and a certain level of communications technology. These are American innovations and are therefore Americanized ways of consuming that are exported worldwide. Ritzer thus tries to accommodate what he calls "the new means of consumption", which include "shopping malls, mega-malls, superstores, home shopping television networks, cybermalls, infomercials and many more" (1998: 1, 117ff.), into McDonaldization. This is a separate argument from the McDonaldization of society or the homogenisation of culture, and indeed from the Americanization of the world generally; instead, it is about the way things are increasingly consumed. Echoing Marx's notion of the ownership of the *means of production*, Ritzer is arguing that the *means of consumption* are increasingly what is at stake, and these are American. Rather than the globalised success of McDonalds, then, the success of Amazon.com and its numerous localised, national affiliates might be a better example – at least until we can buy burgers online with credit cards.

Finally, the discussion of both McDonaldization and Disneyization not only highlights issues of local consumption within globalised frameworks, but also sets the stage for other important areas of consumption. The most significant is the consumption of nature that occurs in tourism and nature-based theme parks such as SeaWorld™ and Disney's Animal Kingdom. In terms of Disneyization, nature becomes reduced to simulation, a magical theme-park ride consistent with a Disney film. In terms of McDonaldization, tourists are offered package tours, with the efficiency and predictability of providing expected highlights and known attractions. This is explored in Chapter 5, 'Nature, Inc.', and so this chapter on McDisneyfications serves as an introduction and companion piece.

4

BODYSHOPPING

THE COMMODIFICATION OF EXPERIENCE
AND SENSATION

INTRODUCTION: CONSUMPTION AS EVERYDAY, EMBODIED EXPERIENCE

There is a well-known philosophical thought experiment that questions how we can know whether our experiences are real. In Descartes' *Meditations on First Philosophy* (1641) he asks whether our experiences are given to us by an evil or malicious demon. Recently this question has been updated to ask: how do we know that we are *not* brains in vats of nutrient material, being fed experiences through the stimulation of neurons and chemicals by aliens, intent on experimenting with us? Something similar is envisaged in the 1999 film *The Matrix*. Everything that we think we feel, such as scratching ourselves, eating chocolate or walking in the countryside, could be entirely artificial, pure simulation. We generally assume that a body is a prerequisite for any experience or sensation that we have, the medium or conduit that translates sensory information from our ears, eyes, nose, tongue and skin into mental events and processes – deciding something tastes good, or disliking certain music. The complex interactions of the senses provide our sense of embodiment, the haptic (tactile) sensation from our feet giving feedback as we walk down the street, for example. Yet, what if all these embodied sensations were merely inputs into our brains, floating without their bodies, in vats millions of miles away?

Provocative as this question is, attempting to answer it reveals not only that our usual conception of experience is embodied, but also how everyday thinking separates the mind from the body. Our brains could be fed simulations of bodily experiences, because our reality might just consist of particular neuronal firings that constitute acts of cognition, memory and perception. Often our brains are seen as the location of our 'real' selves – the person who thinks, acts, feels, makes choices. The separation of mind from body is actually surprisingly common. Going to the doctor we perform this mind–body separation by treating it as a machine, as something to be treated and mended, and even have parts replaced if necessary. A great deal of Western thought has been influenced by this categorical separation of mind and body, and the brain-in-a-vat hypothesis only highlights this. Yet, pushing aside the sceptical implications of being brains in vats, in our everyday interactions and negotiations with the world, our conscious experiences are complex transactions between brain states (mind, cognition) and embodied processes (perception, sensation). This is our everyday experience, what the philosopher Edmund Husserl in 1913 termed the "natural attitude" (1999), and later taken forward by Merleau-Ponty (see e.g. Paterson 2004). Therefore, this chapter proceeds under a similar assumption that fantasy and imagination, although primarily concerned with self-consciousness and mental events, require the raw experience and sensation that comes from having a body. We then consider celebrations of bodily pleasures that attempt to escape any conscious reflection, pure excess and enjoyment. In both cases, this will survey ways that commodities interact with *experiences* and *sensations*, and this will lead us to the final strand of this chapter, the so-called "experience economy" (Pine and Gilmore 1999), the commodification of experiences and sensations.

Throughout this chapter is a motif, a productive tension. Throughout the sections to varying degrees is a dialectic of discipline and transgression, of asceticism and consumption, of tension and release. This dialectic runs throughout discourses of consumption in general, and in particular in terms of food and other bodily pleasures. This dialectic of discipline and trangression, of tension and release, appears in various moments of Western thought. In *The Republic*, Plato considered bodily pain and pleasure in this way, trying to understand the "mental change" that arises from bodily tension and release, and noting that "the majority of the intensest pleasures, so called, which we experience through the body are […] in some sense relief from pain" (1981: 409, or 584c). We need only remember a long journey and the imposition of self-control and the incomparable pleasure of subsequent urination to realise how pleasurable and indeed embodied this release can be, and how mental control over bodily processes occurs. Similarly, Freud's *Beyond the Pleasure Principle* explains the psychical apparatus in terms of the mechanical metaphor of energetic tension and release, an energetic system or "libidinal economics" (1991: 275, 308). In this system, the ego tends towards discharge of libidinal energy, of pleasurable release as much as possible. This 'pleasure principle' is not always possible, and is regulated by the superego which tends to adhere to the opposite of the pleasure principle – the 'reality principle', which tries to keep the energies available to the organism for its survival rather than pleasurable release. Between the tension of the reality principle and the release of the pleasure principle, we have a mechanism of discipline and transgression, and a psychic apparatus that allows fantasy. Freudian formulations of fantasy and repetition will feature later. However, the particular cultural mechanism of bodily discipline and pleasure that will be employed is that of Barthes and Bakhtin, who write of carnival as a time and space for festivity, for bodily trangression from the discipline of social control and hierarchy. Carnival bodies, grotesque bodies, are bodies that celebrate pleasure and excess as compared with the regulated, disciplined bodies of everyday socio-economic entrenchment. Situating the body in relations of both economic and cultural production and consumption, the body is regarded as a consuming body. There are three ways this is the case:

Consuming bodies, producing bodies. Firstly, the treatment of the body in industrial production is seen, in part, as an adjunct or further cog in the machinery, yet the body also consumes (food, education, etc.) in order to produce more, to embed the body ever further in the economic machinery of capitalism. This is an argument about consumption *as* production, an idea that Marx explored in *Grundrisse* (1973). The particular slant I wish to emphasise is the role of the body in this consumption as production, since there are both cultural and economic implications. These ideas will fit into other debates in consumption that we have encountered in the previous chapter, the historical theorisation of consumption, and material in later chapters concerning youth consumption will embellish these ideas.

Consumption as embodied experience. Secondly, and following on from this, is the embodied experience of consumption. Perhaps more straightforward in some respects, our experience of shopping, consuming and display relies on our bodies to effectuate this. Everyday, embodied experience is a crucial aspect to investigate in consumption, since somehow we approach and engage with a multiplicity of different signs, senses and embodied experiences when going shopping, whether it is the mixture of fresh and rotten smells in a street market, or the rather artificially bland spaces of shopping malls. We touch and try objects, manipulate and inspect them, in order to get a better sense of how they look, feel or would fit into our current arrays of goods. The way objects appeal to us, how they are displayed, is often with this embodied experience in mind. This is an idea from retail psychology that will be explored further in Chapter 6, 'The knowing consumer?'. So in this section we will examine how everyday embodied experience is involved in acts of consumption, and how the body is used and conceptualised in retail and marketing. One particular area that will be explored is food and food retailing, as this is perhaps the most literal meaning of 'consumption', cooking and eating being perhaps the paradigmatic example of an everyday practice of embodied consumption.

Consuming sensation. Thirdly, the commodification of experience and sensation is a particularly novel and interesting area. Within management and marketing literature, the engineering of embodied sensations occurs through a variety of different means. This moves our discussion of consumption from the purchase and display of material goods, to consider how actual experiences and sensations, whose prerequisite is having a body to experience them, can be bought and sold. From theme parks to nature tourism (explored especially in Chapter 5, 'Nature, Inc.'), the increasing address to bodily experience is a function of the increasing fluidity of capitalism, and entails a very different form of 'production' as a result (see e.g. Pine and Gilmore 1999; Thrift 2005). We will see that, in consuming sensations, there is a dialectic of discipline and transgression. In certain spaces of consumption, for example health and fitness clubs, the emphasis is on discipline and control; whereas other spaces, for example holiday resorts and dockside bar areas, emphasise excess and transgression, the 'carnivalesque'.

CONSUMING BODIES, PRODUCING BODIES

As a kind of prefatory note, briefly looking at the economics of production and consumption once again will help us to argue about embodied practices of eating, and thence commodifications of experience and sensation. Production and consumption are two inseparable aspects of the production and reproduction of human life, but in modern society these concepts have become separated. Before the socialisation of labour, that is, the separation of labour from the domestic setting to the more general economic sphere, what was produced was for immediate consumption. At this stage, production is identical with consumption, as both are entailed equally in order to preserve life: "in taking in food, for example, which is a form of consumption, the human being produces his own body", says Marx (1973: 91). With the emergence of a social division of labour, consumption becomes separated from production, and must be mediated by a system of distribution and exchange, in other words commerce. So instead of simply exercising our bodies in a healthy lifestyle, we earn a living doing inhuman, unhealthy work to pay for exercise, medicine, holidays, and suchlike, continually bargaining between time and money.

Therefore, it is not simply that production provides the starting point and consumption the end point of distribution and exchange. Marx explores these relations in depth in the first part of the *Grundrisse*, where he argues that: "Production is also immediately consumption" (1973: 90), for several reasons, of which I list three. Firstly, as noted, the body consuming food in order to become effective labour (to produce more, to produce better). Secondly, the inherent creativity of consumption is also a form of production, an idea revisited continuously throughout this book. And thirdly, the notion of consumption as restoring oneself to a previous state, the reproduction of the individual: "The individual produces an object and, by consuming it, returns to himself, but returns as a productive and self-reproducing individual" (1973: 94). These observations by Marx concerning consumption as production will be useful when considering the production of bodies that results from so-called 'industrial food' and the 'McBody', as well as the different notions and metaphors of the consuming body in its interface with the capitalist logic of production.

Cyborg bodies, vampire bodies, zombie bodies

One notion of consumption still feeds back into the notion of the consumer as 'sucker', but in a different, more literal way. The thesis of Rob

Latham's *Consuming Youth* is that young consumers especially are part vampire and part cyborg, since it is these fictional tropes that best embody the "libidinal-political dynamics of the consumerist ethos to which young people have been systematically habituated" (2002: 1). Thinking of these different forms of embodiment as fictional tropes reveals perspectives on human labour, its vitality and depletion within the larger mechanisms of consumption and production, of what happens to bodies when subject to industrial and postindustrial settings of physical machinery (the means of production, factories) and social mechanisms (cycles of innovation, consumption as creativity and expression, upgrade cycles).

Vampire bodies. Firstly, the vampyric element of consumption comes from the fact that, as Marx himself noted in his analysis of labour and production in the industrial age in *Capital*, the flipside of development and progress was inhuman exploitation. Labour power and the incessant need for production and profits meant that the lifeblood was being sucked from the workers. In the Victorian age, people entered the workforce very young. It was not until the 1920s or 1930s that youth was valued separately for its contributions of energy and vitality in the industrial workplace. The valuing of youth in the industrial workplace, based on the capacity for quick learning and adaptability, then culturally valorised youth as a distinct entity. Ewen (2001 [1976]) argues it was a result of this that advertising and marketing directly to the category of youthful consumers and producers could take place. Hence, the sucking of youthful energy and vitality in terms of production is vampyric, as is the reliance of advertising and marketing on the generation of ever-new youth categories and subcultures (teenagers, tweenagers, pre-teens, etc.), sucking their ideas, being parasitic on these youth groups for the creation of new fads, styles and sounds in order to sell these back to them. Or, in Ewen's words, "corporations which demanded youth on the production line now offered that same youth through their products" (2001 [1976]: 146).

Cyborg bodies. Secondly in Latham's account, the cyborg element. In the history of consumption, the notion of Fordist production was crucial. With long production lines, factories with a combination of heavy machinery and human labour that were producing car after car in a continuous process, Seltzer observes a "logic of prosthesis" (in Latham 2002: 14) in operation, the coupling of the human and the machine in complex operations. A prosthesis, such as an artificial leg, is a machinic extension of the human body, and so we can see this as a cyborg coupling of the human and the machine. In the factory, which is basically an organised series of flows of processes, materials and information, and which involves both humans and machines in patterns of feedback and response, it is "cybernetic" (Wiener 1948, 1950).

But what exactly is the relationship between cyborgs, youth and consumption? There are three ways that cyborgs are relevant in the present discussion. Firstly, the adaptability and willingness to learn that made young people become valued in heavily mechanised factories that Ewen (2001 [1976]) noted, above, is a direct result of the organisation of capital and mass production that was Fordism. Young human workers' flexibility and adaptability in working with machines, to be part of the informational and mechanical loops and feedback mechanisms, means that they are literally cybernetic organisms. Secondly, in a figurative sense. Building on Wiener's definition of cybernetic, Donna Haraway argues that "we are all chimeras, theorized and fabricated hybrids of machine and organism" (1991). But the real importance of such hybrids lies not in the combination of human and machine, but in the capacity of reconfiguring, for changing categories and signs. As Haraway defines them, cyborgs are "boundary creatures", having a destabilising tendency within society, and always signifying, making signs, and having the ability to reorganise or redistribute them. The play of gender, the mutability of the body and facial appearance, the tanning of skin, are all things that embodied consumers are doing. Problematising existing boundaries, challenging moral codes, destabilising traditional gendered and ethnic roles are pursued in the application of make-up, the purchase of music, the tanning of skin. Thirdly, based on evidence compiled concerning mobile phone use, the cyborg-like adaptability to the everyday use of mobiles for text messaging means that making social arrangements is often conducted on the fly, so-called "approximeeting" (Hammersley 2005: 24), and the continual use of thumbs for writing such messages is physically altering the body, making the hands more dextrous (Plant 2002). We will return to this aspect of youth culture and mobile telephony in Chapter 6, 'The knowing consumer?'.

Zombie bodies. A possibility not explored by Latham is that of zombie embodiment. Zombies exemplify a particular relation between mind and body, and are used in philosophical thought experiments to highlight the results of mind–body separation. From the introduction to this chapter, mind–body dualism has been prevalent in Western history and philosophy, but zombies are invoked as (un)living examples of what happens to bodies without minds. Inserted into relations of production and consumption, zombies also figure as those whose vitality and higher conscious processes are removed by repetitive labour and uninspiring jobs, in a similar vein to Marx's vampyric bodies, and this is explored in the horror film *Dawn of the Dead* (1978) and, in more slapstick homage, *Shaun of the Dead* (2004). The former is a bleak satire on consumption, where a few survivors take refuge from zombie hordes in a Pittsburgh shopping mall, and scenes of zombies shuffling through the elegant atriums and past immobile mannequins draped in expensive clothes is a powerful visual parody of, literally, mindless consumerism. The latter explores with great comedic effect the fact that the proliferation of mindless McJobs and the incessant need to be cool make us indistinguishable from the actual zombies that start to appear.

Shaping the body

Returning to Bourdieu's ideas about taste, class and 'habitus' (explained in Chapter 2), something of these relations of class, production and the material construction of the body is expressed in *Distinction* (1986a), and follows from the précis of Marx, above. The way that class structure allows the body a different habitus, or set of possibilities for acting and consuming, ensures that these tastes and lifestyles based on class background become literally embodied, helping to materially shape the body: "Taste, a class structure turned into nature, that is, *embodied*, helps to shape the class body" (Bourdieu 1986a: 190). Everything that the body ingests, whether materially or psychologically, he argues, is governed by this class structure. Actual body shapes, material morphologies of bodies over time, are therefore the result of these decisions and possibilities that are a function of class background, Bourdieu argues:

> It follows that the body is the most indisputable materialization of class taste, which it manifests in several ways. It does this first in the seemingly most natural features of the body, the dimensions (vol-

ume, height, weight) and shapes (round or square, stiff or supple, straight or curved) of its visible forms, which express in countless ways a whole relation to the body, i.e. a way of treating it, caring for it, feeding it, maintaining it, which reveals the deepest dispositions of the habitus.

(1986a: 190)

From Bourdieu, Shilling highlights the multiple ways that the body becomes commodified, especially in Western societies. Not only does its morphology alter according to taste and habitus, but the body also becomes a form of 'physical capital', he argues, one that complements Bourdieu's notion of 'cultural capital':

Bourdieu's analysis of the body involves an examination of the multiple ways in which the body has become commodified in modern societies. This refers not only to the body's implication in the buying and selling of labour power, but to the methods by which the body has become a more comprehensive form of *physical capital*; a possessor of power, status and distinctive symbolic forms which is integral to the accumulation of various resources.

(1993: 127)

Different classes emphasise different activities and sports, for example, which thereby shape the body in various ways, showing a relation between cultural capital, economic capital and physical capital. Turner claims that each class has a sport that articulates its particular form of economic and cultural capital: "weightlifting articulates working class bodies, while jogging and tennis produce a body which is at ease in the middle class milieu or habitus" (1992: 88). We are familiar with the cultural representations of the body; in fact, depictions of bodies and bodily ideals are inescapable in everyday life. But Turner shows here how the body is also socially produced, and this coincides directly with the rise of consumer culture from the 1920s onwards, where bodily norms are created and reproduced (Bell and Valentine 1997: 26; Featherstone 2003: 163ff.). Having established such norms and aspirational bodily ideals, bodily maintenance itself becomes a marketable commodity (Featherstone 1991b). From the class-based activities of the habitus we now shift attention back to the consumption of food.

The McBody: Fordist food

Bearing in mind that only those affluent enough in urban industrial societies can truly choose to eat healthily, poverty often means an impoverishment of choice in these matters, and the position that Bourdieu observes – "Plain speaking, plain eating: the working-class meal is characterized by plenty" (1984: 194). Writing about food and the city, David Bell takes a similar approach to Bourdieu, but with a twist of McDonaldization (Ritzer 1993), the double movement of homogenisation and heterogenisation discussed in Chapter 3. Following on from the logic of Fordist industrial production, the standardisation of products and the inflexibility of the production line simply and ceaselessly churning out commodities, Bell talks of "industrial food":

> Industrial food, like modernist architecture, might once have been seen as an answer to social problems, but now seems only to bring new troubles, new indigestions. Of course, abundance-as-sameness still has a prominent place, most notably in fast foods, where it is matched by super-sizing as a double abundance.
>
> (2002: 12)

Industrial food, exemplified by fast-food outlets, bears the legacy of Fordist food preparation, producing abundance, predictability and regularity, under the mantra of McDonaldization. This relation of Fordist industrial production and the consumption of industrial food, obviously, has effects on the body. Fordist food production produces the Fordist consumer, too, the McBody:

> Americans are conscripted to the unseasonable pursuit of abundance. The impossibility of the dream is saved by the translation of quality into quantity and the identification of availability with desirability.
>
> (O'Neill 1999: 49)

Morgan Spurlock's recent documentary *Super Size Me* (USA, 2004) takes this premise of the McBody to its bizarre and logical conclusion. Existing purely on a diet of McDonalds food for a month, and against the advice of doctors and dieticians who regularly monitor him throughout the experiment, Spurlock charts the effects of the regime of fast food on the body. The rules were simple: his three meals a day must all be from the McDonalds menu, and if staff ever offered to 'super size' the order (increasing from a regular size to an extra-large size), he had to agree. The title therefore refers both to the order 'Super size me!', requesting an extra-large meal, and to the actual bodily effects that resulted – a super-sized Morgan Spurlock. The physiological effects charted throughout the film are startling, ranging from weight gain, sugar addiction, 'McSweats', 'McTwitches' and vomiting. "Over the month, he gains 25lb and his cholesterol level goes through the roof" (McKie 2004). Heart palpitations and breathing difficulties start occurring after only twenty-one days, and his doctor equates the effects of the food to an all-out assault on his system. There is no better illustration of the McBody, the physiological effects of industrial food, the notion of how the body responds to the Fordist ethic of abundance, or the equation of availability with desirability. Quite apart from Bourdieu's notion of the effects of habitus or class background on the body, as we have seen, the consumption of 'industrial food' in a regime of Fordist production has noticeable physiological, psychological and material effects on the body. This could usefully be contrasted with more affluent, middle-class concerns with health foods and the rise of the organic movement in the affluent West.

CONSUMPTION AS EMBODIED EXPERIENCE

Consuming food

Cooking and eating are perhaps the most literal forms that consumption as 'using up' can take. The 'McBody' as a result of industrial food has been touched upon, but here the everyday practices of cooking and eating directly relate consumption to embodiment, to accumulation, the growth and shape of individual bodies. "At the simplest biological level, by the act of eating and absorption of food, we become what we eat" (Lupton 1996: 16). As what we eat accrues symbolic and cultural meanings quite apart from merely physiological values, altering our eating regimen similarly alters our body, making it *become* something different. Increasingly, social theory is taking account of the fragmented and changing experiences of embodiment and of subjectivity, such that, in Shilling's words, the body is a project, an "entity in the process of becoming" (1993: 5). Food is one way that the body is experienced and situated in cultural context. But food as literal consumption maps onto more general consumer practices in a number of ways. Firstly, in the way that food and eating are central to our subjectivity, our sense of self, and our experience of embodiment. Secondly, the morphology of self and body and their shifting contexts underlines the fact that, through consumption, we are continually undergoing processes of physiological, psychological, and cultural becoming, and much else besides.

Once we accept that both bodies and subjectivities are dynamic, and that consumption of food and consumption in general are modes of influencing and articulating this process of becoming, then we arrive at something like Foucault's 'practices' or 'technologies' of the self (Martin *et al.* 1988). If Bourdieu's *habitus* was mostly structured from the outside through class and background, Foucault's practices of the self are part of the individual's own project to construct and express their identity, adopting discourses as well as physical phenomena (clothes, commodities) to aid them. As Lupton explains,

> The practices of the self are the ways in which individuals respond to external imperatives concerning self-regulation and comportment, how they recognise them as important or necessary and incorporate these imperatives into everyday life. Such practices 'inscribe' or 'write' upon the body, marking and shaping it in culturally specific ways which are then 'read' or interpreted by others.
>
> (1996: 15)

Consumption practices that involve the body, such as the purchase of clothing and ornamentation, are clearly practices of the self. Food habits and eating preferences are also clearly core practices of the self, in terms of eating culturally 'appropriate' foods, and presenting a persona that is interpreted by others through particular foods, table manners and body shape. There are three other factors worthy of consideration that relate consumption of food to consumption in general.

First, both Lupton (1996: 17) and Bell and Valentine (1997: 49) fix upon what Claude Fischler calls the "omnivore's paradox" (1988). Again, this is an oscillation between states, a movement that characterises much of this chapter and indeed this book. The paradox lies in the fact that, as human omnivores, we need a varied diet and so tend towards innovation and variation in food types. Yet, simultaneously, food is also a potential source of danger, contamination and disease, and so we must be conservative about what we eat. "The omnivore's paradox lies in the tension, the oscillation between the two poles of *neophobia* (prudence, fear of the unknown, resistance to change) and *neophilia* (the tendency to explore, the need for change, novelty, variety)", as Fischler explains (1988: 278). The process of making a food civilised, acceptable and amenable to us is a cultural stamp or imprint onto unknown territory, effectively turning 'nature' into 'culture'. Eating the flesh of other humans is widely unacceptable, yet the flesh of some animals is more acceptable as 'food' than others. There are cultural processes at work in turning what one Chinese man described as the "putrefied mucous discharge of an animal's guts" (Driver, in Lupton 1996: 35) into what Westerners see it as: cheese. This double movement, the paradox of neophilia and neophobia, is a necessary tension in terms of maintaining the individual body (feeding it yet protecting it) and the collective body (defining what is and is not acceptable). In addition, if we were searching for another paradox of consumption in general, neophilia and neophobia could characterise our insatiable desire for novelty yet resistance to commodities and experiences.

Second, Lupton identifies a dialectic of asceticism and consumption (1996: 131), another mechanism in line with the tension and release, or discipline and transgression, that has run throughout this chapter. The inherently embodied experience of eating shows up the dialectic neatly: our self-discipline accommodates the manners of the civilised society that we have been socialised into, whereas our animalistic tendencies would revel in the sheer pleasures of gluttony, and the almost sexual abandon that results. In fact, as Lupton (1996) and Probyn (2000) show, there are continual links between sexual temptation and gluttony, acknowledging the manufactured divide between unfettered desire (Freud's 'pleasure principle') and self-discipline (Freud's 'reality principle'). To separate these tendencies so starkly is also to separate the bodily pleasures (food and sex) from the control of the mind. We thereby revisit the separation between mind and body that started this chapter. This is important because mind–body dualism certainly characterises the anorexic body, the body that is subjugated to the will of the mind that craves food but which fears contamination (of boundaries, of body, of shape). Bordo (1993) acknowledges this mind–body separation in the anorexic body, the lusts and desires of the body being tempered by acts of will and control. Like the anorexic body, we are subject to the "food/health/beauty triplex", argues Lupton (1996: 137), and this is increasingly the case with men, as Bocock (1993: 105) discusses. This nexus of concepts is what makes the slim body a youthful, sexually attractive body, only possible through a continual regime of dieting and/or exercise. Since we are all subject to this triplex to varying degrees, we are similarly subject to the dialectic of asceticism and consumption. In escaping discipline and self-control, by allowing bodily pleasures, animalistic and excessive desires that spill over normal or everyday boundaries, we celebrate transgression, excess, consumption, the carnivalesque, as will be discussed in the following section.

Third, Arjun Appadurai interestingly relates consumption and embodiment with time. There is a periodicity to consumption that is exemplified in eating food, especially when it comes to rituals or rites of passage. We remember the cake at a wedding, the first time we taste alcohol, or the 'last meal' of a condemned prisoner. He characterises contemporary consumption as governed by ephemerality, scopophilia (the love of looking) and body manipulation, linked into "a set of practices that involve a radically new relationship between wanting, remembering, being and buying" (1993: 33). The radically ephemeral and periodic nature of consumption is something that allows the play of identity, a kind of oscillation between wanting, wishing, being and buying that is part of the whole cycle of processes of consumption. The following section, 'Consuming sensation', looks at the notion of phantasmagoria, the dreamlike state of imaginative possibilities in consumption settings. This imaginative engagement with the possibilities that consumption affords is also examined in terms of the concrete spaces of modernity, the arcades and department stores of Paris, in Chapter 7. For now, let us think of the periodicity of consumption as heavily embodied, where the cycle from interest or arousal to the possibilities of the commodity is then tempered by the abject, disgust, contempt and renewal. Appadurai continues the theme of consumption as periodic and ephemeral:

> Ephemerality becomes the civilising counterpart of flexible accumulation and the work of the imagination is to link the ephemerality of goods with the pleasures of the senses.
>
> (1993: 33)

Consuming Sensation

Continuing the theme of the ephemerality of goods, the pleasures of the senses, we move on from food to explore other aspects of embodied consumption. The desiring, wishing consumer who looks at commodities in their luxurious settings is particularly relevant to arcades and early department stores, the spaces of consumption, and this is examined in some depth in Chapter 7. However, aspects of desiring, fulfilment and consummation oscillate between the ephemeral and imaginative and the inescapably embodied, and so the embodied subject's experience of fantasy and fulfilment can be usefully explored here. Firstly, the experience of fantasy, the pursuit of commodities and their representations, allies some psychoanalytic concepts into the process of consumption. Secondly, the disputation and subversion of prevailing social authority and control is examined in the celebration of transgression and excess in festivals and carnival. Both of these being embodied experiences, we will see that they are embodied in different ways, both literal and metaphorical. Earlier, this chapter was concerned with some concretely embodied experiences of food, body and habitus, but later in this section we consider the transition from the consumption of material commodities to that of experiential commodities – consumption of experiences, what Lee terms a "de-materialisation" (1993: 135), and Pine and Gilmore term the "experience economy" (1999).

Mental pleasures of wishing, desiring and fantasy

An important component to our everyday experience of consumption is the wishing for commodities, the daydreaming of possibilities, that comes from window-shopping. As desire, its satisfaction is constantly postponed or deferred, never quite reaching satiation or fulfilment. Previously we noted that a part of 'consumption' resides in 'consummation' or fulfilment, a bringing to completion, and this would imply attaining satisfaction. Closing a deal between shopper and salesperson, making a sale, is often described as "consummatory", as Bowlby (1993: 109) notes. Of course, for the consumer any satisfaction is short-lived, and any sense of fulfilment passes swiftly, furthering this sexual metaphor. We become habituated to a new product and anticipate the next one. We experience a sustained and ever-renewed wishing or desiring that continually seeks fulfilment.

Knowing this, the question concerning desire and consumption is not about a product being "used" (or used up, consumed), but how those "climactic moments" (1993: 110) of anticipation and satiation can be reached. In this way, fantasy culminates in a 'real' event, but is then renewed.

In German, phantasie denotes an imaginative world and its contents, but not necessarily in opposition to any 'real' world. "Fantasy is an imagined scene in which the subject is a protagonist, and which always represents the fulfilment of a wish", as Cowie (1999: 356) succinctly explains. As protagonist, perhaps echoing Campbell's notion of the romantic consumer discussed in Chapter 1, fantasy is experienced from a first-person perspective. True, it is not 'reality' as such, but our familiar experiences of daydreaming and fantasy have an undeniable strength and existence of their own, an existence that runs parallel to our everyday, 'normal' perceptions of concrete reality. Fantasies of identity, of imagining oneself otherwise, are often pursued through consumption and window-shopping, and Angela McRobbie recognises the importance for young women especially of "the space of fantasy ... the state of distractions ... the daydream" (in Lury 1996: 185), as we shall do. Freud for example makes this distinction, between the "material reality" and the "psychical reality" of unconscious wishes and fantasy, explicit:

> If we look at unconscious wishes reduced to their most fundamental and truest shape, we shall have to conclude no doubt that psychical reality is a particular form of existence not to be confused with material reality.
>
> (Freud 1900, in Cowie 1999: 357)

As consumers, the cultivation of unconscious wishes and desires, the endless promise of unattainable fulfilment, is offered to us when window-shopping, browsing, or "just looking" (Bowlby 1985). Advertisements in whatever media pander to the imagination and the "ceaseless consumption of novelty" (Slater 1997: 96). Employing Campbell's (1987) distinction between the romantically inspired consumer and the rational economic subject, advertisements engage our romantic, capricious and hedonistic side, and in Slater's words are "about feeling, imaginative desiring and longing, rather than reason" (1997: 95). We do not habitually confuse psychical reality with material reality, yet in the translation between 'wishing' and 'having', between 'desiring' and 'possession', elements of psychical reality do become material reality. When shopping, the fantasy of owning and possessing a commodity is played through, turned over, explored in our minds. Seeing a figurine within a glass cabinet in a department store, we might ask a sales assistant to 'see' it – meaning to hold, touch, manipulate the object – and we might imagine where the figurine might be placed in our house, how it might fit with other similar objects that we own. Its material properties are browsed, played through. If at last we do purchase the object, its material reality comes home with us, and "that quintessential twentieth-century psychical drama" (Bowlby 1993: 104) that starts with browsing and culminates in the sale, is played out. The sale, the consummation, translates the psychical idea to the physical act; impression to expression; those conscious and unconscious mental events of fantasy into physical, material, embodied reality. In its path from psychical reality to material reality, however, attainment is never equated with fulfilment. Desire renews itself, and wishing begins again.

Nevertheless, this consummatory fantasy does not necessarily entail that consumers are being 'duped', easily led; consumers are often characterised as suckers or dupes, figures with vague sets of desires, unconscious wishes and cravings that can be manipulated or redirected (see Chapter 7). But the relationship between object and fantasy is not so straightforward, and the Freudian model of the consumer in textbooks and marketing manuals certainly has its limitations. Bowlby has analysed numerous historical manuals for sales staff that take pleasure through transforming the "psychical wish into a physiological action" (1993: 115), deploying and misappropriating Freudian terminology. Despite being wishful, fantasies "are not about a wish to have some determinate object, making it present for the subject", declares Cowie (1999: 360). In other words, it is not so straightforwardly object orientated, nor is it reducible to the infamous Freudian mechanism of penis-envy, of absent presence. In my department store example, above, it is the fantasy of what the object *would be*, its possible delights and imagined settings in the home, that is mentally explored, played through. This distinction is important, and means that the creative play of imagination is irreducible to mere mechanism. As Safouan declares, echoing Lacan, "instead of being co-opted to an object, desire is first co-opted to a fantasy" (in Cowie 1999: 361). For, if desire were co-opted to an object, satisfaction would be achieved once the object was attained. If desire is co-opted to a fantasy, then the attainment of an object alters nothing, for the fantasy remains; going from one object to another, satisfaction is deferred. It is vacillation, a wavering movement between psychical desire and its bodily satisfaction, then back again.

In shopping arcades, department stores and malls, what matters as much as the object itself is the *setting*, the window display, the *mise en scène*. These spaces of consumption are examined in Chapter 7, but the effectiveness of the setting of the object is considerable. It is the setting, the arrangement of objects in some luxurious or enviable context, rather than the singular object itself, that perpetuates the fantasy:

> Fantasy involves, is characterised by, not the achievement of desired objects, but the arranging of, a setting out of, desire: a veritable *mise-en-scène* of desire. For, of course, Lacan says, desire is unsatisfiable [...] The fantasy depends not on particular objects, but on their setting out; and the pleasure of fantasy lies in the setting out, not in the having of the objects.
>
> (Cowie 1999: 361, text corrected)

Bearing this in mind, the experience of shopping is one simultaneously of imagination, sensuality, fantasy, wishing and desire. The raw material in fantasy is drawn from everyday embodied experience and sensations, a reworking of previous encounters with objects and settings in the present moment. In a famous article on fantasy, Laplanche and Pontalis state: "The day-dream is a shadow play, utilising its kaleidoscopic material drawn from all quarters of human experience" (1968: 13). The first-person experience is almost heroic yet distracted, a strolling subject who makes and remakes themselves in response to the manifold objects on offer in their often luxurious and exotic window displays (on this subject, the *flâneur* is discussed further in Chapter 7). At once a rich imaginative and embodied experience, both mental and physical, allowing a scent or brush of fabric to distract the attention and, even if momentarily, to open up a space for daydreaming.

Bodily pleasures and the 'carnivalesque'

While daydreaming is an everyday occurrence, the body's constant presence as material reality runs alongside the imagination, the psychic reality of which Freud spoke. The dualism between mental and physical, mind and body, should be familiar, known as Cartesian dualism after the French philosopher and mathematician René Descartes (1596–1650). While there is a long tradition in Western thought of valuing the mind as opposed to the body, in recent decades the importance of the body has been reasserted in philosophy and social theory. In many aspects of consumption embodiment is crucial, the dualism is inverted, and the physical body is prioritised over the rational mind. This is explored in consumer psychology and appeals to pre-reflective sensuality, for example (see Chapter 6). We will follow a different strand of desiring and wishing now, one that is emphatically embodied. In tourist literature, one site where this dualism is inverted but not deconstructed is that of the beach. Rob Shields (1992, after Turner 1974) sees the beach as an example of a "liminal space", where known social orders may be suspended, and different rules apply. For all the writings concerning the body and the gendered politics of embodiment, it is as if the beach reminds us of a different evaluation of embodiment, where the body in its aesthetic obviousness, its physique and physiology, is inescapable. Shields understands beaches as liminal spaces in that they offer some kind of alternative to the disciplines and routines of modern city life. The liminality of the beach functions as a form of disorder, a place of 'desire', contrasted with the instrumentality and bureaucracy of city life. Beaches and the bodies on them provide a cultural space for illicit pleasures, of sexuality, of play, of display, and a place culturally designated as being between nature and culture. In this sense, liminality signifies the difference between a space of discipline and a space of pleasure, where the city emphasises work, labour and industry, whereas the beach valorises the body and its pleasures, not only the play and display of bodies but also 'dirty weekends', the sexual innuendo of music hall, and saucy postcards.

To develop the inversion of body over mind, another related term that incorporates these themes of pleasure, consumption and embodiment is that of the 'carnivalesque'. This notion derives from the work of Mikhail Bakhtin (1895–1975), a Marxist literary critic who wrote about the medieval French poet Rabelais. Bakhtin's concern with carnival was to see how it disrupted the rules of everyday practice and hierarchy in the medieval world. Carnival upended several hierarchies: there was a king of fools, emphasis on bodies and orifices rather than minds or the clergy, and a celebration of excess and surfeit in the face of everyday hunger and lack. The excess and disruption of carnival signifies not only energy and vitality, but also a potential political subversion, a temporary freedom from social control:

> The carnivalesque crowd in the marketplace or in the streets is not merely a crowd. It is the people as a whole, but organized in their own way, the way of the people. It is outside of and contrary to all existing forms of the coercive socioeconomic and political organization, which is suspended for the time of the festivity.
>
> (Bakhtin 1984: 255)

Popular pleasures are not those of the mind but of the body. It is the emphasis on bodily pleasures in carnival rather than the usual bureaucratic, legal and theological order that locates larger social concerns within the individual body, and makes the body a site of struggle and resistance, of power and evasion, of discipline and transgression. These bodily pleasures are unashamedly populist and immersive, not divorcing the spectacle from the observers, but involving all:

> Carnival does not know footlights, in the sense that it does not acknowledge any distinction between actors and spectators [...] Carnival is not a spectacle seen by the people: they live in it, and everyone participates because its very idea embraces all the people.
>
> (1984: 7)

Against the legislature and control over the body politic, the individual body, with its popular pleasures and capacity for excess and trangression, allowed a creative and playful freedom that was potentially a threat. Fiske (1989a: 76) puts this dialectic of discipline and trangression in terms of "recreation" and "release", such that the forms of organised leisure or recreation imposed by authority are opposed by the carnivalesque, focused on bodily pleasures and by nature excessive. During Victorian times, for example, holidays from work were highly organised, based around moral improvement and family values, encouraging temperance and sobriety; whereas spontaneous, bottom-up organisation by participants celebrated the popular pleasures of the body, of drinking, fighting, fornication and excess. Both these are visible in the history of Brighton beach, as Shields (1992) shows, the attractiveness of Brighton lying in its proximity to London.

With bodily pleasures comes release, and rather than the guarded subjectivity and temperance encouraged by the prevailing social order, a loss of self is incurred, a release from "socially constructed and disciplined subjectivity", as Fiske (1989a: 83) puts it. Something exceeds the usual, policed boundaries of practice and decorum in these moments of release, and the emphasis on bodily pleasure entails only a small step to the metaphor of orgasmic release, the form of pleasure exerted from an external source that Barthes describes as *"jouissance"* (1975). With this form of release, the individual body is no longer policed and disciplined but spills over or exceeds; Foucault's (1990: 103ff.) characterisation of medieval bodies is one where orifices open up, sexuality, dirt and disease spread between them. The regulation and disciplining of the body and its practices subsequently in the seventeenth century increased the power of the state over that of the individual through the locus of the body. As Fiske summarises, the body "is where the power-bearing definitions of social and sexual normality are, literally, embodied, and is consequently the site of discipline and punishment for deviation from these norms" (1989a: 90). These social and sexual norms were held by the bourgeoisie, who feared the proletarian body with its popular, bodily pleasures. This is essentially an oppositional account that puts the people versus the power-bloc, as Stuart Hall (1981, after Gramsci 1971) describes. This is discussed further in Chapter 6.

Both Bakhtin (1984) and Barthes (1973) use the example of the Italian *commedia dell'arte*, a band of comic improvisational actors and performers in the sixteenth and seventeenth centuries, who travelled around and performed in town squares and piazzas. Unashamedly populist, the performances were often bawdy, using sexual language and physical comedy to poke fun at society's respectable norms and values. This was effected by exaggerated styles and developing stock characters to be satirised. An important element of this was the *grotesque*, exaggerating characters and situations for comic effect, and the use of masks and props, for the purpose of satire, foolery and laughter. Barthes's innovation is to relate this physical spectacle of bodies to television wrestling, and while this is undoubtedly embodied, exaggerated and possibly cathartic, its satirical content is mostly self-satire. However, the influence of the carnivalesque, its exaggeration into the grotesque, and the improvisational, quick-witted and subversive qualities of the performances, runs throughout the tradition of theatre and performance, and is undeniably present in modern consumer settings of pleasure and festivity such as the beach and the music festival. The carnivalesque, in its Renaissance and more recent incarnations, is emphatically embodied, and as should be clear, celebrates the spontaneity and physicality of 'release' rather than the imposed order of 'recreation'. In the context of modern business management, Pine and Gilmore (1999) are more concerned with the provision of experiences as opposed to services, attempting to describe and indeed engineer an 'experience economy'. It is no accident that the cover of their book features a photograph of a Venetian carnival *commedia dell'arte* mask.

We can easily see elements of the carnivalesque and grotesque in beach settings in old postcards, Donald McGills's notoriously saucy postcards involving fat women and innuendo being the most famous; in practices of eating and drinking, in play and display. But we must exercise caution before unduly celebrating the popular pleasures of the carnivalesque. Mary Russo (1994) for example takes her cue from a phrase heard as a child, "She is making a spectacle of herself", to point towards problems for women in relation to the carnivalesque, for it was often women's bodies (as in McGills's postcards) that were the object of laughter. Arthurs and Grimshaw (1999) also explore this problematic notion of the carnivalesque, and the plethora of reality television shows that show female bodies as spectacle, as transgressing from the gendered norm of self-control and discipline, is discussed by Arthurs (2004). We might ask whether carnivalesque displays of bodies on beaches and on reality television shows such as *Temptation Island* devalue women, making them grotesque, instead of providing a space for their liberation from normal conventions of deportment and behaviour. Similarly, the space of music festivals has increasingly become commodified. Starting from free festivals in the 1960s and 1970s, music festivals such as the Glastonbury Festival of Contemporary Performing Arts, whose first festival in 1970 cost £1 and included a free pint of milk from the farm, have now become vast corporate behemoths. Bodily pleasures are nevertheless emphasised, involving everything from dancing, drug-taking, alcohol-fuelled hedonism to the more sedate pleasures of Reiki massage and Tai Chi. Undoubtedly a temporary space of pleasure and release rather than discipline or mere recreation, it has become increasingly over-subscribed, increasingly organised for reasons of security and crowd control, but also sponsored, commodified and homogenised as a result. This argument is allied to that developed in Chapter 3 on 'McDisneyfication'.

A criticism of the carnivalesque that follows from the above observations is that they are *licensed* moments of the eruption of the grotesque. The challenging of the usual order is permitted, as Eagleton (1981) argues, because the release that is effected works as an important social safety valve, actually strengthening the social hierarchy and the apparatus of social control. The disruptive moment that carnival allows is recuperated or assimilated into the prevailing order. While celebrating popular pleasures, even satirising those in authority, its political effectiveness in terms of challenging or progressively reordering the forces of power and control is limited. In answer to this criticism, Stallybrass and White (1986) argue instead that the truth varies, and that carnival should not be essentialised as either genuinely progressive or as simply another mechanism whereby the prevailing order reasserts itself. As Fiske (1989a: 100) summarises, historically the place of carnival in medieval Europe did, at some key points, have politically transformative effects, with popular uprisings occurring at festival times, and more recently festival can be utopian and counter-hegemonic. Whatever the actual political effects are, these spaces and times of bodily pleasure and excess do expose, if only momentarily, the fragility and arbitrariness of the social order. They are also testament to the vitality and energy of popular forces, the excessive energies that bleed beyond the normal body and the normal social order. The potential to be progressive and disruptive is there, even if this is not always actualised.

CONCLUSION: BODILY RESTRAINT AND EXCESS

It would be all too easy in a chapter entitled 'Bodyshopping' to become literal, turning the discussion towards cosmetic surgery, liposuction, and other ways that bodies are commodified, transformed, exchanged, and bargained with. The popular media's obsession with celebrities and their altering of body parts is consistent with some themes introduced here, but will receive no treatment here. Instead, we have covered a number of themes concerning the immediacy of embodied experiences of consumption, of the way that the body is produced and reproduced through relations of work, labour and class. Throughout this chapter we have explored and revisited a central mechanism, the dialectic of asceticism and consumption, of discipline and transgression, of tension and release, of mental control or fantasy and bodily pleasures. This has been the case with food, with carnival, and with the commodification of experiences and sensations. Writing about the body, even slim bodies, is a gargantuan task since they are implicated in so many forms of consumption, and no book chapter can be exhaustive. By organising some of the ideas and examples around a few central mechanisms of tension and release, of discipline and transgression, of asceticism and consumption, this at least highlights some important areas around embodiment. These counter-tendencies of rationality, stoicism and self-control versus the romantic valorisation of pleasure, emotions and impulses seem to map neatly onto consumption. What Lupton (1996) identified as the dialectic of asceticism and consumption is what Featherstone describes as the two imperatives of consumer culture – the release of control, spending freely, consuming and indulging versus the maintenance of control, saving, producing, the imposition of self-discipline (1990: 13). Although evidently in opposition, the reality is that there is a continual negotiation between positions, and the payoff is this: once we are in possession of the slim, muscular body that requires so much self-control and discipline, then we are more attractive and able to be hedonistic. The one *produces* the other, and in fact the disciplined body can *consume* more in terms of 'healthy' options; diet yoghurts, overpriced water and gym memberships show that this is actually a mechanism of both asceticism *and* consumption, of discipline *and* transgression (Falk 1994: 65; Lupton 1996: 152).

For the remainder of this conclusion I wish to point towards some areas where the "de-materialisation" of commodities (Lee 1993: 135) is evident, whereby it is experiences and sensations that are sold rather than material commodities. This shift is what Pine and Gilmore herald as the arrival of an "experience economy" (1999). The usual organisation of the provision of tangible commodities and material exchange that we think of as straightforward production and consumption is subsequently displaced by the provision of services such as restaurant food and financial advice in our 'service economy'. But the 'service economy' is now supplanted by our hunger for experiences, and an 'experience economy' results. The rise of theme parks, of themed restaurants where everywhere there is a performance, can touch on many other areas of business, they argue. The important element for consumer culture is the acknowl-edgement that we are no longer solely interested in tangible goods, but wish to participate in elaborately constructed spaces of fantasy and day-dreaming, themed enterprises in which we can be immersed and escape the mundane. While food as literal consumption is often an important element of these new leisure experiences, the provision of less tangible experiences and sensations is becoming increasingly important and sought after. Particular rides and rollercoasters in theme parks for exam-ple involve the engineering of complex bodily sensations such as kinaes-thesia (the sense of movement), of balance, of visceral sensations. In Chapter 7 concerning the spaces of consumption, some of these insights of experience and immersion will be applied to shopping malls. In the next chapter, concerning the commodification and consumption of nature, we will examine the way that nature-based theme parks package a series of experiences to be consumed. They are already a part of the experience economy, and signify one of the cultures of nature: as pre-packaged entertainment, to be consumed.

5

NATURE, INC.

For the twentieth-century tourist, the world has become one large department store of countrysides and cities.

(Schivelbusch 1986: 197)

'SeaWorld is like a mall with fish.'

(A student, in Davis 1995: 206)

FROM SEAWORLD™ TO 'SEE THE WORLD': THE SPECTACLE OF NATURE

If the majority of our everyday consumption practices occur within urban settings, this should not obscure the fact that we consume nature in myriad ways. Whether in advertisements, posters, stores like The Body Shop or visiting a travel agent's, even within the densest urban formations nature is offered and sold to us. We avidly consume presentations and representations of 'nature' and the 'wild', and consequently our desire to engage with it more directly is perpetually fuelled. Direct engagements with nature can occur through recreation and leisure pursuits, whether at the beach, a country walk, at a nature-based theme park, or on safari. This chapter is concerned with the consumption of nature, which entails the consumption of images, representations, fantasies and experiences of the nonhuman environment in all its forms. For the purposes of this chapter we consider two popular means of consuming nature: the managed, pre-packaged and heavily mediated form of nature-based theme

Figure 5.1 Let me show you the world in my eyes ... Photo of travel agent's rack of brochures. © 2005 Author photograph.

parks such as SeaWorld™ and Disney's Animal Kingdom™; and nature-based tourism, exemplified by safari expeditions. These two forms of consumption involve an assumed difference between the passive, pre-packaged or Disneyized encounter with nature on the one hand

(SeaWorld™), and the more active, 'authentic' or unmediated engagement with nature on the other ('See the World'). Any such simplistic distinction is problematic, however. Very rarely is the nonhuman
encountered in anything other than a mediated form, whether in zoos,
theme parks or on safari, and so in considering encounters with commodified nature we will be advancing an argument concerning the consumption of nature as spectacle, that is, of spectacular consumption.

The 'gaze' and the fetishisation of nature. Natural phenomena and
events are signposted, our attention is directed to certain things and not
others, and so our consumption is often of particular signs and representations of nature. There is a particular way of seeing that becomes cultivated, partly the result of fantasies and daydreams concerning the
natural world that we wish to buy into, and which are subsequently sold
back to us in commoditised form, as advertisements, theme-park rides
and eco-friendly products. The cultivation of particular forms of attention that occur in recreational activity is what Urry terms the "tourist
gaze" (2002, originally 1990; 2003), something outlined and explored
in this section, where the 'tourist gaze' and the fetishisation of place are
both integral components of our consumption of nature. In addition, a
related concept of the "zoological gaze" (Franklin 1999) becomes pertinent in the case of the blurring of boundaries between zoos and nature-
based theme parks, and the increasing commodification of 'wildness'.

SeaWorld™ and themed nature. The second part of the chapter is
concerned with nature-based theme parks and The Nature Company
stores. Our imaginations and fantasies of nature are engaged through
theme parks such as SeaWorld™ and stores in the mall like The Nature
Company, and we desire and consume particularly idealised versions of
nature. This neatly fits into previous discussions of the McDonaldization
and Disneyization of society in Chapter 3, and is an example of Urry's
'collective gaze'. What better example of dedifferentiation, looking at
both a theme park and a store, both places of consumption and leisure
that fetishise 'nature'? Consequently, theme parks and nature-based
tourism can be seen to offer consumers variously regulated, pre-packaged, predictable and controlled sets of experiences, so that we could
speak of a "McDisneyization" (after Ritzer and Liska 1997) of nature.
However, nature-based theme parks such as SeaWorld™ and Disney's

own Animal Kingdom™ exemplify another concern pertinent to this chapter: the commodification of nature through the staging of nature as spectacle. In other words, nature becomes pre-packaged, managed, re-engineered and re-mediated. Arguably these representations of nature do exhibit the four features of Disneyization that Bryman identifies, namely theming (the management of consistent theming of nature in parks, such as by geographical area of simulated habitat), dedifferentiation (the collapsing of previously separated areas of consumption such as malls and theme parks), merchandising (Shamu T-shirts, posters, caps) and emotional labour (the management of visitors' experiences of these spaces). But there is far more to the consumption of nature than Disneyization, of course, and Susan Davis's (1995, 1997) work on SeaWorld™ will develop some notions not only of the 'gaze' but also of desiring, fantasies of communion with animals, and the imaginations of 'wildness' inherent in the visual consumption of nature, that is, of spectacular consumption. By looking at SeaWorld™ and the store chain The Nature Company, we will move on from the common argument that, through commodification, nature is becoming *simulation*, and instead begin to talk of the *virtualisation* of nature.

'See the World': tourism as desiring nature. It is tempting to think of a more direct engagement with nature, eschewing theme parks and 'tamed' forms of nature, as somehow more 'authentic', more 'real'. The tourist's motive in seeking a less mediated encounter with nature, one that exemplifies Urry's 'romantic gaze', is the concern of the third part of the chapter. The romantically inspired desire to be in communion with nature must contend with the fact that most tourist experience is structured and organised to varying degrees, despite our best intentions. MacCannell's influential work on the tourist (1976) and the notion of the "post-tourist" (Feifer 1985) directly confront this tension between authenticity and the mediation of experiences. Along the way, Edensor (1998) and others will show us that, if speaking of the McDonaldization of tourism is reductive, tourist experience and the management of tourist expectation is structured in a number of ways. We shall apply this to various tourist encounters with nature. Examples could range from the beach (as a site of nature/culture) to adventure tourism to ecotourism. Instead, to advance the point that spectacular consumption may also fetishise place and timeless nature through first-world/third-world colonial histories and exploitation, the example will be safaris. Roughly, this is proceeding from the management and packaging of *commodities* to the organisation and packaging of *experiences*, and therefore from Veblen's notion of *conspicuous consumption* to that of *spectacular consumption*, the primarily visual form of the consumption of a staged nature, characterised by the tourist gaze.

THE 'GAZE' AND THE FETISHISATION OF NATURE

> The idea of nature contains, though often unnoticed, an extraordinary amount of human history.
>
> (Williams 1980: 67)

The gaze

The idea of the 'gaze' is extremely useful here, referring in general to the way we organise or enframe phenomena through our acts of looking. There is certainly a visual bias, although other senses are obviously involved in experiencing natural phenomena. But since it is dominant, it is the visual sense which organises experience and is invested with power, since the powerless are subject to the gaze of the powerful. Foucault identifies this practice of the power-inflected gaze in the history of medicine as the 'medical gaze' that separates doctors from patients (1973), and Mulvey in the context of the movie camera objectifying passive female bodies as the 'male gaze' (1981). It is from this genealogy that Urry develops his notion of the 'tourist gaze', applicable to experiences of natural and cultural phenomena. In addition, Franklin's 'zoological gaze' (1999) refers to the way that confined animals become objects of analysis within both scientific and recreational modes, making them at once recreation on the part of the zoo-visiting public, and also part of a larger educational concern with conservation and the preservation of species. Just as tourists desire to have authentic encounters with 'genuine' natural and cultural phenomena, Franklin notes a genuine curiosity and concern to appreciate animals *as* animals, and not as surrogate humans (1999: 86). Yet, the tendency for zoos to theme animals in their supposedly naturalistic settings is evidence of the opposite, of anthropomorphism. Remembering (from Chapter 3) that 'theming' is a major element in Bryman's notion of 'Disneyization', this allows Beardsworth and Bryman to talk of the "Disneyization of zoos" (2001).

The tourist gaze

The 'right to roam', 'getting back to nature,' 'getting away from it all' are popular expressions that allude to the way that we desire to leave our domiciles, our sites of quotidian human domesticity, and encounter something other, something outside. For the majority of us in the developed world, being a traveller (or tourist) means going to a previously unvisited place. Be it populous, vibrant urban centres, or environments with a diversity of nonhuman plant and animal species, when going 'away' we become receptive to the spectacular shapes, sounds, smells and colours of a burgeoning nature, teeming with extraordinary and inspirational life-forms. To become travellers or tourists, to cultivate this newly receptive attitude, is to seek departure from everyday life, thinks Urry. Tourist practices "involve the notion of 'departure', of a limited breaking with established routines and practices of everyday life and allowing one's senses to engage with a set of stimuli that contrast with the everyday and the mundane", suggests Urry (2002: 2). Later in the same volume he continues this idea: "Central to much tourism is some notion of departure, particularly that there are distinct contrasts between what people routinely see and experience and what is extraordinary" (2002: 124). Our modern experience of nature, agrees Green, "has largely to do with leisure and pleasure – tourism, spectacular entertainment, visual refreshment" (1990: 6).

If tourism is a key mode of encountering and consuming nonhuman nature, however, it is not necessarily dialectically opposed to everyday consumption practices. With their multiple roaming gazes and sensory (mostly visual) receptivity, with the dedifferentiation of consumption spaces such as malls and theme parks (a crucial element in Disneyization), and with the collapse of spaces of production and consumption, work and leisure, we may consider tourist practices as simultaneously extraordinary and mundane, as a form of both conspicuous and spectacular consumption. Central to this mode of heightened receptivity is the consumption of particular signs, markers or representations, the tourist's attention being directed to them through an anticipative engagement with discourses of travel and nature through brochures and advertisements for example.

Tourism is a complex form of consumption that involves a particular way of seeing, therefore, what Urry (2002, 2003) terms the 'tourist gaze'. It is the consuming of images, representations, and predominantly visual experiences at first hand, yet also involves the consumption of a vast supporting network of resources in order to facilitate this gaze, such as use of transport systems, accommodation, finance and monetary circulation, and much else besides. "A gaze is after all visual, it can literally take a split second, and the other services provided are in a sense peripheral to the fundamental process of consumption, which is the capturing of the gaze", he explains (2003: 119). Add to this the political economy of the gaze, where the tourist gaze is most often performed by those from the most developed countries, whereas the supporting services, the landscape and the natural world being consumed, especially in the case of safaris and 'exotic' nature, are those of less developed countries. Tourism is predominantly a first-world pursuit that often involves the consumption of third-world resources. It therefore exemplifies the idea of *conspicuous* consumption on the one hand (Veblen's term, discussed in Chapter 1), and *spectacular* consumption (the consumption of representations, spectacle and mediated experiences) on the other. It is in tourism more than any other form of consumption that the hidden conditions behind what we expect in place – the supportive systems of finance, transport, legality and government – are made most visible, and the underlying systems of exploitation that perpetuate poverty are most revealed. In terms of goods or products, their packaging and placement within a retail environment obscures the relations of production and exploitation behind them, which Marx termed 'commodity fetishism' (discussed in Chapter 1). In terms of tourism and the gaze, we have instead a fetishisation of place, with no tangible commodity being purchased; there is only visual consumption and the fantasy of place, a fetish co-constructed by the consumer and by brochures and advertisements:

> Places are chosen to be gazed upon because there is anticipation, especially through daydreaming and fantasy, of intense pleasures, either on a different scale or involving different senses from those

customarily encountered. Such anticipation is constructed and sustained through a variety of non-tourist practices, such as film, TV, literature, magazines, records and videos, which construct and
reinforce that gaze.

(Urry 2002: 3)

We might add to this list other tourist practices that reinforce the gaze,
such as listening to fellow travellers' tales or browsing through
brochures in travel agents.

Urry distinguishes between two types of tourist gaze, the 'romantic'
and the 'collective' (2003: 119). As a product of the Western European
romantic tradition, the ability to view the natural world in all its undisturbed, pristine glory means it is usually a solitary experience, a deeply
personal and even semi-religious experience. Landscape paintings often
adhere to this principle, with the gaze of the painter as viewer overlook-
ing an undisturbed vista of natural beauty, without ugly man-made
buildings, and often unpolluted even by fellow human beings. The
romantic gaze is such a historically pervasive tradition that current
tourist practices are inevitably shaped by it, in the propensity for walking or cycling holidays, for hill-walking and mountaineering. The
romantic gaze is consistent with that erstwhile figure of modernity, the
flâneur (see Chapter 7). As Urry explains, the *flâneur* was "the modern
hero, able to travel, to arrive, to gaze, to move on, to be anonymous, to
be in a liminal zone" (2002: 126). If historically the *flâneur* was an
urban, male phenomenon, who loses himself in the crowd and wanders
around the city in a mode of aimless distraction, the tourist is a continuation and makes the figure an everyman (and everywoman):

The strolling *flâneur* was a forerunner of the twentieth-century tourist
and in particular of the activity which has become emblematic of the
tourist: the democratised taking of photographs – of being seen and
recorded, and of seeing others and recording them.

(2002: 127)

On the other hand, the 'collective' tourist gaze is the mode of mass
tourism, the way that certain tourist sites are designed and consumed as
public places, and it would be difficult to think of their existence without an influx of people. "It is the presence of other *tourists*, people just

like oneself, that is actually necessary for the success of such places which depend on the collective tourist gaze" (Urry 2003: 120, original emphasis). The seaside resort in summer, or stately homes with their material opulence and extensively crafted gardens, represent the collective gaze of nature or natural settings, but of course the collective gaze is equally applicable to cities, where crowds, bustle and noise are inextricable from the urban experience and form part of the attraction to those from elsewhere. When the collective gaze is applied to natural settings, however, there are environmental implications, and the expectation by large numbers of tourists that they all see particular places entails erosion, an important corollary.

Dedifferentiation, the collapsing of different forms of consumption (one of Bryman's 1999b criteria for Disneyization), also occurs in tourism. Urry for example writes how tourism has historically been separated from other activities, such as shopping, sport, architecture, music and so on, but these distinctions are now dissolving. People travel overseas to go clubbing, or visit galleries such as MoMa in Bilbao – the city, the building, the gallery and the paintings are all being consumed, along with Spanish food and wine. The result of these collapsing distinctions is a "universalising of the tourist gaze" (Urry 2002). This universalising of the gaze, the dedifferentiation of consumption, can be applied to nature-based theme parks like SeaWorld™ especially, "a mall with fish" (Davis 1995: 206), since along with any consumption of spectacle or educational content is the straightforward consumption of related merchandise such as Shamu T-shirts.

Tourist nodes

Sitting in a *gaijin* (foreigner) bar in Hiroshima, Japan, listening to backpackers' tales in 1995, particular places or nodes would recur in these exchanges. From the usual beaches in Thailand, to clubs in Bali and street restaurants in Hong Kong, it was only a matter of time before someone told the story of walking along a street in Kathmandu and recognising an old schoolfriend. Amidst mild cries of surprise, the true shock is how few and restricted the tourist nodes, those places that become attractors due to either nature or culture, actually are. If the expectation of a large number of tourists is to see a particular site because of guidebooks, word of mouth, and therefore tradition, the circulation of a series of signs or markers points towards a number of 'tourist nodes', particular places where tourists are channelled, despite other places being equally rich culturally or naturally. "There are markers which identify what things and places are worthy of our gaze. Such signposting identifies a relatively small number of tourist nodes", explains Urry (2003: 120). These nodes are important attractors for any collective tourist gaze, and they range across a continuum between the mostly cultural (Disney World) and the mostly natural (Macchu Pichu, the Grand Canyon). It is based on this notion of signposting of natural phenomena within tourism that we can talk about the packaging of tourism, where so-called 'package tours' notoriously cover well-trodden sites as a collective gaze, before quickly moving on. However, as we shall see, questions of authenticity of tourist experience are raised when distinguishing between the romantic and collective gazes. As in my Hiroshima story, backpackers are no less susceptible to tourist nodes, although their selection will be different to that of their package-tour compatriots.

Spectacular consumption

Spectacles are rich, complex visual images and environments which convey cultural meanings that are then integrated into consumers' understandings of reality. From zoos, theme parks, Disney movies and totemic images or icons such as team badges or logos, we can see the way that experiences are shaped or organized by previous exposure to images. In the natural world, our responses to killer whales might be shaped by the memory of Shamu the killer whale at SeaWorld™, or the movie *Free Willy* (1993), or both. Our encounters with deer, whether actual or as simply more imagery, might be shaped by Disney's hugely successful *Bambi* (1942). In this way, exposure to already existing imagery shapes the cultural meanings of natural phenomena, and therefore influences our present experience.

Building on the groundbreaking and influential 1967 work of Parisian intellectual Guy Debord's, *The Society of the Spectacle* (1995), we can make a distinction between Veblen's conspicuous consumption as a marker of social positioning, to spectacular consumption, consumption of – and domination by – image or spectacle. Debord was a guiding member of the Situationist International, a collective of urban theorists, artists and activists who were influenced by Dadaism and Surrealism, and who sought to uncover previously hidden aspects of everyday urban experience through innovative methods, taking long 'dérives' (walks through the city) and mapping out 'psychogeographies' (see e.g. Plant 1992). Adding to Marxist ideas of the alienation inherent in modern industrial capitalism, and understanding that the shift since Marx's time is from the site of industrial production to the points of individual consumption, the Situationist addition to Marx is the recognition of 'pseudo-needs', created by capitalism to continually ensure increased consumption. This is in keeping with the critique of mass culture of the Frankfurt School.

Consumption of the image and spectacle acknowledge a complex visuality, where all events, behaviour and commodity transactions become reduced to spectacle. So the spectacle is the domination of everyday life by images, which subsumes all other forms of domination. Debord attacks the usual Marxist targets of wage labour and commodity production, but claims they continue to wield power only in their subsumption into the spectacle. Images, predominantly visual although capable of exhibiting other sensory qualities, are thereby the currency of contemporary consumer society. No matter how visually literate we consumers become, it is through increasingly sophisticated spectacle that the prevailing institutions and power structures are maintained. Consequently, as we become increasingly dominated by the spectacle, our agency becomes devalued, and even political protest becomes mere spectacle. Clearly, Debord's sworn enemies would include advertising and marketing. Yet these are also areas that benefit, not just from the visual literacy that perpetuates the society of the spectacle, but also by using Debord's critique to become more effective, for example in terms of marketing studies of Nike Town (e.g. Penaloza 1998) and zoos. A spectacle, in its usual definition, has a performative element (street theatre, protest, display) and must somehow be staged or enframed, taken out of the context of everyday life. These elements will later be examined in the case of nature-based theme parks and safaris, so that our consumption of nature as spectacle will be discussed as the consumption of a variety of staged signs and (not only visual) experiences.

The nature of semiosis

This section on semiosis, the way we create meaning through the production and consumption of signs, will focus on the visual, although the consumption of non-visual experiences is discussed later in the chapter. Part of the performance of being a tourist involves taking photographs and visually chronicling the events that are experienced. "As everyone becomes a photographer so everyone also becomes an amateur semiotician", as Urry (2002: 128) puts it. The history of photography and its place within leisure and tourism entails that the main mechanism for the capture and active recirculation of signs for tourists is the camera, and therefore that these signs are visual (see e.g. Crawshaw and Urry (1997) on how tourists photograph). The way certain photographs are framed accords with learned ways of seeing and representing, whereby the thatched cottage within an English village signifies traditional values and Olde England, or the reflections of other buildings in the glass of skyscrapers in New York signifies urban modernity, entirely in keeping with decades of posters, Sunday newspaper supplements, magazines and holiday brochures. In this way, signs beget signs. Rather than talk of the proliferation only of signs, MacCannell uses the word "marker" (1999: 110ff.) to expand the notion of signs across a whole range of media, including brochures, signposts and advertisements, both on and off site. However, following Urry, we can use 'sign' in this expansive sense as part of the way the gaze is maintained and reproduced.

"Involved in much tourism is a hermeneutic circle", as Urry puts it (2002: 129), where the tourist goes in pursuit of these images and captures them for themselves. If a certain landscape, scene or building has been portrayed in a particular way, to show that one has actually been there it is incumbent on us to portray that scene in a similar way – especially if we can be pictured in that scene too. Increasingly, just as in art galleries, what is captured and photographed is the sign or signpost as much as the actual scene. Not just as a place-marker, to be photographed in front of a sign shows to oneself and others that we have genuinely been there. Urry argues that these attractors or nodes are separated off from everyday experience, lingered over, and then visually captured or objectified through photographs, postcards, camcorders, and so on. The gaze is therefore endlessly reproduced, recaptured and recirculated. As Culler argues, reminding us of Urry's notion of the tourist as amateur semiotician,

> the tourist is interested in everything as a sign of itself ... All over the
> world the unsung armies of semioticians, the tourists, are fanning out

in search of the signs of Frenchness, typical Italian behaviour, exemplary Oriental scenes, typical American thruways, traditional English pubs.

(1981: 127)

Culler's examples are mostly cultural phenomena, but equally signs of nonhuman nature are sought in terms of landscape (jungle, beach, mountain), flora (extraordinary, colourful flowers) or fauna (savagery, wildness). For instance, nature documentaries on television respond to, and reinforce, anthropomorphic stereotypes concerning particular animals. The 'pathetic fallacy' is to ascribe human characteristics to nonhuman nature, and this form of anthropomorphism belongs not only to the audience of such documentaries but also to the producers and editors (see e.g. Lindahl-Elliot 2001). Peter Conrad rather amusingly reviews one such documentary in a newspaper:

[W]e insist on thinking of our fellow creatures as retarded replicas of ourselves. The naturalists on *The Animal Zone* (BBC2), studying Tanzanian chimps or Kenyan elephants, fondly indulge the pathetic fallacy. [Presenter] Charlotte Uhlenbroek's video diary about an extended family of chimpanzees treats the animals as if they were the cast of [Australian soap opera] *Neighbours* in gorilla suits. There's a matriarch, as in all soap operas, and some frisky youngsters to capture the teen demographic; despite all the gratuitous tantrums and furiously uprooted shrubs, nothing much ever happens. Charlotte's humanising viewpoint betrayed itself when commenting on a young tearaway as he sulked in disgrace after a rumpus she said: 'Galahad looks sheepish.'

Even sheep don't often look sheepish, which is a specifically human facial expression. However can a chimpanzee manage the feat?

(Conrad 1997: 8)

Authenticity and simulation

Haraway (1997) talks of the 'implosion' of nature and culture, as they each become increasingly interpolated with each other. Other theorists of postmodernity such as Latour (1993) and Jameson (1995) have argued similarly that the difference between 'nature' and 'culture' has been elided so that 'nature' exists no longer. Franklin *et al.* acknowledge this process, and in terms of the 'natural' and the 'artificial' realise that we are left only with 'artifice'. Their book is an account of "how nature is being commodified, technologised, re-animated and rebranded in ways that expose its artifice" (2000: 10). The implosion of nature into culture, then, is one answer for what happens after *The End of Nature* (McKibben 1989). If we were to accept nature as pure artifice, as sign without referent, it would be tempting to think of all nature as simply simulation. In *Simulacra and Simulation* (1994b), Baudrillard defines "third order simulation" as a simulation where the 'real' (the referent) is no longer present, or presumed unimportant. If the real disappears, only simulation remains. Examples that might explore the 'nature of simulation' can easily be found, in computer-generated imagery of extinct species or natural phenomena (*Jurassic Park*, the BBC series *Walking With Dinosaurs*), computer games (*Unreal*, *Myst*) and VR, as well as nature-based theme parks. In these cases the 'real' either no longer exists (and is therefore simulation) or never existed (simulacra). Yet Baudrillard's claim for simulation is stronger, applicable to many more contexts and experiences, and Hayles shows this in the case of supposedly 'natural' scenes:

> Ironically, then, many of the experiences that contemporary Americans most readily identify with nature – mountain views seen from conveniently located lookouts, graded trails traversed along gurgling streams, great national parks like Yosemite visited with reservations made months in advance – could equally well be considered simulation.

> (Hayles 1995: 411)

Hayles's observation starkly shows the implosion of 'nature' and 'culture' through the crumbling distinction between 'nature' and 'simulation'. Baudrillard famously argues that "the age of simulation thus begins with a liquidation of all referentials" (1994b: 4). In any sign system, the referent is the object to which the sign refers. If the referent is liquidated then signs refer to nothing originally there or present. There is nothing 'authentic' or 'real' in this case. So what happens to nature in the age of simulation? Baudrillard acknowledges that in an age of simulation and simulacra, "There is a proliferation of myths of origin and signs of reality; of second-hand truth, objectivity and authenticity" (1991: 12). The search for an original, an 'authentic' object that grounds the image or representation, is continual. What could be more authentic than untouched, pristine nature? Of course, imaginations of nature as an original referent are tinged with romanticism, as we have seen. Paul Shepard in *Reinventing Nature* comments:

> As fast as the relics of the past, whether old growth forest or downtown Santa Fe, are demolished they are reincarnated in idealized form.
>
> (in Wills 2002: 409)

This idealisation of the original in an age of simulation partly explains the popularity of stores like Pastimes, selling historical goods, and The Nature Company in shopping malls. Against these movements of simulation and simulacra, a common strategy in the presentation of spectacle is to reinject 'realness' and referentiality everywhere, to stress authenticity. This might even involve a knowingly fake authenticity, like Buffalo Bill's Wild West Show which captivated audiences all over America and Europe at the turn of the twentieth century, a time when the Wild West technically no longer existed. "Yet it is the simulation, not the firsthand experience, that often enters popular consciousness as the operative cultural signifier", observes Hayles (1995: 410). History and genealogy become disproportionately important in an age of timeless, digital simulation. The famous prehistoric cave paintings of Lascaux are behind glass, and what the public see is actually only a copy. But it no longer matters, argues Baudrillard, since "the duplication is sufficient to render both artificial" (1994b: 18).

The depiction of nature in David Cronenberg's *eXistenZ* (1999) entertainingly exemplifies this ambiguity between 'real' and 'simulation', since the film is set within a series of ennested videogames where the 'actual' world is arguably never shown. Nature is shown in Technicolor, as hyperreal, and the film continually plays with ideas of the original, the actual. "Are we still in the 'game' or is this 'real'?" both audience and characters in the film ask at various points, desperately seeking a referent. The accentuated colours and almost hallucinogenic reproduction of the natural world is perhaps an electro-romantic depiction of nature, to borrow a term from Wills (2002). The unusual blending of organic and machinic, of nature and artifice, is also shown in the film through the depiction of the videogame consoles themselves which live, react, squirm and breathe, directly plugging into our nervous system. Throughout the film, therefore, questions are raised concerning what is 'real', 'natural', organic or machinic. For Baudrillard himself, it is Disneyland which is the perfect model of the variously entangled forms of simulation. Disneyland represents a third-order simulation in which it is so hyperreal, so obviously a simulation, that by contrast other things *seem* real but are not. It becomes impossible to isolate the process of the 'real', to prove the 'real' (1994b: 41):

> Disneyland is presented as imaginary in order to make us believe that the rest is real, when in fact all of Los Angeles and the America surrounding it are no longer real, but of the order of the hyperreal and of simulation.

> (1994b: 25)

We shall apply this analysis to SeaWorld™ and develop it, where nature as it is perceived is so obviously a simulation that it obscures the fact that there is no 'nature' as such. Simulation is only one step towards a more complex construction of nature as virtualisation. Following from the arguments of Haraway (1991), Hayles (1995) and Franklin *et al.* (2000), the virtualisation of nature may be more useful in thinking of the consumption of nature as spectacle.

SEAWORLD™: 'A MALL WITH FISH'

Susan G. Davis has written perspicaciously about theme-park versions of nature as *Spectacular Nature* (1997), and in 'Touch the magic' (1995) she describes television advertisements for the Anheuser-Busch theme park SeaWorld™, a way of mediating human–nature relations, selling representations of nature as benign, friendly, within reach, to vast audiences. Davis analyses these mediated representations as simulations: superficially, they seem diverse, and the different dioramas – the plastic settings, simulations of a natural environment – are not only highly artificial, but also standardised between the different parks. So the 'Penguin Encounter' (sponsored by Arco) is a living diorama that simulates part of the Antarctic environment. A moving walkway conveys people to shark exhibits in Orlando and San Diego, proceeding through a Plexiglas tube in order to arrive at the 'Terrors of the Deep'. At the 'Shark Encounter' there are no Pacific Islanders to be seen, observes Davis, yet the mysterious and exotic sound of drums enhances the carefully painted and sculpted set (simulation). So far, so fake. Shamu, the killer whale in the advertisement, is a registered trademark, no longer an animal but a commodified product. But the advertisement also promises something else: the fantasy of a nature within reach, that like the children in the advertisement, you can have actual contact with nature, being nose to nose with a benign animal – that you can 'touch the magic'. Despite the Plexiglas, despite the physical separation, you are sold the fantasy of "a total merging with wild nature" (1995: 211).

Previously we noted the way that spectacular consumption involves the domination of the image, and that we bring to natural phenomena pre-existing cultural references and representations. SeaWorld™ creates and displays versions of nature that are modelled on our expectations, hopes, fears, and fantasies. In some cases, for the sake of the visitors, nature must be re-engineered or remediated. For example, Davis found that in creating the Penguin Encounter, "designers thought they had to keep the penguins from appearing overcrowded to their public" (1997: 108). Because of anthropocentric concerns, it was held that visitors would feel uncomfortable at the sight of swarming, crowding animals, despite this being the penguins' behaviour in their original habitat. Crowding might indicate mistreatment in captivity, thought the designers, but also evoke uncomfortable feelings of stressful or crowded environments within the visitors. Remodelling the artificial environment to suit public sensibilities, remediating the 'real' conditions of the habitat, somewhat paradoxically manages therefore to "connect customers to nature", argues Davis, and "gives the domination of nature a gentle, civilized face" (1997: 35). At the same time, she argues, these manufactured spectacles create "a process of reflecting on our own experiences" (1997: 108).

The morally improving discourse of nature, a bastion of nineteenth-century romantic thinking such as Ruskin and Wordsworth, is also evident in SeaWorld™. In these accounts, experiences of nature supposedly educate us to become a better person. "To make contact with nature is to have real feelings and to become someone different and more desirable", Davis summarises (1995: 211), reflecting the concerns of most visitors. This can also be identified in the rhetoric of nature in zoos, the origin of the 'zoological gaze' (Franklin 1999) being in self-improvement, moral instruction and education. The nature-based theme park consolidates aspects of the zoo, by combining the search for private profits through entertainment with an attempt to occupy the cultural space of the publicly funded zoo or museum. Because animals are turned into spectacle, in zoos and theme parks, and because they are made both passive and captive, this underlines the marginalisation of nature from human post-industrial everyday experience. The aesthetic of the new zoos, with their increasing emphasis on conservation and wildlife management (see e.g. Conway 1996; Mullan and Marvin 1999), and of nature-based theme parks like SeaWorld™, is to override that distance, to present animals in more natural-looking environments. These environments, if re-engineered for the sake of human visitors or nonhuman inhabitants, adapt 'nature' and virtualise it. The virtualisation of nature allows adaptation, mutation according to visitor expectation or animal need, and redeploys it elsewhere if necessary.

The virtualisation of nature, just as Franklin *et al.* (2000) show, is a corollary of its commodification. It allows the synergy of an educational discourse (protecting the oceans) along with the corporate attitude ("SeaWorld is like a mall with fish", in Davis 1995: 206) that equates with the selling of our own fantasies about nature back to us, at extortionate prices. SeaWorld™, in Davis's words, "profits by selling people's dreams back to them" (1997: 244), but the dreams and the desire are already in place (see 'Desiring nature', below). Like other nature-based theme parks, SeaWorld™ utilises artificial habitats and remediated environments as stage settings for the presentation of nature as spectacle. This is only possible through the virtualisation of nature, where nature is simultaneously simulation, spectacle, educational discourse and commodity.

The *virtualisation* of nature

> Is it possible that people in our culture have become so estranged from nature that their only avenue to it is consumerism?
>
> (Dunne 1989)

The Nature Company. It is a short step from theme-park nature to nature at the mall. Jennifer Price analyses a chain of stores called The Nature Company, mostly in shopping malls across the US, which seem to sell an idiosyncratic range of products. What should such a store sell, exactly? From rocks to Native American crafts to bat puppets, in their brochures they explain the ethos: "Each product introduces customers to an aspect of the natural world" (in Price 1995: 189). But, asks Price, *what* meanings of nature does The Nature Company market? And *whose* nature is on sale? Her answer, in short, is a child-friendly, morally instructive idea of nature, distinctly middle class, a version of 'nature' that we enjoy as a leisure pursuit. Fitting perfectly into Urry's romantic gaze, it is a fetishisation of nature that only makes sense if our jobs do not involve the grime, sweat and toil of actually working outside. The Nature Company markets "authenticity", "uniqueness" and "simplicity", all within those most unnatural of settings, shopping malls, places of conspicuous consumption that notoriously involve artifice or simulation. Price argues that the new malls, as they incorporate place-based themes such as rainforest, New Orleans or ancient Rome (see Chapter 7), *simulate* place (1995: 192). Likewise, The Nature Company markets a version of nature that is mostly simulated. Just like Hayles, Price argues that "encounters with nature ... have become as simulated and disconnected from place as 'the mall' itself" (1995: 193). Later, she succinctly summarises her position:

> I use 'nature' like a vessel for all my middle-class generational angst about urban life in the nineties. I encounter nature most often out of place, in the city, through artifice and simulation. And I am a consumer.
>
> (1995: 201)

Offering us authenticity, simplicity and a timeless sense of place, nature would seem to oppose that feeling of placelessness that mall modernity represents. The difference, of course, is that The Nature Company connects us not to nature itself, but to what nature 'means' to a particular segment of the population, and hence those circulated meanings, associations, representations and simulations that we take 'nature' to be. If "'Nature', many of us like to think, is antonym and antidote to modern materialism" (1995: 197), why is business so brisk, and next door is

Emporio Armani? Visitors to the store reported they feel "manipulated", that "it feels inauthentic" or "fake" (1995: 187). So the unavoidable question is why we shop for nature with our credit cards, why visitors are inside the mall *buying* it rather than proceeding outside and *experiencing* it?

To pose this question is a little misleading, for up to this point there has been a simplistic opposition of 'nature' and 'artifice', of 'real' and 'simulation'. Even within the concept of simulation, too often it becomes equated with 'representation'. But a true simulation, like a computer program, involves a series of dynamic processes rather than static representations. The difficulty with the hermeneutic circle of signs and representations discussed earlier is that, too often, it ignores the experiential element. Thus, it would be better to talk of *virtualisation* of nature rather than *simulation*. Unlike simulation per se, virtualisation is irreducibly experiential, incorporating not only signs or representations, but also more dynamic processes and imaginations. For example, if global consumption is actually buying into an imagination of the global through commodity consumption, then buying nature at the mall is equally an imaginative engagement with nature and natural processes. Rather than dealing solely with representations, therefore, nature remediated, re-imagined, commodified and available to experience is better described as a virtualisation of nature. This reframes Davis's discussion of SeaWorld™ somewhat, and we should bear this in mind when looking at other commodified, experiential forms of encounters with nature such as safaris, below.

'Virtual' nature is consequently the way that nature becomes commodified and globalised (Franklin *et al.* 2000: 112) just like The Nature Company and The Body Shop. This virtualisation need not be restricted to the heightened experiential encounters of theme parks, then, since it also applies to everyday shopping experiences at the mall. Buying creams and lotions that are marketed as being 'natural' from The Body Shop, contemporary Western consumers can 'go native', can become 'a bit like the Other' (that is, non-white indigenous peoples) as a means of "getting closer to nature, of finding a community and of achieving self-knowledge", argue Franklin *et al.* (2000: 115). Similarly, Sara Ahmed (2000) examines this need to be like the 'other' through incorporating 'natural' products within a postcolonial context. Involving an imaginative engagement with 'nature' through aggressively marketed commodified forms, an identification with a more 'connected' people and more 'authentic' pre-industrial knowledges is as much a virtualisation of nature as SeaWorld™ or safaris. However, the commodification of nature entails the inescapable paradox of getting 'closer to nature' literally by consuming it: to do this, nature is taken out of its temporal and spatial contexts, becomes decontextualised, detemporalised – even, as we have seen, Disneyfied. As Franklin *et al.* state,

> the contradiction in terms of a 'decontextualised nature' is held up to confirm its power as magical sign: nature is reinvented as history in a different place at a different time, thoroughly out of context, *and yet the very mutability that facilitates such a cultural change demonstrates its universality.*
>
> (2000: 115, original emphasis)

This hints at a more sinister virtualisation of nature, since it becomes abstracted, mobile, mutable, able to be reduced to a set of immediately recognisable signs and then attached to any commodity. In this way, even environmentally unfriendly petroleum companies gain green credentials through advertising and public relations. There are numerous examples of the commodification and commercialisation of nature in a more literal and politically dubious sense, for example the patenting of seeds (in Franklin *et al.* 2000: 78ff.), and the patenting of mice with a cancer-inducing gene for the purpose of animal experimentation (Haraway 1997).

'SEE THE WORLD': TOURISM AS DESIRING NATURE

> The tourism industry provides a structure within which tourists view, experience and interact with nature.
>
> (Wilson 1992)

Tourism as desiring nature happens in two significant ways, I argue. The first is the straightforward way that 'nature' as commodity is packaged, turned into a set of mediated signs, representations or markers in advertisements and brochures for tourists to consume. The second is a more complex use of the term 'desire' that is more psychoanalytic, and which plays on the identification of self with nature. Wanting to be at one with nature, to commune with the natural world, is consistent with the Western romantic tradition. Either a complete erasure of ego investment, or conversely perverse self-aggrandisement, the desire for nature is a major factor in tourism. Yet, as the quotation at the beginning of this section suggests, these desires must be mediated and structured in various forms, and it is this tension between imaginative constructs of nature, and the necessity to package and offer particular tourist sites, scenes or 'nodes', that is dealt with here. The staging of tourist sites, the formation of spectacles in nature, would hint at a "staged authenticity" (MacCannell 1999).

What follows from both of these kinds of desiring nature is something that returns us to that original definition of 'consumption'. While the majority of this chapter has been concerned with the predominantly visual consumption of spectacle, the other definition of consumption as 'using up' or being destroyed is all too applicable to the case of mass tourism. What were once isolated and beautiful spots become over-run by trampling tourists as a result of the collective gaze. The idea of desiring nature, whether to consume nature or commune with it, obviously entails a cost, that those sites we most desire to see are destroyed by our very desire to see them. The question of the sustainability of mass tourism, although not addressed specifically in this chapter, is an extremely important consideration nonetheless.

Consumption and communion

> But still we feel the need for pristine places, places substantially *unaltered* by man. Even if we do not visit them, they matter to us.
>
> (McKibben 1989: 58)

The first way of desiring nature is the immediately interpretable and straightforward way that 'nature' as commodity is packaged, transformed into a set of mediated representations, for us as tourists to consume. Being an extension of the tourist gaze, we need only look at photographs, brochures and Sunday supplements to recognise this, but the mediated set of representations seek to package and enframe a way of thinking about nature that encourages us to think about our actions as 'getting back to nature'. Thus a set of touristic practices are then engaged, a performative mode of being within nature, that is derived from our consumption of the images and representations. The institutions of tourism such as travel agencies and tour companies seem to perpetuate, maintain and mediate these attitudes to nature. Kevin Markwell for example argues that:

> tourist-nature interactions are constructed and mediated by the tourism industry and associated agencies – nature within tourism is predominantly experienced through contrived or mediated encounters, with the guided tour itself a prime source of mediation.
>
> (2001: 41)

These mediations and enframing practices of nature can only exist, paradoxically, by sustaining the more romantic or naïve view of nature-tourism relations, in which tourism allows for "an unmediated and intensely personal relationship between the person and the natural world" (Fine 1992: 166). This is the myth of the promise of encountering 'real' nature. The ways that nature becomes mythologised find resonance in tourism through significations that reproduce and perpetuate themselves, what Urry had explained as a hermeneutic circle. Selwyn (1996: 1) describes tourists as those who "chase myths", and argues that the tourism industry actively mythologises places and cultures. Myths pervade tourist brochures and websites, helping to confirm existing beliefs about places, cultures and nature. And, increasingly, popular ethnographic tourism means there is an increasing market eager to consume images and performances of indigenous peoples and who want to understand their relationship with the environment. Zurick (in Nuttall 1997: 229) says:

> If contemporary Western society no longer holds a valid myth … then that might be why people search other cultures – to discover that which may be lost in their own.

This illustrates what is meant by 'desiring nature'. Desire is a "letting go of the self-conscious will to knowledge and the disappearance of ego investment", as Fullagar explains it (2000: 63). Just as in

SeaWorld™, rubbing noses with Shamu and so 'touching the magic', it naïvely promises a profound sense of communion or interconnection, erasing the boundaries between subject and object, human and nonhuman. Seeking one moment, a flash of intensity that flattens the relations between human and nonhuman, predator and prey, exposing what Tennyson called "nature red in tooth and claw" in his poem *In Memoriam*. It hints at pure animality, the sublime revelation of larger biotic networks of power, energy, vitality of which we are only a (tiny) part. Bachelard's phrase "intimate immensity" (1994: 183) seems appropriate here. Val Plumwood for example speaks of an 'intimate' encounter with a crocodile in Australia that leapt out at her, and frames this as a brush with true wildness and savagery that few members of industrialised countries experience (in Fullagar 2000). In a predominantly urban, industrialised world where contact with nature is limited or becomes a segregated leisure activity, the fantasy of an intimacy with nature is seductive. Just as in window-shopping and the purchase of commodities, daydreaming and imaginative anticipation are elements in the consumption of nature as spectacle (Campbell (1987) and the romantic spirit of consumption are discussed in Chapter 1; daydreaming, wishing and fantasy in Chapters 4 and 7). Imaginations of nature and the anticipation of its consumption therefore feed into the circulation of the signs and markers previously discussed. The romantic imagination and anticipative pleasures of nature entail the reassertion of fantasies of pristine, Edenic nature, predominantly to an industrialised – or postindustrial, service-sector – bourgeoisie (e.g. Smith 1984; Evernden 1992). One form of this desiring nature, sold as exotic vacation, occurs on safari, and this will be discussed below.

The desire for the 'authentic'

If the desire for nature is present then tourist guides and tour operators are willing to seduce tourists by offering their romantic imaginations of nature back to them, in packaged and saleable form. This leads to a number of paradoxes. Firstly, only through artifice can the locals meet the tourist demand for authenticity. If tourists demand to see authentic nature, it will be an artificial form of 'authentic' nature, since only through pre-packaging as a tourist site or node are tourists confident that a natural site is worthy of attention. A $50 chimpanzee walk in western Uganda is inherently more attractive than walking down the road to encounter butterflies, baboons, old-growth equatorial forest, and occasionally local human inhabitants. Natural sites, just like tourist nodes, come to be framed. Just as a work of art becomes interpreted as a work of art through a framing process, whether it be the covers and titles of a book or the actual gilt frame around a painting, a natural site becomes framed by gates, permits and supportive interpretive texts (brochures, leaflets) to set them apart. Complicated staging and framing mechanisms allow the tourist to recognise, at last, the 'real thing', whether that is to catch site of the chimpanzee eventually, or to take that walk to arrive at the famous waterfalls. Even when told at the outset there is no guarantee of sighting the chimpanzees, this only adds to the dramatic quality of seeing the 'real thing', especially if you have travelled extensively to get there. Rob Shields has argued also about these enframing mechanisms of representing nature to us tourist-consumers:

> Tourists generally – and certainly those at Niagara – encounter a package of previously validated and even staged events and artefacts.
>
> (1991: 126)

Niagara and other places are theme-park versions of nature, sometimes literally when amusement rides are attached, but even in more 'natural' tourist sites there are degrees of staging and manipulation. Edensor (1998) for example provides a detailed account of the regulation of a tourist space and the practices of photography there. National parks regulate and control tourist interactions with nature by establishing clearly demarcated boundaries, and these boundaries separate tourists both physically and metaphorically from nature, for example the edges of walking trails, raised concrete walkways in the Peak District, viewing platforms, or the wire fronts of animal exhibits. The boundaries formalise the relationship between nature and tourist, enframe and reinforce nature as 'other', as object of the tourist gaze.

MacCannell assumes that all tourists are in search of authentic experience, and following Goffman he recognises a difference between 'front' regions, where tourists are allowed to go, and 'back' regions, such as kitchens or dressing rooms, where they are not. For a tourist, being granted entry to a back region offers a taste of the authentic. The

Universal Studios theme parks for example are full of a series of 'behind-the-scenes' back regions that provide a tantalising taste of the 'authentic'. Of course, these back regions are intentionally part of the show. MacCannell calls this "staged authenticity" (1999: 98). It follows that:

> Touristic consciousness is motivated by its desire for authentic experiences, and the tourist may believe that he [sic] is moving in this direction, but often it is very difficult to know for sure if the experience is in fact authentic. It is always possible that what is taken to be entry into a back region is really entry into a front region that has been totally set up in advance for touristic visitation.
>
> (1999: 101)

Rather than reproduce the distinction between 'sucker' or 'savvy' tourists, this debate centred around authenticity is often couched in terms of 'tourists' and 'post-tourists'. Rojek argues that, along with recognising these boundaries, the tourist is aware of the commodification of the tourist experience, and even in package tours is not necessarily "a passive consumer of staged experiences" (1993: 176). It would not be instructive to engage in debates concerning the relative definitions of 'traveller', 'tourist' or 'post-tourists' at this point. However, while MacCannell argues that the tourist desires to consume only authentic experiences, primarily through visually capturing particular nodes as we have discussed, the 'post-tourist' acknowledges no such concern with authenticity or, in fact, the meaningfulness or otherwise of the experience: "For the post-tourist there is no particular problem about the inauthentic. It is merely another game to be played at, another pastiched surface feature of post-modern experience", explains Urry (2003: 121). If the tourist is still motivated by a romantic impulse, to encounter nature as a form of self-improvement or moral instruction, Rojek argues that the post-tourist

> is attracted by experience as an end in itself and not by what the experience teaches about one's inner resources, or whether the attraction is authentic. Axiomatic to this mental attitude is the recognition that the tourist experience may not, and often does not, add up to very much.
>
> (1993: 177)

Seen as a foil against the romantic desire for nature outlined previously, this is a conception of experience of cultural or natural otherness as flattened, as mundane, that seeks no magical transformation through experience.

On safari: wild nature as spectacle

Consider this newspaper description of a safari, which references other mediated forms of the experience (photographs, television), explicitly refers to a natural event as a "spectacle", suggests particular tourist nodes, and acknowledges that tour guides help structure the experience for you:

> September [...] starts with nature's most photographed spectacle, the wildebeest migration across the Serengeti plains. However often you've seen it on television, nothing can compare to being there in the Masai Mara, within metres of the trail that leads two million animals (zebras and gazelles as well as wildebeest) through the crocodile-infested waters of the Mara River. With the help of a tour operator you can see the procession at various points along the route.
>
> (*The Independent on Sunday*, 20 January 2002)

Safaris typify some of the important themes concerning the consumption of nature already raised, then, and will help to tie these disparate themes together. Safari, from the Arabic meaning 'journey', epitomises the romantic gaze and the desire for nature or wildness. There is the signposting or tourist nodes (you are driven and confined to a jeep), the notion of 'wild' nature as image or spectacle (the watering hole and the migration of wildebeest are not only tourist nodes but familiar through television), and the fetishisation of place (Africa and Africans become associated through mediated representations more with 'nature' than 'culture'). In addition, the fetishisation of natural place often involves making it timeless, what Anne McClintock calls "anachronistic space", a site existing in "a permanently anterior time within the geographic space of the modern empire [...], the living embodiment of the archaic 'primitive' " (1995: 30). An example of this occurs in another, more extensive piece of travel journalism. Doug McDougal travels from the famous Ngorongoro nature reserve, an extinct but fertile volcano, "across the vast Serengeti plain where we hope to see one of the most humbling spectacles in the natural world – the migration of two million wildebeest" (2002: 14). But this is no 'ordinary' safari, the kind offered by enterprising Kenyans in Nairobi when you first land. It is a luxury safari offered by an exclusive specialist travel agent, unashamedly reminiscent of colonial conditions, with talk of sundowners, butlers and canapés. The rest of the article proceeds to frame the rawness of nature within this context of refined luxury:

> As darkness descends, we head towards our lodgings high on the rim of the crater. Our tour operator Abercromby & Kent has excelled itself, providing us with a private tented safari that harks back to the days of Africa's big game hunters.
>
> The camp, set up 24 hours before we arrive, is extraordinary. At its heart lies a huge camp fire where we are greeted by liveried butlers brandishing trays of wine and canapés. Our private tents with showers and real beds, each have a butler – dinner, we are told, will be served on china in a dining tent – surely not even Hemingway had it this good.
>
> After a heavy night of Tusker beer, we arise bleary-eyed with the dawn and take our first look at the crater floor in daylight. Today our aim is to tick off the big five on our list, rhinos, elephants, lions, chee-tahs and water buffalo, and a smaller sixth – the elusive honey bad-ger, which, despite its cute name, has a reputation for viciousness and is even known to attack safari jeeps. Ngorongoro is a conserva-tion area, rather than a national park; today farmers live here and the Masai graze their cattle. The foothills around the extinct volcano are fertile – mangetout and avocado country, supplying many UK super-markets – and the slopes are covered in montane forest.
>
> (McDougal 2002: 14)

The last sentence unexpectedly illustrates the commodity fetishism behind these exotic fruit and vegetables (see Chapter 1). The mundane shopping experience of buying mangetout not only obscures third-world/first-world relations of exploitation and production, but fetishises the natural setting from which they derive. Whether the experience is luxurious or more basic, a safari provides an opportunity to see 'raw' nature, 'live' and supposedly unmediated, but with clear reference points to previously enframed and represented nature from television documen-taries. This is not to deny the sheer excitement and the engagement of all bodily senses, the smells and sounds accompanying the now-familiar sights, and the kinaesthetic experience of being off-road in a jeep or on horseback. Nor is it to deny the emotional intensity of seeing nonhuman nature living, eating or fighting in its natural habitat, which is more 'authentic' than the presentation of similar animals within zoos. But, in looking at the safari as an example of the consumption of the spectacle of nature, it should be clear that it fits into previously raised themes in this chapter, such as the structuring and organising of tourist experience, the 'nodes' of attraction, and the circulation of the same signs – from film, nature documentaries, brochures, and even ways of describing the experience, whether by word of mouth or in travel journalism, as we have seen. Safaris also exemplify the type of romantic gaze that relies on the fantasy of communion with, connection with, or being 'at one' with nature, only in this case with overtones of colonial history and the mastery over nature.

EXPERIENCING NATURE VS. THE IMPACT

If commodity fetishism makes the patina on our desired object shinier, precisely because we cannot see the hidden histories of production and labour behind it, the object in its smart packaging and label only increases in appeal. But whether we are luxury tourists or shoestring backpackers, it is inevitable that poverty and exploitative relations will be encountered at some stage, if only in passing. The gnawing feeling, that twinge of consciousness when we glimpse the abject, unties the smartly packaged experience, forcing us to confront poverty and the whole exploitative system that enables this first-third world encounter. To conclude this chapter I want to raise some issues that arise from mass tourism and the collective gaze: the economic impact and the environmental impact. Firstly, if place and nature become fetishised by tourism, at least the inequalities of first-world visitors encountering third-world cultures and natures are glimpsed. It is a given that one path to development is tourism, a nation effectively staging its natural resources as spectacle. Secondly, the need for development and foreign investment has unintended consequences on those same natural resources, as there is an obvious environmental impact in mass tourism. Two alternatives to mass tourism, ecotourism and 'native tourism', promise more environmentally sustainable paths to economic development through tourism, and could be considered here as an ethical rejoinder to the mass consumption of nature. As a result, they both rely on the romantic gaze.

6

THE KNOWING CONSUMER?

Sucker:
(a): a person easily cheated or deceived; (b): a person irresistibly attracted by something specified e.g. a sucker for ghost stories.

Savvy:
alteration of *sabi* know (in English-based creoles and pidgins), from Portuguese *sabe* he knows, from *saber* to know, from Latin *sapere* to be wise

(Both adapted from Mirriam-Webster Dictionary, 2004)

INTRODUCTION

> If we went into stores only when we needed to buy something, and if once there we bought only what we needed, the economy would collapse, boom.
>
> (Underhill 2003: 31)

So far we have outlined two competing views of the consumer. Firstly, the consumer as rational agent who crafts their sense of personal identity, positioning themselves within a social group through the use, abuse and display of certain commodities. The second view is the relatively mindless consumer, unwittingly compelled by the mass media to buy goods incessantly. The same dialectical tension, between our assumed freedom of expression and the manipulation and control of the mass culture industry, we have previously referred to as the 'consumer paradox' (after Miles 1998). We have also characterised consumption as a 'using up', a destruction (*consumere*) while simultaneously being a bringing to completion, a fulfilment, a creation (*consumare*). These are tensions that have persisted throughout the book so far, and can be characterised for the purposes of this chapter in a simpler way: are we *savvy*, knowing consumers, or *suckers* to the marketing and advertising industries? If the economy relies to such a large extent on consumers buying things they don't actually need, are we being manipulated for the larger purpose of the economy and existing power structures, or does the importance of our choice and identity render the situation otherwise? The debate between rational agent and consumer pawn reaches back into the historical context of the Frankfurt School, and then to the theorists of the creativity and power of everyday life, such as Henri Lefebvre and Michel de Certeau.

This chapter therefore sets these arguments against each other, to divine how we negotiate these positions, finding somewhere in-between. What we have discussed in previous chapters, about our relatively optimistic sense of freedom, identity and choice through acts of consumption, is contrasted with the rather sceptical and deterministic outlook that we are manipulated and controlled. By setting the positions so manifestly and crudely in opposition, at least initially, we can generate a more fine-tuned set of tactics or negotiations that characterise our travels through the system. We find a path in-between, that is, we *make do*. Improvising, appropriating, making up and making do, are all everyday ways that we negotiate multiple sets of rules and systems, structures and spaces. The use, purchase, display of objects, commodities, things is an inextricable part of this process. The structure of this chapter therefore is essentially threefold:

Suckers

Firstly, the notion of the consumer as 'sucker', as mindlessly manipulated by larger forces, is reviewed. Its familiarity stems from Marxist and neo-Marxist conceptions of the consumer, and reconnects with the Frankfurt School's deeply critical evaluation of consumption as the perpetuation of "false needs", discussed in the first chapter. Subsequently we find allies for this critical approach in more recent ideas about consumption, such as the beginnings of consumer psychology, as detailed by Bowlby, and retail psychology, the diverse ways that retail spaces are organised to make us consume more. Famously this includes the use of artificial scents such as bread smells in supermarkets, and aerosol sprays of 'new car smell'. Such smells and other subliminal cues imply the manipulation of the consumer's unconscious motivations, in shopping malls and showrooms. This will allow some interesting stories to be told garnered from journalism and journals of retail psychology, furthering the view of the programmability of consumers in retail spaces.

Savvy

Secondly, considering the 'savvy' or 'knowing' consumer, aware they are manipulated to a certain extent by large corporations and the mass media, but able to reclaim their own sense of identity in some way. The use of mass-produced objects in ways unintended by the manufacturer reveals a sense of irony and creative use ('appropriation') by the consumer, being a tacit acknowledgement of mass media manipulation but simultaneously an unwillingness to blindly comply. In this section, a brief introduction to Michel de Certeau's *The Practice of Everyday Life* (1984) explores such individual 'tactics' within a larger corporate 'strategy', and contrasts this with the critics of the mass culture industry, such as the Frankfurt School (especially Adorno, Horkheimer, and Marcuse). Similarly, Lefebvre's 'appropriation' of space by gatherings of people makes a former capitalist-consumer space (a market) into an emancipatory, shared social space, an idea examined further in the following chapter.

'The art of being in-between': consuming youth

In order to track some of these ideas through more specific case studies, histories and examples, we can look at the beginnings of youth cultures after the Second World War to the present day. This is particularly useful because it illustrates the origins of a unique market directed specifically at young consumers, how it was targeted in terms of marketing and advertising, and how 'taste' and 'authenticity' have been negotiated and performed through consumption practices. Importantly, post-war youth cultures coincide with developments of Fordism and mass consumption, and are at the forefront of disputes and issues of subcultures, smaller social groups based on affinities and interests as opposed to more traditional structures such as school, workplace or family. Of course, consumption is central to these subcultures, as it is through the unique style and aesthetics of black clothes and purple lipstick that we 'become' Goths, or by purchasing and displaying knee-length trousers and hooded tops that we 'become' Skaters. Thus, whichever subculture we identify with in industrial or postindustrial societies, it will inevitably involve a negotiation between mass-produced goods and a creative 'appropriation' or misuse of them in order to reclaim a sense of authenticity and identity.

Putting these three together, we can look to more recent examples, including the fluid forms of communication, shifting identities, and tentative flirting made possible through mobile phones, to raise the same question in an everyday context: are we 'suckers' for taking part in an obvious form of conspicuous consumption, or 'savvy' in wanting to reclaim a technology and use it for our own ends? The context of everydayness is an important underlying theme to address in this chapter, as these complex negotiations occur within everyday activities and spaces of consumption. Whether it is purchasing jeans in order to rip them later, or buying pre-ripped jeans, our performances of self- and social identity occur as a complex set of negotiations within the everyday. Forging and maintaining our shifting and multiple identities between spaces of discipline – of home, work, or school – and spaces of leisure and consumption – such as pubs, clubs, or malls – requires sophisticated understandings of the presentation of self in everyday life, and nuanced understandings of the shifting relations between self, space and consumption. The particularly spatial contexts of these relations will be examined in the following chapter, 'Mallrats and car boots', while this chapter concentrates on the tensions between attempts at manipulating and structuring the consumer, and the freedom and appropriation of these commodities and practices; and subsequently, between formations of self-identity and especially social identity, our place and status within groups or subcultures.

THE SUCKER

(a): a person easily cheated or deceived; (b): a person irresistibly attracted by something specified e.g. a sucker for ghost stories.

Constructing the consumer

We have already looked at the Frankfurt School as exemplars of a more deterministic structure in which we are compliant in the imposition of culture and commodities from what Adorno and Horkheimer in 1947 called the "mass culture industry". The imposition of homogeneity and predictability, they argued, led to a depoliticised social conformity. An updated version of this same idea was discussed in Chapter 3, concerning the McDonaldization of society. The argument is powerful because it limits political and social transformation or alternatives only to those realisable within the framework of capitalism, which is by definition exploitative. As we saw in Chapter 1, Marcuse had pronounced that, through the culture industry and the newly emerging mass consumer society, capitalism promotes an "ideology of control" that limits the powers of the individual. The monolithic control and exploitation of populations by the mass culture industry – the State, advertising and the mass media – all united in generating "false needs", he thought (1968: 26–27), needs which were themselves forms of social control. By buying into false needs, so the story goes, we become passive consumers, manipulated by larger forces beyond our control. In other words, we become "mindless dupes" (Mackay 1997: 3), "pitiable dupes" (Bowlby 2000: 132). We are taken in. Suckers. This construction of the consumer, the engineering of tastes, desires and (false) needs, is what Storey (1999: 19ff.) terms the model of "consumption as manipulation".

Most contemporary theorists of consumption no longer take this view, attributing to consumers a more active, creative role. Before examining this in the next section ('The savvy'), it is worth engaging in more recent developments that continue in the same vein as the Frankfurt School and their legacy. For the same dialectic between individuality and conformity, between freedom and determinism, between resistance and domination, persists through more modern retail methods. The construction of the consumer continues with retail psychology, with psychoanalysis, and with the engineering of consumer desire and instinct that is orchestrated through advertising and marketing. Part of this history could be told through Freud's nephew, Edward Bernays, who contributed considerably to the rise of public relations and marketing in the USA after the Second World War. In 1928 he argued: "If we understand the mechanism and motives of the group mind, it is now possible to control and regiment the masses according to our will without their knowing it" (2004: 71). This scientific technique of moulding public opinion, used for public relations and marketing in its early days, he called the "engineering of consent". Similarly, new techniques of marketing and the rise of retail psychology continue this theme of the engineering of consumer behaviour, and are briefly surveyed below.

Retail psychology – manipulating the consumer

The construction of the consumer can similarly be seen as the manipulation of the group mind, the engineering of desires and needs. A few examples will suffice to further the view of the programmability of consumers in retail spaces, the manipulation of the consumer's unconscious motivations, in shopping malls and showrooms. The structuring of spaces and the appeal to the senses within a retail environment heavily influences consumer behaviour, and has emerged as an area of academic study. If consumer behaviour can be manipulated, however subtly, are we essentially trapped within the iron cage of consumption? Are purchasing decisions made by ourselves, or engineered by other factors?

Retail psychology, a burgeoning branch of psychology, researches the various conditions under which consumers are more likely to purchase. Attempts at influencing the decisions of buyers started in the 1930s, when the self-service supermarket was becoming a retail phenomenon very separate from the local 'store'. For the first time, the scientific organisation of retail space was combined with aesthetics, the sensory appeal to the shopper. As Bowlby shows, this combination was reflected in a series of influential books by Carl Dipman for example, who envisioned a new epoch of modern, progressive retailing:

> The old-fashioned store was to a large extent a storeroom. The dealer was a storekeeper. But the modern grocery store must be a scientific salesroom. The grocer must be a modern sales engineer.
>
> (1931, in Bowlby 2000: 143)

Unlike the general store, where visits only replenished items that were regularly required, the ethos of the modern grocery store was to actively promote new things, to try them out, treating the customer not as a known entity with predictable needs but, as Dipman wrote in 1935, as "a bundle of sales possibilities" (in Bowlby 2000: 144). This could only occur through a "modern sales engineer", employing elementary retail psychology to disrupt previous habitual patterns of consumption and to persuade the customer to pick up and try out new items. To encourage this, thought Dipman, aesthetics must come to the forefront. Beauty, sensory appeal, these were the factors that mattered to mostly female customers:

> The grocery store today must be both pleasing to the customer – a thing of beauty – yet so constructed that work and labor are reduced to a minimum ... The application of sight and touch, coupled with efficiency of operation, are the most important factors in the new retail salesmanship.
>
> (1931, in Bowlby 2000: 144)

The American housewife was therefore partly constructed in the imagination of modern sales engineers like Dipman as discriminating, yet open to new possibilities and aware of the aesthetics and sensory appeal of objects and packages. American housewives were therefore educated in aesthetics, and their position as consumers was to change – "They were not seen as blameworthy, but as the pitiable dupes of a malevolent environment called 'consumer society'" (in Bowlby 2000: 132). Continually looking for value in order to fulfil the role of dutiful household shopper, they were also a bundle of sales possibilities. After the Second World War, the abundance of items on American supermarket shelves was arranged in vast, sometimes overwhelming displays. The pressure to buy partly arose from the sheer impressiveness of display, but also by appeal to the customer's "whims and fancies", which emanated from the customers themselves (Bowlby 2000: 144). The older grocery stores merely replaced what was consumed in the everyday household's usual stock of items. The modern store, by combining aesthetics and organisation, and now with the abundance of items available after the war, was to pander to the whims and fancies of the customer, steadily encouraging impulse purchases.

In modern retail environments, more sophisticated appeals to the senses are made, such as ambient lighting, the subtle use of smell, music of the right tempo, and the visual appeal of window displays. The particularly fascinating innovations however are at the preconscious or subliminal level. It has long been known that certain smells for example trigger moods or feelings. As Marcel Proust famously realised in *Remembrance of Things Past*, smells can trigger emotions and memories, and the limbic system is the part of the brain responsible for these. But it was the British supermarket Tesco that pioneered an artificial smell of freshly baked bread that it pumped throughout its stores. Underhill, in his pop-

Are you reeled in?
By Beth Neil, *The Evening Chronicle*

… Jim gets even more enthusiastic as we come to the kitchen section. "Just look at the difference in lighting here. So much brighter."

He's right. Extra spot lights hanging above the fridges and towels make everything look a beautifully crisp, pristine white. It's the same story over at the fruit and veg. Jim looks at a pile of shiny, glowing red apples. "See underneath here there's a strip light which is reflecting on the apples making them appear lovely and red," he says.

He takes an apple and pulls it slowly away from the rest. As the fruit moves out of the light, the colour dulls and the shine virtually disappears. Of course, shoppers don't notice the difference as they quickly gather what they want from the shelves and chuck it in the trolley.

The smell of freshly baked bread drifts seductively towards us. But Jim remarks that all might not be quite as it seems.

"A lot of supermarkets pump out the smell of bread to entice customers and whet their appetite.

"Most of the bread will be baked early in the morning, so it's impossible to keep those lovely smells going throughout the day."

Clever, or sneaky? I can't decide.

Jim rejects any accusations that customers are being duped. "Absolutely not. Customers aren't stupid [*sic*] they know stores are there to make a profit …"

Source: *The Evening Chronicle* (Newcastle), 26 September 2003, Features, p.26.

ular book on retailing, *Why We Buy*, describes this as the "olfactory trail" from aisle to bakery, the piped smell of bread being "warm, homey scents" (2003: 164). The warm, welcoming feelings evoked by the smell, especially by the entrance, either enticed customers inside or made customers feel more positively disposed towards the store. This new trend in retailing, 'atmospherics', attends to aspects of the atmosphere like this (music, smell or appearance) in order to influence consumer behaviour.

Read the extract from the boxed newspaper story, which concerns a visit to a Tesco store with a consumer psychologist, Jim Goudie. The article follows the usual circuit of the shopper, from start to finish, detailing some of the mechanisms whereby customers are guided in particular directions, and noticing some of the 'atmospherics' being used to attract customers towards certain commodities.

The comment "Clever, or sneaky? I can't decide" could be a refrain that applies to the whole history of retail psychology. Tesco's artificial bread smell idea later encouraged prospective house sellers to ensure the smell of roasted coffee or baked goods was present during the inspection, to better dispose the visitors to the property (e.g. Doig 1999). Similarly, a psychology experiment concerning smell in retail environments conducted using business studies students is revealing. Responding to the diffusion of various scents and evaluating responses within a simulated store, it was found by the researchers that the evaluation of the store and environment by the students was more positive in the scented conditions; these conditions were rated as more favourable, positive and modern. The students wished to revisit the store and regarded the merchandise as more up to date, varied and of higher quality. According to the researchers, "the presence of an inoffensive scent in a store is an inexpensive and effective way to enhance consumer reactions to the store and its merchandise" (Spangenberg *et al.* 1996). Smell works as an incredibly powerful trigger to associate an environment with a mood or feeling, and thereby impact on sales, and other atmospherics promote other associative properties.

The so-called 'new car smell' is held to be one of the most popular smells, despite being a possibly carcinogenic cocktail of chemical treatments to upholstery and materials. Nevertheless, it is desirable and powerfully evocative, and may enhance the purchasing decision. For example, a used-car showroom employed Oxford's The Aroma Company to produce an aerosol spray of the smell, and applied it to used cars in a trial:

> In the short space of time in which a person decides whether they like the car the smell plays a big part in whether they bond with the vehicle and can be a small but important factor when it comes to buying.
>
> (*Daily Post* 2004)

Of course, smell is a particularly powerful way of guiding or influencing the consumer, its effectiveness lying in the association between scents and memories of warmth and homeliness, in the case of bread, or the brash, crisp, modern smell of the new car. In retail psychology, whether it is cunning or conning the consumer, or as the *Evening Chronicle* article asked, being "clever or sneaky", there are various sensory cues and associative mechanisms, and practical ways that customers can be channelled through space, past the special offers aisles and into luxury items in a distant corner of the store. The spatial arrangement of early supermarkets was similar to conventional stores. The introduction of turnstiles and the separation of entry and exit was initially a method of lowering lost sales through pilfering, as Bowlby (2000: 141) shows. Subsequently the space within most supermarkets became similarly demarcated, where the inner aisles of the store were self-service, a free space to pick up and examine anything you like, and the exit as a 'control' point, where everyone must pay to leave. More on the spaces of

IT'S PSYCHOLOGICAL WARFARE OUT THERE

The moment they walk into a US store, potential customers are bombarded with trickery and messages – subliminal and direct – all designed to lighten purses and wallets [...]

The governing principle of US retail psychology is to concentrate on creating an environment conducive to spending. This involves making shoppers happy (nice music, lighting, free samples), and then convincing them to buy certain products [...]

So next time you dive in to a shop determined to grab just bread, milk and an evening newspaper and come out carrying nail varnish, Christmas crackers, six two-litre drums of ice cream and a case of wine, remember – it's not your fault, they made you do it.

Source: *The Scotsman*, 21 February 2001, p.4.

consumption and the management of retail spaces will be discussed in Chapter 7, 'Mallrats and car boots'.

Yet it is one thing to describe the mechanisms employed in influencing customers to pick up, touch and try a particular product, and another to actually compel the customer towards the purchase. The process leading up to the moment of decision can be influenced, but the actual decision belongs to the customer. Underhill writes about the experience of clothing store The Gap where, rather than clothes being on hangars, they are folded and arranged on tables within a large, open salesfloor. In traditional retail lore this means less stock being available within a given retail space. But the picking up of clothes, the unfolding and refolding, increases tactile contact with the commodity, and encourages staff to approach and offer human contact. "We buy things today more than ever based on trial and touch" (2003: 162), he argues:

> It's the sensory aspect of the decision-making process that's most intriguing because how else do we experience anything? But it's especially crucial in this context because virtually all unplanned purchases – and many planned ones, too – come as a result of the shopper seeing, touching, smelling or tasting something that promises pleasure, if not total fulfilment.
>
> (2003: 162)

To see all this as an 'iron cage' of consumption, where consumers are locked into patterns of behaviour not of their own choosing, where their decisions are not their own, would be the logical development of the creation of, and compulsion towards, "false needs" that the Frankfurt School decried. Yet one of the criticisms of the Frankfurt School and the Leavisite critics of popular culture and mass consumption is that it grossly oversimplifies the workings of the mass culture industry. As Storey (1999: 32) argues, there is not always the total and successful manipulation of passive subjects. Consumption occurs in cultural contexts, as we shall see in the following section, as well as social spaces (in Chapter 7). Instead, the sciences of retail psychology with its sensory appeals and spatial arrangements may encourage us to touch and to *try*, but not – as yet – forcing us to *buy*. And, even when bought, items can be used in unforeseen and imaginative ways.

THE SAVVY

> alteration of *sabi* know (in English-based creoles and pidgins), from Portuguese *sabe* he knows, from *saber* to know, from Latin *sapere* to be wise.

If the post-war abundance of commodities, the emergence of retail psychology and the rise of impulse purchasing encourages us to touch and try products, actually buying them takes us into different territory. Without denigrating the practices of 'just looking', the browsing, trying on and non-purchasing of products for recreational purposes, purchased commodities not only help to articulate our sense of identity, but can also be used in ways unintended or unforeseen by the manufacturers. Being a 'savvy' consumer is not about continually finding the best bargains, although that is a useful skill. Being a savvy consumer is to be aware of the contradictions between the marketing and advertising imposed on us, but still consuming items in intended and unintended ways in order to articulate something else – a sense of self-identity, of difference, or to express a social identity, that sense of belonging to a group based on shared tastes and values. Often the sense of belonging to a group is defined in terms of resistance, as Stuart Hall argues, this being a pervasive or even seductive attitude. Using a notion from Antonio Gramsci concerning the contested "terrain of culture", wherein ideological struggles take place, Hall continues:

> The people versus the power-bloc: this, rather than 'class-against-class', is the central line of contradiction around which the terrain of culture is polarized. Popular culture, especially, is organized around the contradiction: the popular forces versus the power-bloc.
>
> (1981: 238)

Popular culture, especially music, often encourages this collective sense of resistance against an ill-defined yet omnipotent force such as 'big business', 'capitalism' or the forces of commercialism. And it is only in resistance that identities and subcultures can form, despite the fact that these identities also involve consumption, the music and clothes are still bought. Nevertheless, looking at youth subcultures and the way they are often organised around patterns of consumption entails a recognition that consumers are 'active' and even creative, rather than the suckers the "passive 'dupes'" (Storey 1999: 54) of much social theory.

Michel de Certeau

Whether we sympathise with the Frankfurt School's harsh critique of the mass culture industry, or even aspire to the celebrations of aspiration and material success that was *Dynasty* in the 1980s or *Sex and the City* in the late 1990s, we can acknowledge the viewpoint that our consumer choices are engineered by a culture industry that enforces homogenisation, conformity, a single model for us all to aspire to. George Ritzer's 'McDonaldization' thesis explores this in terms of the modern business of leisure, seeing this homogenisation as a template being applied to ever new areas, as we saw in Chapter 3. Again, consumers become 'dupes' or 'suckers' by falling for this. But theorists such as Michel de Certeau (1925–1986) have suggested the opposite. In *The Practice of Everyday Life* (1984), de Certeau forthrightly wishes to claim instead that consumption practices can be reclaimed. Consumption can be creative; consumption is a way of asserting freedom or challenging the systems of power; and consumption can be a way of fighting back at capitalism itself. In other words, instead of simply being duped we can exercise our creativity, not merely straightforwardly using the products imposed on us, but misusing or altering them for our own purposes. There is a creativity in consumption that de Certeau wishes to reclaim, and this forms something of the fabric of our everyday micropolitics.

Rather than attempting to write and represent the totality of social relations in a grand theoretical mode, as does Lefebvre and others in their Marxist-influenced revolutionary backgrounds, Michel de Certeau is content to celebrate the more mundane moments of creativity and festivity within everyday life, including consumption. There is a different orientation to his more revolutionary brethren, the acknowledgement that consumer capitalism simply cannot contain the spontaneity and energies of the people, and that mass culture never contains the activities of the consumer, nor the *use* they make of commodities:

> The consumer cannot be identified or qualified by the newspapers or commercial products he assimilates: between the person (who uses

them) and these products (indexes of the 'order' which is imposed on him), there is a gap of varying proportions opened by the uses he makes of them.

(1984: 32)

There is a perpetual "anonymous creativity" that persists, indicative of more pluralistic, spontaneous and unsystematic forms of culture that continually arise. The creativity involved in consumption in everyday life implies that there is a *production* in the acts and processes of consumption. "Consumers 'produce' through the adoption of errant or non-formalised practices, which obey internal logics that are often unintelligible to the outsider", summarises Gardiner (2000: 170). In fact, consumption is *the* locus of production for the majority of the population, especially in late capitalism. Rather than being passive, victim-like suckers, consumer-producers exercise cunning, trickery, are truly savvy in their creative appropriation of mass-produced commodities. Economists, advertising executives, marketing people will translate the singular act of purchasing as significant, and this can be captured by statistical study, tracing only the "material used by consumer practices – a material which is obviously that imposed on everyone by production". What cannot be captured is the *ways* of using those products, "the very activity of 'making do'" (de Certeau 1984: 34).

In a way, de Certeau echoes Stuart Hall's observation, above, that popular culture often defines itself in opposition to the power bloc. For there to be any resistance to the dominant forces of our culture, thinks de Certeau, we must be like guerrillas. As such, consumption is likened to a tactical raid upon the system, the dominant forces:

In reality, a rationalized, expansionist, centralized, spectacular and clamorous production is confronted by an entirely different kind of production, called 'consumption' and characterized by its ruses, its fragmentation (the results of the circumstances), its poaching, its clandestine nature, its tireless but quiet activity, in short by its quasi-invisibility, since it shows itself not in its own products (where would it place them?) but in an art of using those imposed on it.

(1984: 31)

In acknowledging that we no longer make our own products so easily, and therefore we must rely on products "imposed" upon us, a fundamental aspect of the culture of everyday life is therefore to be found in "adaptation", in *"ways of using* imposed systems"; and this he likens to "trickery – (ruse, deception, in the way one uses or cheats with the terms of social contracts)" (1984: 18).

As Fiske shows, the language de Certeau uses contrasts those that have power, the "cumbersome, unimaginative and overorganized", with the weak, who are "creative, nimble and flexible" (1989a: 29). The contrast couldn't be clearer. Much like military interventions in so-called rogue states, a lumbering but mighty military force is pitted against a weaker but more mobile and underground set of disparate forces that remain hidden. The larger forces of domination are over-organised, and must utilise a *strategy*; we, on the other hand, are weaker and, like guerrillas, must use *tactics*. A strategy is a long-term plan, where resources are expendable in the attainment of a long-term goal (e.g. capturing a nation, maximising profit), whereas tactics are short-term plans, to resist a dominant force (e.g. an occupying army, the imposition of mass-marketed commodities) through skirmishes, raids, ambushes, smaller-scale opposition. A weaker force will simply lose against a larger force if direct confrontation happens in the open; hence the fight must be taken underground, must rely on surprise in smaller-scale attacks, and must occupy territories in a more fleeting and temporary way. We are reminded most recently of these tactics and strategies in the conflicts between the US and Vietnam, Nicaragua, Afghanistan (delete according to age). But these metaphors will also be useful in considering the ways we react to, and resist, imposed meanings, ordered spaces of consumption, and mass-marketed commodities.

The art of appropriation

In terms of ways of adapting the goods imposed on us through consumer capitalism, or *"ways of using* imposed systems" (1984: 18), de Certeau introduces the term 'appropriation'. We appropriate mass-produced consumer goods or alter their meaning through *use*; we do different things with them, make them mean different things. In this way we negotiate our cultural identity and our politics through this use (or misuse) of standardised, mass-produced products, as Lunt and Livingstone explain:

> The process of negotiation is one in which the consumer transforms
> or appropriates the mass-produced object. They do not necessarily
> take on the meanings which are publicly associated with the object
> but work symbolically on the object's meaning, bringing objects into
> the home and under control, giving them local meanings, translating
> the object from an alienable to an inalienable condition.
>
> (1992: 84)

Unlike the Frankfurt School, the acknowledgement that commodities and the products of the culture industries are woven into the fabric of everyday life is central to de Certeau. Sometimes the use of these mass-produced standardised products is artful, cunning, unusual, and transforms their meaning. In describing the art of appropriation, we can look at examples that show consumption is part of a dialogic process as opposed to the simple act of purchasing and display. This dialogue continues between consumers and producers, but also between consumers and other consumers. In terms of subcultures, one stylistic innovation does not exist in isolation. Imitation, mimicry, mutability and eventual transformation characterise this ongoing dialogue within, and between, subcultures. An example of this is described in the 'Subcultures' section below, which details the transformation of the scooter from democratic, unisex transport device to male Mod style icon.

Any analysis of consumption within subcultures is to a certain extent one of *homology*, that is, the recognition of patterns of similarity. Storey (1999) in looking at cultural consumption realises this similarity within a group and between groups. The way that subcultures or groups dress similarly and share core values clearly identifies them, whether they be Mods, Goths, Punks, Skaters or whatever. Yet while recognising the internal coherence of youth subcultures, we can also acknowledge a *heterology*, the patterns of difference and the accommodation of otherness. This heterology is clear when we notice that no one member of a group is exactly alike, and that there are stylistic traits or the innovative use of objects or decorations that mark out a member as different from another. The production of difference, the stylistic innovation, de Certeau thinks of as a process of *bricolage*. *Bricolage* is to acknowledge the plurality of meanings of commodities, even if mass produced, through their use, misuse and appropriation by a subculture or group. In a sense, as Lury (1996: 197) remarks, this is a double movement, the homology of subcultures yet the heterology of the different uses of products to mark out the differential practices of the subculture. The heterology, the marking out of difference between groups, is consequently pursued primarily through consumption, then. Following de Certeau a number of researchers have found that young consumers are active, creative and critical in their use and appropriation of commodities. "In a process of *bricolage*, they appropriated, re-accented, rearticulated or trans-coded the material of mass culture to their own ends, through a range of everyday creative and symbolic practices", summarises Mackay (1997: 6). Appropriation, this artful, creative process of transforming commodities from their intended use into a sign-system of a subculture's own making, is examined in terms of motor scooters by Hebdige (1988, 2000), and in terms of ripping jeans by Fiske (1989a). Thus paradigmatic examples of artful appropriation occur within youth culture.

'THE ART OF BEING IN-BETWEEN': CONSUMING YOUTH

This section will take the debate concerning consumers as 'suckers' or 'savvy' into more complex territory, using the historical creation of youth cultures and their often ambiguous but necessary reliance on consumption to articulate these cultures as a continuous negotiation between positions. Steven Miles's book *Consumerism – As a Way of Life* flags up what he calls "the consuming paradox":

> the fact that in terms of our individual experience consumerism appears to have a fascinating, arguably fulfilling, personal appeal and yet simultaneously plays some form of an ideological role in actually controlling the character of everyday life.
>
> (1998: 5)

In other words, this is to ask whether we are being creative and expressing ourselves and our identities through consumption, or whether we are being manipulated and controlled by a mass culture industry. Or, we could rephrase this into Gramsci's (1971) language, where the form of ideological control occurring through culture is hegemonic – perpetuating hegemony – and any cultural resistance is counter-hegemonic. It is to ask whether we are seducers or the seduced, or as we have portrayed it in this chapter, whether 'suckers' or 'savvy'. Perhaps, as in any sexual encounter, a bit of both. Being a savvy consumer is therefore to be aware of Miles's 'consuming paradox', the knowledge that our tastes and desires are manipulated by the mass media, yet simultaneously the belief that we still find satisfaction and articulate our identities through consumption. Contrary to the Frankfurt School and its explicit notion that we become assimilated into what the mass culture industry dictates, we can 'poach' or 'appropriate' things for our own ends, ensuring that commodities can be assimilated into what *we* are, rather than the other way around.

Yet we should be wary of de Certeau's romanticised view of guerrilla consumption, the translation or appropriation of objects. Celebrating the everyday creativities that help fabricate culture is fine, but does lead to naïve and unrealistic claims concerning the importance of these acts. de Certeau is culpable of this in certain passages:

> Dwelling, moving about, speaking, reading, shopping and cooking are activities that seem to correspond to the characteristics of tactical ruses and surprises: clever tricks of the 'weak' within the order established by the 'strong,' an art of putting one over on the adversary on his own turf, hunters' tricks, maneuverable, polymorphic mobilities, jubilant, poetic and warlike discoveries.

> (1984: 38)

In addition, the dramatic language of 'poaching', ruse, trickery is oppositional, still adhering to what Hall (1981) had declared, that popular culture is always defined against the power bloc. Gramsci himself uses military analogies too, yet his emphasis is not on the side of the minor victories of popular culture:

> In war it would sometimes appear that a fierce artillery attack seemed to have destroyed the enemy's entire defensive system, whereas in fact it had only destroyed the outer perimeter: and at the moment of their advance and attack the assailants would find themselves confronted by a line of defence which was still effective.

> (1971: 235)

In the contested terrain of culture, some "superficial concessions" within culture may be allowed (Strinati 1995: 167), but this does not significantly alter the power balance. In other words, minor victories against a larger foe may have the dramatic appeal of a war movie, but may just be the insignificant and sneaky victories of teenagers getting one over on the teacher. As Clarke puts it in his essay 'Dupes and guerrillas: the dialectics of cultural consumption' (2000), the polarisation of the debate into 'dupes' and 'guerrillas' tends to romanticise the political character of these acts of resistance. "While this approach correctly gets rid of the pessimism of seeing subordinate groups as 'cultural dupes', the alternative vision of guerrilla armies of cultural activists seems excessively celebratory", he argues (2000: 293). And how these cultural resistances fit into any identifiable political direction is uncertain. Is it playful or revolutionary? Anticapitalist, or symptomatic of 'postmodern' consumption?[1] McGuigan's criticism of Fiske also applies by extension to de Certeau: that their theorising, "focused so narrowly as it is on the micro-politics of consumption and the local victories and defeats of everyday life, provides little space for transformative struggle of any kind" (2000: 295).

One problem about romanticising the guerrillas rather than the dupes, is that there is an unsophisticated understanding of the economic and ideological model as monolithic or singular. This criticism is familiar from the Frankfurt School. But even for De Certeau, commodities are first imposed on us, and only then can we transform them. Yet the economic impetus behind the culture of consumption, Clarke argues, has always involved the use of alternative or oppositional creative practices; in short, it is simplistic to argue that cultural uniformity or homogenisation results, since the economic drive is towards increasing diversity in terms of objects and services for consumption (2000: 288). New production technologies have left the uniformity and standardisation of the Model 'T' Ford behind, enabling a range of highly differentiated and tailored products to be manufactured from the same production processes. Similarly, consumer culture being increasingly homogeneous is one of the myths of consumption that Miller wishes to puncture. The forms of diversity and sociality produced through consumption are diminished with respect to earlier forms, which are usually held to be more 'authentic'. Miller argues that this "myth of cultural erosion" refuses to regard new forms of diversity as 'culture' (1993: 22). True, consumers desire innovation yet also the reassurance that a product fits into their expectations, so there is a conventionalising process. A new recording artist might be described as "the new Norah Jones", for example. But this is not the same as homogenisation or uniformity. One strategy to accommodate these tensions or contradictions is to move away from the polarisation of the debate, from 'dupes' and 'guerrillas', suckers or savvy, and to think instead of the practices of cultural consumption, the way their negotiations reveal social relations, and the way that strategies for surviving these processes are constructed. This is clearest in the analysis of youthful consumption, where the selection and display of commodities is most exposed.

Youth culture means dwelling at the edges of competing tendencies. In the case of consumption, this may be consumption with a 'knowing' or ironic edge. The competing or even contradictory tendencies between work and leisure, between the hard-working ethos of production and the hedonistic or pleasure-seeking ethos of consumption, as Lee observes, are particularly prominent in youth culture. Fordism essentially

> developed and defined the social category of youth which became the most prominent materialisation of the new mass consumption ethic … [Fordism] opened up fertile new youth markets and made available for youth the now familiar material and symbolic objects by which they could objectify a common structure of feeling.
>
> (1992: 106–107)

Thus Fordism, the logic of mass production and mass consumption, introduced a notion of group identity and solidarity based on purchasing goods, and rewarded the flexibility of the youthful workforce by granting them not only their own culture but also the money to buy into it. It is not a one-way street, however. As boundary creatures, youth consumers are indeed ideal consumers, being representative of "Fordism's strategic enshrinement of consumption", but also "its most telling site of cultural contradiction", as Latham (2002: 19) points out. In other words, the consumer paradox is never so keenly exemplified as in the complexities and contradictions of youth consumption.

Post-war consumption and the invention of the 'teenager'

The market research company Datamonitor in their report 'Teenage Consumers' claimed that, in US dollars, the "total European market value is 6.0bn for tweens and 10.5bn for 14-to-17 year-old teenagers in 2002" (Datamonitor 2003). Along with the identification of distinct youth categories and their relative spending power, the report compiled trends in spending and suggested strategies for more effective marketing to this group. In an earlier report entitled 'Tweenagers' they advise: "One of the most effective ways to market to tweens will be to introduce 'step stone' brands that extend the appeal of more adult-orientated products to include tweens" (Datamonitor 2002). The separation and maintenance of distinct categories for marketing, such as 'teenagers' and 'tweenagers', along with appropriate strategies for approaching such target markets, is historically a result of the explosion of post-war consumption.

The 'teenager' as a distinct category was coined in the mid-1940s by market researchers in the US, and took a few years to be imported into the UK. Once imported, however, the new term 'teenager' became rooted, and central to this category was the idea that "traditional class boundaries were being eroded by the fashions and lifestyles of newly affluent 'gilded' youth", in the words of Osgerby (1998: 35). This rise in youth identities and subcultures based largely on consumption meant that other categories of identity, such as the workplace or role in the household, became less meaningful. Whereas one's identity was predominantly given by one's economic status and role in the workplace or household before the Second World War, emerging youth groups placed the emphasis first on *social* identity (identity within the social group) as opposed to *economic* identity (within the workplace). Bocock describes this shift from "work-role identity" (1993: 105), where work instead provides the money for buying the consumer goods required to construct and maintain other, more self-directed forms of identity. Rather than being bound by class-based formations of identity derived from the workplace, the rise of youth subcultures was elective, a matter of lifestyle choice that could escape previously rigid and entrenched class-based and social divisions. The shift from workplace identity even hinted at a new 'classlessness', where post-war economic growth and new consumer freedoms ameliorated social divisions.

As an example of Bourdieu's distinction, where 'taste' is always set up in opposition to bad taste, to the objectionable, the lowly or unimaginative, in post-war affluence we have a particular sort of "conspicuous, leisure-oriented" consumption, in the words of Osgerby (1998: 31), driven by youth tastes and centred around competing forms of consumption. Rather than the domestic consumption of their parents' generation, this expenditure on entertainments and display of commodities was public, flamboyant even. To the youth participating in these subcultures based on consumption, and to the increasingly important areas of marketing and the mass media, the clear association was of youthfulness with ebullience, affluence and a rejection of the seemingly dull conformity and primitive pleasures of previous generations. So clearly identified and distinct as a marketing category, post-war youth culture's need to express itself through conspicuous consumption, and to forge separate subcultures within which one found social status and a sense of identity, was ripe for economic exploitation, as shown by this astonishingly candid report from 1966:

> The quality of life lived by the average young person of today is much affected by the realisation by commercial interests that the age group fourteen to twenty-five represents, in economic terms, a vast multi-million pound market; a well-defined consumer group, affluent and innocent, to be attracted and exploited and pandered to; second only to the housewife in potential spending power.
>
> (Hawes 1966, in Osgerby 1998: 38)

As a result, the media industries and marketing helped to popularise and accelerate changes in youth fashion, music and style, and took distinct subcultures such as the Teddy boys and Mods nationwide so that even provincial areas had their versions.

Subcultures and the aestheticisation of everyday life

What is a subculture? A social group that uses the "detritus of a dominant culture to affirm a counter-culture", say Clarke *et al.* (2003: 136). The usual history of post-war consumption emphasises the emergence of youth cultures based on consumption. Subcultures were an attempt after the Second World War to hold on to the traditional working-class community of the 'parent' culture, while using the opportunities afforded by the so-called 'affluent society' of post-war Britain and America that J.K. Galbraith had famously identified. As such, they started as working-class phenomena, positioned between old values and new affluence. Subcultures in Dick Hebdige's formulation are "concerned first and foremost with consumption" (1979: 94–95). The purchase of certain commodities such as records and clothes, aimed at emerging youth markets, entailed an increasing identification of the consumer with a chosen lifestyle pattern. This occurs in something like a *bricolage* process, where commodities from the various culture industries are appropriated for their own purposes or meanings. A simple commodity can be transformed by an act of cultural resistance, such as the ripping of jeans as Fiske (1989a) shows. But this act of resistance often leads to 'incorporation' – that is, the manufacturers will then sell the transformed commodity as a commodity, such as pre-ripped jeans. The analysis of the subcultural patterns of consumption in this way reveals the active nature of consumption, almost as part of a dialogic process, as opposed to the passive form of consumption that the Frankfurt School and other cultural critics assume. Consumers are not "passive dupes", as Storey (1999: 54) remarks. An example of this is the scooter.

We usually think of the 'Mods' and the 'Rockers' as quintessential post-war youth subcultures, and indeed they neatly show the divide in terms of consumption. While the Rockers were more traditionally rebellious, basing their consumption on Americanised motorbike culture and rock music, the Mods were more attuned to the increasing aestheticisation of everyday life of continental Europe, receptive to modernist (hence 'Mod') design influences, especially from Italy. As Hebdige explains, "Mod was predominantly working-class, male-dominated and centred on an obsessive clothes-consciousness", and therefore, according to sociological and marketing literature, "was largely a matter of commodity selection" (2000: 154). This is reflected in their consumption of soul and rhythm and blues music, their prominent ownership of mopeds such as Vespa and Lambretta, their wearing of suits, often Italian in origin, displaying their taste and setting them in opposition to the Rockers, with their motorbikes, rock music, leather jackets and denims. If the motorcycle was resolutely masculine, the scooter was gendered as female. It was an aestheticised object, initially marketed to teenagers and women, as Hebdige (2000: 131–132) shows. As its design progressed, the engine became increasingly hidden behind panelling, the design and streamlining coming to the fore. Hence, its use by young, working-class, predominantly male Mods showed their preference for aesthetics rather than functionality, and placed progressive style and design as a badge of belonging to that particular subculture:

> As an everyday artefact invested with some standards of style and utility but which still managed to satisfy all the key criteria – elegance, serviceability, popularity and visual discretion – the scooter fulfilled all the modern ideals.
>
> (Hebdige 2000: 150)

The appropriation of such an object, the unique use of a commodity outside its intended target market, assimilates a seemingly arbitrary object into a sign-system of the subculture's own making, and constitutes the object as emblematic, a badge signifying identity and belonging to a particular cultural group. "Value was conferred upon the scooter by the simple act of selection", is how Hebdige (2000: 155) describes it, and the process of transformation of the scooter from a democratic mode of transport to a Mod style statement entailed its appropriation and subsequent modification. In a process of *bricolage* or hybridisation, out of the styles, images and material culture available to a subculture like the Mods, autonomy and uniqueness were pursued. Pennants, whip aerials, mirrors, and horns were added to the original design, separating the object from its original target market, and just like Bourdieu's notion of distinction, using the object as a signal or marker to others with similar tastes. To differentiate both object and owner from the mainstream, through the purchase and transformation of the scooter, is simultaneously to bind consumer and commodity into a singular articulation of taste, style and identity.

The competition between such groups was not limited to transport or the boutique, of course, as newspapers often sensationally portrayed their violent confrontations en masse in seaside towns, as both Hebdige (1988, 2000) and Shields (1991) describe. This excessive energy was partly fuelled by the media. Cohen famously characterises the clashes at beach resorts like Clacton as a "moral panic" and shows how "folk devils" or deviants from the norm are portrayed in exaggerated form in the media, as a threat to institutions and normality, and which must be neutralised (1972: 40ff.). And partly this excessive energy was accommodated by cycles of consumption, and has since spread to teenage consumption where the buying of commodities and the formations of identity within subcultural groups (Mods, Rockers, Punks, Goths, Skaters and so on) is an index for the sheer, unbridled hedonistic pleasure in consumption that youth could enjoy after the stringent restrictions and rationing of wartime. The Mods are an exemplary hybrid, a subculture whose more European, upwardly mobile and aesthetically aware sensibility was still rooted in British working-class life in urban housing estates, while their music taste included the black American urban soul of the Stax and Motown labels, and also the music of recent Afro-Caribbean immigrants, such as ska. Colin MacInnes's 1959 novel *Absolute Beginners*, filmed by Julien Temple in 1986, shows the aestheticisation of Mod culture, the centrality of music to the formation of the social identity, the iconicity of the Vespa scooter, and the beginnings of the 'teenager' as a cultural entity and, later, as marketing category. The novelty of youth culture as a distinct category, represented by shiny espresso machines and coffee bars, away from the prosaic adult world of squalid pubs, is shown in this passage:

> Everyone had loot to spend, everyone a bath with verbena salts behind them, and nobody had broken hearts, because they were all ripe for the easy summer evening. The rubber-plants in the espressos had been dusted, and the smooth white lights of the new-style Chinese restaurants – not the old Mah Jongg categories, but the latest thing with broad glass fronts, and dacron curtainings, and a beige carpet over the interiors – were shining a dazzle, like some monster telly screens. Even those horrible old anglo-saxon public-houses – all potato crisps and flat, stale ale, and puddles on the counter bar, and spittle – looked quite alluring, provided you didn't push those two-ton doors that pinch your arse, and wander in. In fact, the capital was a night-horse dream.

(1961: 87)

The emblematic scooter takes its part in a more generalised context of affluence, progressive design, the cultivation of style and distinction, separating this from the tawdry, the banal, the unimaginative. Hebdige calls this the 'aestheticisation' of everyday life: "The perfection of surfaces within Mod was part of the 'aestheticisation' of everyday life achieved through the intervention of the Image, through conflation of the 'public' and the 'personal', consumption and display" (2000: 156).

While this section has concentrated on a particular historical era in order to exemplify the aestheticisation of everyday life, the appropriation and transformation of scooters within Mod culture, we can easily transpose this to a more recent subculture and set of objects. Unsurprisingly, in some respects little has changed. The fixation with Italian culture still persists in some echelons of the new 'Casuals' subculture, British working-class male groups organised around fashion, fighting and football, as described by Thornton. Reminiscent of Mod's fixation with style, a Portsmouth fan describes the uniform of his peers: "The knitwear was Italian; Armani and Valentino were the main labels" (in Thornton 2003: 125). Of course, the range of commodities has diversified greatly, and footwear has featured prominently as an articulation of subcultural style and identity, as well as ethnicity. Bobbito Garcia's historical account of the role of trainers in popular culture in New York from the 1960s onwards in *Where'd You Get Those?* (2003) illustrates this, as does Nick Heard's book *Trainers* (2003).

From 'Generation X' to 'Generation Text'

'Generation X' was the title of a nationwide study of youth attitudes and opinions that Charles Hamblett and Jane Deverson conducted between 1963 and 1964. Originally commissioned for a British women's magazine, asking the nation's youth their opinions and printing chunks of the transcripts meant that their frank findings did not sit well with the magazine's editor, so the study was published in book form. In a variety of typefaces presumably indicating the variety of views, the cover has young people "talking about Education, Marriage, Money, Pop, Politics, Parents, Drugs, Drink, God, Sex, Class, Colour, Kinks and Living for Kicks" (1964). The timing was apposite. British youth was just emerging into the world's spotlight, with the Beatles as the epitome of cool. Mods were fighting against Rockers, sexual liberation was in the air, and as we have seen, black music was fused with white lower-middle-class art-school style. There was a sense of optimism in popular culture, and a plural but clearly identifiable voice of British youth.

The term 'Generation X' was therefore coined before Punk and before Douglas Coupland's eponymous novel of 1991. Yet so much has changed since both books were written that current youth no longer have the naïve nihilism of 1960s teenagers, nor the fashionable *weltschmerz* of Coupland's 1990s. Arguably, contemporary youth has blended teens, tweens, twenty- and thirty-somethings into a single blob of consumer credit and status anxiety, and these 'kidults' or 'adultescents' are complicit with creative and innovative forms of the mass culture industry as never before. One example of this is in the use of mobile telephones, their appropriation and involvement in symbolic innovation. Hence we can call them 'Generation Text', as Hammersley (2005) does, rather than 'Generation X'. Mobile phone use does lead to symbolic and linguistic innovation, such as the commonly understood forms of abbreviation of the 'txt messg', which has certainly eclipsed email in terms of spontaneity and instantaneity of communication. Frank Furedi (2003) offers other examples of a creeping infantilisation of consumption, such as twenty-somethings watching *Teletubbies*, the popularity of Sony's PlayStations amongst twenty- and thirty-something professionals. Childish joys that are derived from childish toys represent a form of nostalgia that is experienced at an earlier life stage than before, and this nostalgia can easily be commodified. Some advertisers in the US have coined another term, 'Peterpandemonium', and explain: "People in their twenties and thirties are clamouring for comfort in purchases and products, and sensory experiences that remind them of a happier, more innocent time – childhood" (in Furedi 2003). One historical continuity between 'Generation X' and the kidults of 'Generation Text' is that the celebration of youth involves consumption of key products that serve as markers of mutual belonging to a youthful, vibrant and energetic culture. Kidults, however, comprise a large market that involves age compression – everyone from 5 to 45 can enjoy *Teletubbies*, *Bagpuss*, PlayStation games or Hello Kitty, but for different reasons.

A PARTING SHOT

There is no clearly identifiable third way between the manipulation and control of the consumer and the consumer's own expression of freedom and identity through consumption. There is no such neat resolution. In part, we messily use and misuse the commodities that are within reach of our spheres of everydayness, sometimes being co-opted and compelled, at other times consciously willing against it, according to our level of awareness at the time. And so, in terms of our experiences of everydayness, the true promise of endless choice and the ability to freely articulate who we are never quite materialises, remaining shadowy, elusive. As soon as something is incorporated into an altered semiotic-material system, and hence enters the realm of a different cultural economy, the meaning is taken back, transformed again, and sold back to us. What made us so confident in terms of giving a spin or articulating something of ourselves within a commodity is then taken away, temporarily no longer ours. Until we step forward and reclaim it again. A continual oscillation, one that we will see in particular with the ethnic appropriation of branded goods in Chapter 8.

Moving away from the descriptions of subcultures, we will pursue some of these themes of the transformation of spaces in everyday life, especially the spaces of consumption, in the next chapter. Something of the mobility of individual and social identities has been suggested in previous chapters. Here we have considered how post-war youth subcultures have used and appropriated commodities as a way of negotiating their cultural identities, both within the group and between groups. But the history of youth cultures is not about fixity or enclosure. As we shall see in the following chapter, not only do the commodities change, but so do the subcultures and the populations that constitute them. Social groups that are partly defined by consumption are not in fixity but in flux, leading Maffesoli (1996) to argue that social groups are neo-tribal in formation, meaning that they are often loose, mobile arrangements of members, often centred around particular forms of consumption (see also Muggleton's notion of "post-subcultures" (2000), and edited volume (2003)). We will see how this fluid identity of the individual and the group translates not only into ways that commodities are used and appropriated, but also the way that spaces of consumption – shopping malls, department stores and the like – are used and appropriated.

NOTE

1 These issues will be raised in more detail in the final chapter, 'Where do we want to go today?', on postmodern consumption.

7

MALLRATS AND CAR BOOTS
THE SPACES OF CONSUMPTION

> Someday it may be possible to be born, go from preschool
> through college, get a job, date, marry, have children ... get a
> divorce, advance through a career or two, receive your medi-
> cal care, even get arrested, tried and jailed; live a relatively full
> life of culture and entertainment, and eventually die and be
> given funeral rites without ever leaving a particular mall com-
> plex – because every one of those possibilities now exists in
> some shopping center somewhere.
>
> (Kowinski 1985)

INTRODUCTION

We are aware historically how commodities have been intricately bound up
with self-identity and social identities, and how consumption can alter the
intended use or meaning of an object in order to articulate something else.
As we saw in the previous chapter, subcultures and social groups have
complex dialogic relations with objects that try simultaneously to resist
and modify the straightforward patterns of consumption that are imposed
on us. Michel de Certeau has termed this "appropriation". We have seen
how advertising and marketing respond to such resistance, aping, second-
guessing or even encouraging their own resistances as a marketing strategy,
with commodities such as jeans and trainers. Looking at youth consumption

and subcultures in particular, we explored how consumers can be active creators of meanings (savvy) rather than passive dupes (suckers) in terms of using the imposed objects of mass production. The "art of using" such objects (De Certeau 1984: 31), that is, the creative impetus behind consumption, helps to articulate not only identity within a group but also the differences between groups. Now we shift attention from the commodities themselves to their spatial contexts.

The spaces of consumption include *where* commodities are sold and consumed, from impromptu markets or souks to more purpose-built department stores, supermarkets, shopping centres or malls. This chapter will concentrate mainly on department stores and shopping malls, since there is an historical unfolding of one into the other which opens up questions concerning the structure and use of such spaces. Malls in particular have been characterised as homogeneous and identical spaces across the world. Shopping malls, like theme parks, are held by some to be symptomatic of the McDonaldization of society, as we saw in Chapter 3. As usual, we can problematise such 'top-down' theories by focusing on the intricacies of the practices of everyday life, taking a 'bottom-up' approach that looks at how, exactly, these spaces are used, appropriated and, if only temporarily, taken over. Just as in identity, such spaces are subject to a dialectic of flux and fixity, at once given or imposed and fluid and malleable.

The structure of this chapter is threefold, and connects with the questions of cultural geography just raised. Firstly, 'Histories of shopping spaces' looks at the development of those archetypal spaces of consumption, department stores and shopping malls, through history. We ask what this reveals about the way they are structured today and the forces that have shaped them. Secondly, 'Consumption spaces and everyday life' moves from historical considerations to ask how and where we consume now, and the shifting identity of both consumers and the spaces in which they consume. We also ask *how* spaces of consumption help influence both what we do and the meanings of the products and activities created. Thirdly, 'Spaces of fake, fantasy and control', particularly in relation to big shopping malls, follows on from the last chapter about the engineering of choice (sucker) or the creative arts of appropriating mass-produced objects (savvy) to ask how we negotiate the discipline and control that regulate our behaviour in such spaces, and to what extent we establish ownership and identity within them. Again, we will argue that there is a negotiation between these positions by the users of these spaces, but that this involves temporal elements alongside spatial ones.

Questions of culture and space

These questions are the concern of cultural geography, that branch of human geography after the so-called 'cultural turn' (see e.g. Pile and Thrift 1995; Crang 1998; Barnett 1998). Cultural geography examines the spatial productions of such things as power, subjectivity, identity, gender and ethnicity, and has paid increasing attention to theories of everyday life and consumption. Implicit in cultural geography are several notions, of which three are relevant to this chapter. Firstly, that culture is ordinary, about everyday life. We continually produce and reproduce our culture through activities, some of which are reflective and some unreflective, and this certainly applies to consumption. Secondly, that it's not just *what* we do, but *where* we do it, so that the spatial contexts of cultural practices often help structure the activities occurring within them. The design and planning of spaces of consumption actually alter consumer behaviour, both intentionally and unintentionally. And thirdly, the *places* in which everyday life occurs are important. This point is crucial. The *spaces* which are given or imposed on us, the shopping malls and supermarkets designed from architectural blueprints, come to be *places* through the uses and activities of the people within them. Just like the use of commodities, the use of a space might significantly alter its intended meaning or purpose, and may change over time. Shopping malls are famous for being the hangout for pensioners, walkers, mallrats and housewives at different times of the day, consuming to varying extents and using the given space in manifold ways. A large part of this chapter will examine these questions of cultural geography, exploring our everyday signifying practices within spaces of consumption.

HISTORIES OF SHOPPING SPACES

The nineteenth-century French novelist Emile Zola described the department store, then a novel and developing space of consumption, as "the cathedral of modern commerce" (see Crossick and Jaumain 1999). The geographer Rachel Bowlby has described them as historically "a 'palace' for the middle classes" (2000: 9–10). This epithet could now be attached to the large out-of-town shopping malls and sprawls of retail parks that mushroom in the more developed nations of the world. It is apt to explore the spatial metaphors of cathedrals and palaces within the spatial contexts of consumption. For example, like Lauren Langman (1992) suggests in passing, we could see malls as performing the same function for communities, the same maintenance of hierarchies of power and control, as cathedrals did in feudal times. This would be to understand the historical secularisation of society, the long process of separation of Church and State, to observe that consumption (literally) takes the place of the Church in the formation of citizenship, participation and community. For many years in Britain, virtually all shops were closed on Sundays by law. A change in the law on Sunday trading in August 1994 meant that, suddenly, Sunday became one of the busiest trading days of the week, easily observable by turning up to the nearest mall.

This section will briefly outline the historical development of these spaces of consumption for the purpose of commerce, trade, community and shopping. Along the way are observations concerning the changing architecture of such spaces, the different weighting of the senses as new materials and mechanisms of display become utilised, the increasing tendency to make spaces of consumption not only sites of purchase but also places of recreation and leisure, and the historical responses to gender in these spaces.

From medieval marketplace to industrial revolution

If the industrial revolution significantly accelerated the manufacture of commodities and threw up new spaces in which to consume them, pre-industrial spaces of consumption centred around the marketplace. In cities and towns throughout medieval Europe for example, farmers and artisans met to trade wares and barter at specific places and times. To this day, market days continue in a large number of these places, although the commodities sold are markedly different. While these activities could not be characterised strictly as 'shopping', the buying and trading of food, especially, was the focus of the pre-industrial city (see e.g. Dyer

1994), often linked to festivals, fun and revelry. As we saw in Chapter 4, the notion of festival and carnival celebrated bodily pleasures and became differentiated from the everyday reality of work, hunger and impoverishment. Often political events or pageantry were tied to such market days, and as such they performed important functions. Market days concerned not only trade, then, but also those things that happen when people commune, for example recreation, entertainment, fun; also a civil aspect in terms of the maintenance of communities and regional identities. By painting this picture in such broad strokes we can see historical continuities with more modern spaces of consumption.

The invention of the cotton-spinning jenny in 1765 by Thomas Hargreaves roughly signals the beginning of the industrial revolution, although its origin is complex. Overcoming bottlenecks in production through rudimentary machinery entails a massive increase in available commodities, what was bought and sold. These were the products of the new industries, a proportion of which were exported to the colonies and traded for an increasingly vast range of exotic goods such as spices, foods and drinks. The consumption of meats, tea and sugar rose significantly as the relative price of these commodities decreased in relation to wages (although see debates in Taylor (1975)). As agricultural populations moved to urban centres to become factory workers within these new industries, towns and cities grew ever larger. These two developments, the massive increase in available commodities alongside a burgeoning urban population, set the conditions for a fundamental change in *where* people shopped and what *social meaning* shopping had. Relations between producer and consumer altered, and the notion of shopping as a distinct recreational activity, albeit for an affluent minority, began to occur with the massive proliferation of commodities. Following the migration of worker from agricultural to industrial forms of production, the significance of spaces of consumption altered accordingly. Sketching roughly for the sake of historical argument, if villages were served by a number of small shops, each being distinct and delimited according to the commodity or service sold (grocer, butcher, blacksmith), the shopkeeper often knew the producer, and was the personal intermediary between producer and consumer. The origin of most products was known, and circulations of commodities were primarily local or regional. The retail experience was participative, conversational even, as Rudolph Kenna shows:

The typical [...] shopkeeper was a retail tradesman, living on or near his premises. Each shopkeeper had special skills: grocers had to blend weight, grind, weigh and package much of their stock, and butchers were frequently their own slaughtermen. In those days the modus operandi of shopping was very different from that of today. Stock was stored in cupboards and boxes, many articles had to be made to order from designs in pattern books, and it was customary to haggle over prices. Cash sales at fixed prices would have struck the average trader as a very eccentric way of doing business, and he would have marvelled at the docility of the modern shopper.

(1996: 3)

This was to change massively in the mid-nineteenth century, as two big technical innovations fundamentally and irreversibly altered the material construction of shopping spaces, their architecture, and thereby the activities within them.

The transformation of the shopping experience

While straightforward incremental advances in material construction, the use of iron and glass in the mid-nineteenth century transformed the whole retail experience, as Walter Benjamin (1892–1940) described in his famous *Arcades Project*, written between 1927 and his death in 1940. Iron, steel and plate glass made possible the formation of three extremely important spatial sites of consumption: the arcades, which were built from 1822 onwards; then department stores, the first of which was Bon Marché in Paris in 1852; and more currently the vast and decontextualised structures that are shopping malls, the first of which was arguably the Country Club Plaza in Kansas City in 1922.

Arcades were small shops with plate glass windows and glass-covered streets protected from the weather. For Benjamin, the arcades of Paris were "*the* defining buildings of the 19th century" (Shields 1989: 148). At first lit by gaslight, and then by electricity, the buildings were often ornate. This was a dry, warm retail environment that could be strolled through, and made buying commodities a much more leisurely pursuit. The large glass roofs allowed natural light through, and the iron super-structures and manufacture of large sheets of glass meant that the buildings could be large. At night they were riots of electric colours, and during the day skylight poured through the roof. The *atrium*, an internal courtyard lit by natural light, was a feature of Roman architecture. With these large iron and glass structures, arcades could follow the same route. It allowed a large, central, almost theatrical interior, around which smaller shops could be organised, and elegantly designed balustrades and ornamental balconies which only increased the sense of being in a theatre or museum. Rather than fill all available space with shops and goods, the atrium "created, in its vaulted interior, the impression of an infinitely extended space, filled with an inexhaustible supply of commodities" (Ferguson 1992: 31). The most famous arcades were in Paris, celebrated by Walter Benjamin's compendium of writing about modernity and street life, *The Arcades Project*. The Parisian arcades, he says,

> which get their light from above, are the most elegant shops, so that the arcade is a city, a world in miniature, in which consumers will find everything they need [...] all this is the arcade in our eyes [...] radiated through Paris [...] like grottoes. We [the inhabitants] are pointed now and then by signs and inscriptions which multiply along the walls within, where here and there, between the shops, a spiral staircase rises into darkness.

> (1999: 873–876)

Department stores, like the arcades, employed building materials that allowed a central glass-covered atrium, but this time on numerous floors with a vast range of goods. By using metallic frames to provide structural strength, in combination with plate glass, the glass-covered atrium was possible and allowed much more light through. This architectural feature was exploited very effectively in subsequent shopping malls, where instead of a series of consecutive small shops, the glass and metal structure permitted one vast single space, and the customer was free to wander and browse through.

In both arcades and department stores, the technical innovation of manufacturing sizeable sheets of glass transformed shop architectures, which were previously small buildings with small windows. Plate glass transformed the shoppers' experience, allowing natural light through large roof panels, and vast window displays where passers-by could browse the array of commodities on display. As Ferguson explains, "The department store opens itself to the passer-by. Its windows are larger, better lit, and fuller of merchandise than earlier, specialized shops" (1992); even Freud was impressed when visiting the Parisian arcades, and in 1885 he wrote of "the infinite variety of attractively displayed goods" (in Ferguson 1992: 29), succumbing to the atmosphere of sensuous luxury. A seemingly straightforward and commonplace architectural feature, the shop window allowed something more than the passage of light, as Rachel Bowlby describes:

> The window can be variously a source of pleasure, surprise, dreaming absorption, curiosity, desire, disturbance, and more, in all sorts of combinations. It elicits the attention and inattention, the passions and the boredoms, of single strollers and gathered crowds and distant onlookers.
>
> (2000: 51)

Shop windows basked the goods in mixtures of artificial and natural light, and provided an almost theatrical backdrop or setting for their display, as we will explore. Combined, the developments of iron construction, plate glass, the growth of urban populations and the proliferation of industrial commodities changed the nature of consumption within distinct spaces. An elementary 'before' and 'after' comparison of the shopping experience reveals the difference these innovations made, and cements the notion of the transformation of the experience of consumption to concrete spatial innovations. *Before*, the shopper entered a small shop and asked the shopkeeper for the desired commodity, which was a personal matter, conducted through conversation and salesmanship. The shopkeeper brandished the goods, the price was haggled over, and the shop was visited according to *necessity*, to replenish stock. *After*, shopping trips were more pleasant, dryer and warmer, more convenient, and everything was now in one place. The shopper was left alone, allowed the freedom to wander, browse, and fantasise. As Mica Nava explains, space and environment were key to a new type of shopping experience:

> The new [department] stores modernised retailing not only by offering a wide range of cheaper, mass-produced fashionable clothes and other commodities, but also by rationalising the use of space, making economies of scale, introducing clear pricing systems and displaying

goods in a safe and pleasant environment so that customers could look and compare without obligation to buy.

(1997: 65)

Around the mid-nineteenth century, architectural innovations therefore transformed the actual experience of shopping, especially for the emerging middle classes, and started to alter the types of consumption taking place. We can identify four trends or tendencies to this transformation of the shopping experience, which start to unhinge the activity of 'shopping' from actual purchasing, allowing the wider definition of 'consumption' that is utilised currently. Shopping then becomes about, firstly, *looking* rather than *speaking*; secondly, *entertainment* and *leisure*; thirdly, *desire* rather than *need*; and fourthly, about *women*.

Looking rather than speaking

Rather than the personal contact and conversational style of shopping which emphasised speaking, shopping became less about speaking and more about looking. But there are two ways that 'looking' became more central to the experience. Firstly, there was a *new emphasis on display* in department stores and arcades. Iron and plate glass windows offered large displays, and passers-by could look at commodities while walking down the street. In the arcade shops commodities were arranged carefully, and in the department stores were big window displays. Passers-by were free to peruse, compare them visually at leisure without engaging the salesman in conversation. The carefully arranged window displays therefore flaunt the commodity, offering it to the casual passer-by as incomplete, tantalising. More than about trying or touching, it is about visual display, which forms

an enclosed area, at the same time totally exposed to the gaze and inaccessible to the hands, impenetrable and yet without secrets, a world you may only touch with your eyes but which is nevertheless real, in no way illusory like the world of photography.

(Tournier 1988: 144)

Secondly, alongside this growth in display and arrangement was a concern with *aestheticisation*, with *how commodities look*. This concern was also reflected in the buildings, created to look pleasing by utilising decorative features such as mosaics, ornate ironwork, marble walls, or big domed ceilings. Instead of being simply distribution centres, these spaces of consumption worked hard to be *settings* for the commodities. They became stage sets to show objects off, and to evoke the sense of luxury along with the simple display of the commodities for purchase. In fact, the sumptuousness, luxury and abundance of goods meant that an increasing amount were simply there for display, for example in the food halls of Harrods and in Selfridges, in London. There were increasing attempts to be exotic, for example through the use of lush fabrics and Eastern carpets. The immersion in luxury for consumers was perpetuated in the provision of heating and lighting. Strangely, these spaces of consumption were the first public places to use heating, and the first to provide electric light in the 1880s. Altogether, these helped the aestheticisation, not only of the commodities but also of the retail environment, by setting up an atmosphere of luxury within which consumers could bathe.

Historical developments in these spaces of consumption have resulted in different activities being pursued within them, some of which are pertinent to current spatial practices of consumption. For example, 'shoppers' not only looked at the commodities themselves, but also at the retail environments, the stores and arcades too. This, it could be argued, is an extension of commodity fetishism (see Chapter 1), where the spaces of consumption become fetishised just like the commodities themselves, disguising the real economic conditions such as the low-paid sales clerks and security staff. As a result, some of this added value transfers to the commodities, so that *where* one buys a product matters almost as much as *what* one buys. Place therefore confers upon commodities an added value, like a halo effect. Something purchased in a particular mall or store, just like a souvenir bought on holiday, becomes associated with place, and in the words of Ferguson

> may thus acquire, by virtue of the network of confirming architectural and cultural messages which are a permanent feature of the physical and social structure of the building, a different 'value' to an identical item bought elsewhere. It will absorb, in spite of being mass-produced and widely distributed, a certain glow of exclusivity, an association with the 'right' sort of place.

(1992: 37)

Similarly, Morris also concludes that even in everyday suburban shopping practices, "it isn't necessarily or always the objects consumed that count in the act of consumption, but rather the unique sense of place" (1999: 408). The uniqueness of place is something actively encouraged by tourism and souvenir shops, as we have seen in Chapter 5, in everyday retail spaces, and also in flagship stores for global brands. Such stores are designed as an extension of their goods and their brand, such as Niketown in Atlanta, which Olins enthuses about: "Niketown isn't a retail outlet; it's a three-dimensional expression of Nikeness" (2004: 67). Similarly, the flagship Apple Store in San Francisco continues the sleek modern design of their computers, and so the retail environment itself as fetish is visible today. Where do the commodities for sale end, and the shop begin?

An activity of *leisure* and *pleasure*

Returning to the historical development of shopping spaces, shopping was not just about buying and selling but became a pleasurable activity in itself (subject to qualifications of class and gender, discussed in more detail in 'Women', below). In a similar vein to theatre foyers and hotels, the new shopping spaces placed an emphasis on theatricality, sometimes organising live entertainment with orchestras and fashion shows. The Marble Palace in New York used fashion shows in the 1850s to display clothes they imported from Europe. With such activities embellishing the shopping experience, these were the beginnings of shopping as a distinct leisure activity. Multiple entertainments were on offer: looking at and being entertained by the goods themselves; looking at and immersing oneself in the place where the goods are sold; and, increasingly, being looked at by other people. And so the fetish extends ever further, to include not only the space of consumption but also the consumer themselves. Shopping becomes about fashion, by making yourself as good-looking and magical as the commodities on show.

Shopping as an *activity* was predominantly something that only middle-class women could afford to do. Nevertheless, these activities and pleasures of shopping have in recent times percolated to all socio-economic groups, where the visual pleasures of shopping that surround the commodities are evident. Echoing the elite consumption of luxury goods in the eighteenth century, today people often visit town to look and be looked at, not just to buy, to enjoy looking at how commodities look, and to enjoy the ambience of the shops. Such activities of *non*-consumers in shopping spaces are examined later.

Desire rather than *need*: window-licking

The historical shift in the shopping experience also reveals how shopping became linked to ideas of *fantasy* and *desire*. We have seen how consumption has historically been considered mostly in economic terms, involving the construction of the consumer as based on needs and rational decisions. But now the need to replenish stock, the larder or storeroom was only one part of the story. These spaces actively promoted the opposite: *fantasy* and *irrationality* rather than rational economic decisions. Through the aestheticisation of the commodity, as we have seen, the visual appeal and the setting became prominent. Appeal to bodies, to *sensuality*, where goods could be touched, felt, picked up, smelt, and generally manipulated, entailed promoting the other senses; arresting the attention of the consumer through the object's reaching out and appealing to them.

The notion of consumption as *consummation* as well as *consommer*, running throughout this book, involves the recognition of desire as an explicit and clearly identifiable element of consumption. For example, the phrase 'window-licking' is a translation of the French 'faire du lèche-vitrines'. The English equivalent, 'window-shopping', has more staid and seemly connotations, as if the objects behind the display can be looked at, dreamed about, but not touched. 'Window-licking' instead implies more urgency, more desire, an attempt to decrease the distance between consumer and commodity on display. Desire and the female consumer were increasingly intertwined, as novelists such as Zola observed; the coincidences of bourgeois women being affluent consumers and the new spaces of consumption being increasingly feminised, as we shall see, became a powerful combination. Along with the unleashing of desire is also an appeal to *fantasy*, especially fantasies of identity, as the usually female consumer was offered an immersion in exoticism, refinement and luxury when visiting these spaces. As Ferguson summarises, the notion of a sovereign, individuated self underlying the variety of 'wants' has been an historically pervasive idea. "The inner 'needs' or 'wants' of the isolated individual were held to be the sovereign and irreducible basis of consumption" (1992: 27). But this self was not static, unchanging; it could become activated or made conscious through specific events or desires: "The 'self' which exists *potentially* within us, it was held, becomes *actual* through the process of consumption" (1992: 27, emphasis added). The encounter with commodities in settings of exotic luxury, such as arcades and department stores, perpetuates the wanting and wishing, the fantasies of the self and the almost endless possibilities of its actualisation.

This is entirely in keeping with the department stores of the nineteenth century, but also with the Great Exhibition in London (1851) and the Great Exposition of Paris (1900); retail spaces and grand exhibitions of commodities which inspired each other into ever greater settings of sensuousness and luxury. The merchandise can no longer be simply a collection of items for sale, but part of a larger stage setting. The Trocadero exhibit at the Paris Exposition was notable for its "sumptuous orientalism", displaying "unusual and distant" objects in a way that suggested the décor of the harem (Ferguson 1992: 30). The sheer volume of commodities, plus the sumptuousness of their settings, had the effect of overwhelming the ego, assaulting the senses, just like Zola's *Ladies' Paradise*. The consumer within such exhibitions and department stores is, in Bowlby's words, "seduced, driven crazy" (1985: 74–75) by the superabundant luxury of the vast displays and sensuous settings of commodities. These are real spaces of wishes, wanting and desire. Walter Benjamin had analysed such places of pure entertainment as the Paris Exposition, claiming that they transformed visitors to the level of the commodity, that the visitors enter a truly "phantasmagorical world" (in Urry 2000: 25).

Women

Building on the observations above, we note that department stores were created mainly as a feminine environment. While this section is entitled 'Women' to denote the increasing feminisation of retail spaces, it is important to add the proviso that this applies almost entirely to *middle-class* women, and sales staff were correspondingly usually working-class women. The new department stores incorporated tearooms and restaurants within them, and encouraged an association with domestic spaces in terms of furniture and lighting. These were increasingly female *social* spaces, and some women routinely met with friends and socialised in these stores several times a week, signifying some new-found urban freedoms for women who were previously bound to their domiciles. As Benson (1986: 84–85) and Ferguson (1992: 30) show, American stores in particular were endowed with such spaces as nurseries, writing-rooms, art galleries, and meeting places for women's clubs. The use of the store as social meeting place was actively encouraged, and reflected in the shops' advertising. The feminisation of consumer spaces, advertising and marketing became extremely pervasive. Bowlby reminds us how big a step was taken when *male* shoppers were recognised by marketing and advertising: the shopper was no longer seen as only female, "passive, exploited and dim" (2000: 7).

The above comments concerning the feminisation of spaces of consumption are in need of qualification, and I will outline briefly some historical connections between women and shopping before going on to analyse the everydayness of shopping spaces.

Why women were born to shop: connections between women and shopping

There are two factors to consider here. Firstly, the construction of the female shopper that results from male economic rationalism, and secondly feminist critics of this position who argue that female shopping was a form of liberation, if only for a lucky minority. For this section there is a mixture of observations, from feminist theorists of consumption to male social commentators, such as the novelist Emile Zola.

Male economic rationalism

Previously we have identified the historical legacy of male economic rationalism and its attempt to see purchasing decisions as rational and informed. Abandoning the strict replacement of necessities at the best price, in the male economic mindset shopping by women is about irrationality, being fooled by commodities, being distracted by fake promises of luxury; in other words, being duped. The irrational and uncontrollable lust for luxury that is ascribed to women shoppers, presumably by male shop-owners, is noted by Laermans:

> The female customer was intended to feel like a real queen or at least a lady while she was shopping because she walked in a palace-like atmosphere that was thoroughly imbued with luxury.
>
> (1993: 93)

Evidence of women's supposed concern with triviality and frivolousness can be found in marketing literature and even in novels. In *The Ladies' Paradise* (*Au Bonheur des Dames*), Emile Zola was writing about the 1860s, and describes women shoppers entering after the displays had been seasonally redone:

> The crowd had reached the silk department [...] At the far end of the hall, around one of the small cast-iron columns which supported the glass roof, material was streaming down like a bubbling sheet of water [...] Women pale with desire were leaning over as if to look at themselves. Faced with this wild cataract, they all remained standing there, filled with the secret fear of being caught in the overflow of all this luxury and with an irresistible desire to throw themselves into it and be lost.
>
> (1998: 103–104)

The themes in this passage are clear: display, spectacle, desire and novelty. But of course this positions women as irrational victims or dupes. As we have seen in the extensive discussion on consumers as 'suckers' or 'savvy' in the previous chapter, the positioning of the consumer as irrational and easily swayed has a long heritage, but here we consider it as explicitly concerned with female shopping. This is part of a tradition of feminising consumption, that has considered consumption as trivial or frivolous, and therefore essentially feminine. The serious academic study of consumption is so recent precisely for this reason.

Feminist critics and shopping

Against this view of the identification of women with shopping due to irrationality and triviality, some feminists concerned with consumption (e.g. Benson 1986; Wolff 1990; Friedberg 1993; Radner 1995; Lury 1996; Bowlby 2000; Morris 1999) argue instead that shopping is historically important as a way through which women can create their own freedom, and celebrate their own social spaces. This view gains currency when we consider that the nineteenth century was one in which respectable women were not only associated with domesticity, but were more forcefully confined to the home. Baudelaire's celebrated notion of the *flâneur*, the aimless stroller through the city who typifies the experience of urban modernity, looking and being looked at, being socially promiscuous, is an emphatically masculine experience. Wolff attempts but fails to find the female equivalent, a *flâneuse*, because

> The line drawn increasingly sharply between the public and private was also one which confined women to the private, while men retained the freedom to move in the crowd or to frequent cafés and pubs.

> (1990: 40)

Respectable middle-class town women rarely ventured out to public places alone, so unlike their male counterparts they "could not stroll alone in the city" (1990: 41); although presumably working-class women and children were not so restricted. In response to Wolff, Griselda Pollock confirms the class divide in terms of socialisation and mobility, stating: "Bourgeois women [...] obviously went out in public, to promenade, go shopping, or visiting or simply to be on display. And working-class women went out to work" (1988: 69), she concedes, but women's appearance in public did not constitute the kinds of freedom of looking, socialising and flirtatious or sexualised encounters that true *flâneurie* promised. With new shopping spaces however came an excuse to leave the house and gain personal freedom without threat. With tearooms and restaurants, these were spaces where middle-class women could socialise, outside the confines of the domestic regime. There was the potentially thrilling possibility of secret liaisons, of extra-marital affairs, of flirtations; they became another space of looking, being looked at, of desire and seduction. Thus, in enabling women to escape the confines of domesticity, and to engage in a social space of their own, was shopping not a form of empowerment? In this view, consumption was historically one way women could assert themselves, take control over their everyday lives.

Against these feminist critics' arguments in terms of freedom, desire and self-expression, they acknowledge some difficulties, however. As we have suggested and Lury (1996) shows, female consumption is class-bound. The commodities and freedoms alike were only significantly available to middle-class women, and working-class women had to work or even live in these same spaces, suffering from low pay, hard work, and a strictly regulated social life. Lury also questions the extent that these spaces were truly liberating for the middle classes, since shopping could also be seen as part of domestic labour. One problem in celebrating consumption as a space of freedom and self-control, then, is that of differing resources and orientations. For women and men alike, the freedom and self-expression possible through consumption was a class privilege not guaranteed to all. This harks back to the lingering problem of commodity fetishism, since any freedoms can only be contextualised in a wider, unjust economic system based on exploitation, with widely varying distributions of wealth and spending power.

CONSUMPTION SPACES AND EVERYDAY LIFE

Shopping spaces: then and now

The historical development of shopping in the mid-nineteenth century shows clear parallels between the arcades and early department stores, and the pedestrianised precincts and indoor malls of today. We will continue the historical parallels in order to consider more current consumption spaces and consumer behaviour. Even now, modern retail spaces such as shopping centres and malls architecturally mimic the iron and glass architecture of the Parisian arcades of the nineteenth century, as does the behaviour of shoppers. In modern shopping centres and malls there is usually a central atrium area, and shoppers are promenading, window-shopping, looking. Likewise, there are still strong elements of entertainment, places to look and be looked at by others, but the associations with women have been extended to other groups:

> Whatever one's status or job in the world of work or even without a job, there is an equality of just being there and looking at the shows

of décor, goods and other people. Malls appear democratic and open to all, rich or poor, young or old.

(Shields 1992: 5)

'Actual' shopping, the purchase of goods, is likewise as important as the *experience* of shopping, and the meaning of buying an object is constructed as much by the environment in which it is bought as by the object itself. And, as will be explored in more detail below, there are currently similar issues concerning empowerment, of fantasy, of fetishism, of display and leisure, as pertinent today as 150 years ago. Continuous with the arcades of the nineteenth century, the practices within shopping centres and malls are similar – "a new indoor *flâneurie* (strolling), the habit of window shopping as much as 'hanging out' or being an onlooker enjoying the crowds", observes Shields (1989: 149), are features of contemporary life in spaces of consumption.

Yet while these new spaces and worlds of consumption *appear* democratic, no longer limited to the privileged male *flâneur* but open to all, their everydayness hides something coercive, that seems to refer to the opposite of everydayness; fantasies or playful imaginations that lie beyond the quotidian. Langman writes:

> Like the carnivals and fairs of old, these worlds are outside the ordinary, indeed may reverse its values and often mock and parody it. Everyday life has thus become the realm where ordinariness has been transformed into an unending series of mass-mediated fragmented 'spectacles' and carnivals that celebrate the universalization of consumption.
>
> (1992: 47)

Shopping malls construct themselves as a public space open to all, a mundane or everyday experience that is simultaneously extraordinary, festive, a series of fantasies that range across a multitude of times and places. They make an attempt at localisation, sometimes trading on the idea of community, often standing in as a leisure resource for the city by hosting fashion shows or Santa's grottos. Thus the civic aspect of medieval market life is emulated, but not quite attained. As Shields argues,

The enclosed mall environment of shopping centres attempts to reproduce the vicarious pleasures of the market square or hall, presenting itself as the continuation of the tradition of such public spaces.

(1992: 104)

This returns us to the old medieval idea of the marketplace as an important civic space with a political aspect, of festival. Bakhtin (1984: 8–9) refers to this feeling of communion with others in a group as *communitas*, and elsewhere Shields sees the experience of *communitas* in shopping malls as being "harnessed for the benefit of consumption" (1989: 157). In being currently tied to the idea of shopping as a distinct leisure activity, this legitimates collective consumption as a healthy, moral, community activity, a rare occurrence of a social collective in operation. We will now think more closely about these issues and the kind of critical and political questions that modern shopping spaces raise: *placelessness*, as *spaces of fake and fantasy*, and as *spaces of subversion*.

Placeless spaces: the mall as 'non-place'

Malls offer an elsewhere to the city streets outside. They remove traffic and noise, urban disorder, and seem to represent a new vision of social cohesion, since there is no crime, only harmonious order. There are rarely any local characteristics, meaning that at a global level retail spaces are equally fake, equally homogeneous. As a consumer you could be anywhere – Kuala Lumpur, Chicago, Dubai or Cape Town – since all have a Body Shop, Gap and Starbucks. This is the familiar charge, as we saw in Chapter 3 on McDisneyfication: of homogeneity, of uniformity, that they devalue local culture and local history. In other words, they are retail *spaces* but not real *places*. Anthropologist Marc Augé defines 'place' as "relational, historical and concerned with identity" (1995: 77). The 'non-place' is the absence of those things, dead or inert spaces that are filled with everyday movements of people who do not live or dwell there. Non-places such as transit zones, airports, malls, motorway service stations and supermarkets proliferate the accelerated condition of 'supermodernity' – characterised, he argues, by an over-abundance of times, of spaces, and of emphasis on the individual. These non-places mushroom everywhere, making the visitor live within a "perpetual present" (1995: 105), always en route elsewhere. They involve a new architecture of transit and impermanence, are temporary holding bays for human activity such as hotel chains, holiday resorts and refugee camps, supermarkets, airports, car parks and highways. Of course, shopping malls exemplify non-places too. As a frequent visitor or consumer within non-places, it is rare to recognise anyone else. There is an anonymity that is comforting, and Augé terms this the "paradox of non-place" (1995: 106) – the feeling of being at home within these anonymous non-places.

Shopping malls therefore seem to exemplify both Rob Shields's notion of "placelessness" (1992), and also Augé's "non-places" (1995). As a result of the increasingly imposed uses of space due to the demands of global capitalism, "supermodernity produces non-places, meaning spaces which are not themselves anthropological places and which, unlike Baudelairean modernity, do not integrate with earlier places" (1995: 78). In other words, as Benjamin strolls along the arcades and passages of Paris as an archetypal *flâneur* he would notice, as did Baudelaire, that the new shopping spaces were being integrated with older buildings. The neon signs and electric streetlamps were added onto the cobbled, winding streets of an earlier age. The Moulin Rouge and flashy department stores take their place amongst the Gothic churches and period housing. This cosy picture is complicated by the process of Haussmanisation of Paris, for example, where the architect Haussman was called in to destroy the older, slum parts of the city to make way for broad boulevards and the new department stores. Similarly, Augé's 'supermodernity' produces whole new environments that are isolated and removed from previous historical and spatial contexts, as we can recognise. Malls as non-places act as a kind of cultural vacuum. Having little unique identity of their own, whatever surrounding culture exists is simply sucked in. Reference is made to different places and different cultures, but only in a superficial way. Mall food courts exemplify this, a bland space being populated with numerous fast-food emporia from various nations – an Italian panini joint, a French café, a Thai noodle bar. It becomes *pastiche*, the familiar postmodern motif of unreal imitation. "The real-space relations of the globe are replaced by imaginary-space relations. The events of different epochs, cultures and settings are to be combined in a Disneyland-esque 'pastiche' of scenes", summarises Shields (1989: 153). Along with pastiche it is another example of commodity fetishism, since a fantasy of other cultures is constructed, offered for sale, only by emptying out any local meaning or local experience. References to other cultures are made as a stage setting, to fabricate a context for commodities. If these are indeed depthless, raceless, placeless spaces, they suck in whatever is around, creating a montage of novelty, luxury and exotica. Unlike the nineteenth-century arcades, however, shoppers are now no longer limited to the female middle classes.

Examples of such placelessness, racelessness and depthlessness include the Forum Shops in Las Vegas, a themed mall based around an ancient Roman marketplace. The theme is pursued architecturally, the atrium being revisited in this crash of ancient and postmodern consumption spaces, along with marble floors and white pillars. On the hour, statues of Caesar and other Roman figures magically come to life and bellow "Hail Caesar"; Centurions periodically march, appropriately enough, towards Caesar's Palace casino. Even the stores' interiors feature scrolls, tablets, Roman numerals and gold draperies. As Pine and Gilmore remark, showing the effectiveness of luxurious and exotic settings for commodities: "The theme implies opulence, and the mall's more than $1000 per-square-foot sales in 1997 (versus less than $300 at a typical mall) suggests that the experience works" (1999: 47).

Similarly, British high-street store The Pier, which sells exotic luxury interior design goods, also exemplifies the retail space as commodity fetish. A fascination with the Orient is revealed with displays of Chinese and Moroccan furniture and vases, and the store is furnished with dark wood and exotic spot lighting, immersing the shopper in the exotic setting of a North African bazaar. The store therefore operates as one large commodity fetish, since there is no real connection to Moroccan or Chinese culture, and no actual experience of these cultures is being represented. No mention is made of the colonial history and exploitation that made these commodities desirable or available. Instead, the commodities and the settings are reduced to a set of signs, 'Chineseness' or 'Moroccanness', a stylistic rather than an authentic relation between the origin of the commodity, its original context or setting. Even the online store (The Pier 2005) allows you to "Find Products Inspired By" and then offers a drop-down list: "Africa/America ... Far East/India/Indonesia/Morocco", relating to a distant, orientalist imaginary of exotic and luxurious products. Online and in stores the consumer can find "things which will transform the ordinary into the extraordinary", even if it is simply furnishing your kitchen or bedroom with Oriental goods. So although stores like The Pier, the department store Selfridges (e.g. Nava 1998), shopping centres and malls appear to offer a wealth of experiences of different cultures, different periods and different cultural experiences, they actually mask a profound homogeneity, reducing complex sets of relations between objects and material culture to a set of signs which can be selected, clicked or bought. As such it becomes pure surface without depth.

Everymall

Like the exotic commodities and settings of the Parisian arcades, in stores like The Pier and in shopping mall food courts, local culture, tradition and experience is emptied out under the bland space of global capitalism. Such global/local spaces – locals instances of global phenomena such as shopping malls – exhibit commodity fetishism, therefore, by not only masking the relations of material production of the commodity itself, but also by placing those commodities in non-native settings that evoke luxury and exotica. But also this commodity fetishism extends to the retail space itself, which hides its relation to the *local* context in order to become the bland, homogeneous space of everymall – a *global* phenomenon. In 1988 the West Edmonton Mall was the largest shopping mall in existence, a mixture of theme park and retail space, and Shields wrote that what was being asserted is "a new collective sense of place founded on the notion of having transcended the barrier of distance", that conflates the fantasies of the global with no actual reference to the real setting or history of Edmonton, so that this "displaced sense of place also rests on a denial of locality" (1989: 153). Obviously, the same denial of locality applies to every mall.

Nevertheless, in an influential and self-reflective essay by Meaghan Morris on Australian shopping centres, there is much variation between individual structures, partly as a result of capital, where "the display of difference will [...] increase a centre's 'tourist' appeal to everyone else from elsewhere" (1999: 398; see also Urry 2000: 23). And partly this variation is a result of aging and the need to maintain aesthetic appeal, since malls do get renovated, need facelifts and change their image. She concludes that "shopping-centre identities aren't fixed, consistent or permanent" and that each centre has a "spatial play in time" that is variable and complex (1999: 393).

In addition, there is a tension between the relative fixity over time that shopping centres and malls endure as structures, and the continually shifting spectacle within, and around, the mall that appeals to shoppers, that persists in drawing us in, absorbing us into the spectacle. Another tension that Morris identifies is that between the imposed, intended use of the designers and corporations (i.e. as *space*), and the *place* as it is performed and actually utilised. It also cuts to the heart of the issue of 'everymall', since each one is heavily differentiated not only through architecture and localised themes, but also the variety of uses that are made of it by the local populations:

> A shopping centre is a 'place' combining an extreme project of general 'planning' competence (efforts at total unification, total management) with an intense degree of aberrance and diversity in local performance. It is also a 'place' consecrated to timelessness and stasis (no clocks, perfect weather ...) yet lived and celebrated, loved and loathed, in intimately historic terms: for some, as ruptural event (catastrophic or Edenic) in the social experience of a community, for others, as the enduring scene (as the cinema once was, and the home still may be) of all the changes, fluctuations and repetitions of the passing of everyday life.
>
> (1999: 399, text corrected)

As such, this cuts into the distinction between space and place from before, and revisits the territory of Michel de Certeau. It is also a useful observation to take us into considerations of malls as spaces of *freedom* (of fantasy and fake) and *control*, in the next section.

SPACES OF FAKE, FANTASY AND CONTROL

Writing about the Parisian arcades, Walter Benjamin called them a site of "collective dreaming" and fantasy (in Shields 1989: 152). Both these elements, of collective feeling and fantasy, are equally applicable to malls. To remind ourselves, malls are not just places to buy goods, but spaces of fantasy, a "new dream-like order of commercial reality", as Langman describes it (1992: 48). The fact that malls are isolated and controlled makes them blank spaces (or non-places) that can be over-written with a variety of themes or fantasies. Their isolation from the larger environs of the city and its street life entails separation from our ordinary spatial contexts and their usual meanings. They are also controlled, where everything from temperature, smells and muzak to shop window displays are managed with precision, the elaborate free-flowing space of fantasy paradoxically maintained through rigid mechanisms of observation and control. These mechanisms are at once familiar and insidious:

> 'No Loitering', as the signs in the mall say. Certain types of comportment are expected. The emotions linked with boisterous behaviour are smothered under a flood of continuous, calming, psychologically tested 'music'.
>
> (Shields 1989: 149)

More generally, Lauren Langman describes some design processes occurring in US malls, but the mall being a local/global phenomenon, with multinational developers imposing particular designs and themes around the world, means the same is happening everywhere:

> The design and layout of malls attempt to create a utopia of consumption situated between a mythical past of the pre-automobile Main Street of Smalltown where one walked from store to store, and the future night-tech world of neon, holograms, lasers and space travel as malls come to resemble the space station of [Kubrick's science-fiction film] 2001, the Starship Enterprise or high-tech future cities. They create nostalgic memories of neighbourhood and lost community, or at least Christmas-card images of a past abundant with goods and social cohesion.
>
> (1992: 49)

Langman brings out the element of utopian fantasy in malls, with the powerful myth of social cohesion and material abundance that they appeal to. This fantasy entails a world in which everyone belongs to a single community, brought together through the harmony of shopping.

This utopian wish makes the mall so appealing, promising the meaningfulness of the experience, but reveals it to be ultimately fake, ersatz. The fundamental irony is that such spaces of desire and fantasy, of collective community (Bakhtin's *communitas*), must rely on isolation and control, so that the environment is regulated and security guards eject undesirables – non-consumers, or those unlikely to consume, such as the homeless or troublemaking teenagers. Malls are accordingly spaces of simulation and fantasy without genuine imagination, and this factor is only enhanced by looking at the definition of 'utopia', which literally means 'without place'. Placeless, depthless, they are spaces of fake and fantasy.

But what of other fantasies, of freedom and feelings? In describing the mall as utopia, it is unnecessary to revisit the 'sucker'/'savvy' debate. Rather than thinking of shoppers or mallgoers as unfulfilled, merely seeking out ersatz fantasies based on consumption while actually being manipulated and controlled, there is a negotiation of freedom and selfhood that occurs, the ability to try out goods, settings and feelings. Arguably a space is made for experimentation and play with different styles of the self, and to respond individually and socially. Just as some feminist critics have argued that department stores were feminised, social spaces of liberation from domestic duties and control, malls extend the freedoms and playfulness to other social groups. This process is part of what Langman terms 'malling', where

> malls then are places to purchase the goods of gratification and/or to be something, to *realize fantasies* located outside of the usual constraints of time and place. Malling thus exists as a dialectic between doing something and being someone, a fantastic someone whose selfhood brings recognition and gratification.
>
> (1992: 54, emphasis added)

Spaces of subversion

Malls are recognisably spaces of control that promote a singular vision of citizen-consumers, yet there are also recognisable forms of resistance to this. As spatial sites, malls allow a degree of contestation, of reinterpretation, of mobilisation, if not in *fact*, then in *fantasy* as we have seen.

The question then becomes one of the *reception* and *mediation* of the mall by its users, since not all shoppers are happy, and not everyone can celebrate these spaces of consumption in the way intended. "What ironic reversals and hijackings of intended perceptions are being made", asks Shields, and "how do these dialectically relate to and inflect the modes of spatial practice present?" (1989: 154). If we have characterised malls as spaces of fake, fantasy and control, in other words, what oppositional spatial practices are evident? John Fiske (1989a) suggests that although malls are structured by power, subordinated groups such as youth and the unemployed succeed in subverting them. They find ways of appropriating mall space for their own purposes, thereby creating new meanings and new identities. Speaking of the unemployed, for example, and using the guerrilla warfare metaphors of resistance of Michel de Certeau (see Chapter 6), Fiske argues:

> With no money but much time to spend, they consumed the place and the images, but not the commodities. They turned the place of the mall into their space to enact their oppositional culture, to maintain and assert their social difference and their subordinated but hostile social identities. They would cluster around store windows, preventing legitimate consumers from seeing the displays or entering; their pleasure was in disrupting the strategy and in provoking the owner-enemy to emerge and confront them, or to call in the security services to move them on.
>
> (1989a: 38)

Of course, other groups use the mall for their own purposes, such as walkers or pensioners. Unlike the reverence that churchgoers had for the priesthood in the days of the great cathedrals, mallgoers ('mallers'/mallrats) can find "microspheres of empowerment" in malls, from the products they obtain there and the meanings and pleasures the person can choose. Fiske (1989a) gives the example of young mothers who go into the mall to use its heating, with no intention of going shopping; and two secretaries who spend their lunch hour browsing and trying on clothes with no intention of buying anything. He sees these activities of non-purchasing as a form of stealing, using the system for their own ends. Because they are not officially breaking any rules, they cannot be ejected. Therefore, he claims, "The place of shopping malls is turned into numberless spaces temporarily controlled by the weak" (1989a: 40). This might strike us as too optimistic, a naïve view of oppositional culture. Taking the view that the secretaries are 'stealing' ignores the way that shopping spaces make fantasies, and the secretaries' fantasies concerning femininity and glamour are entirely consistent with the ideology of consumerism. However, it does hint at loopholes in what might otherwise seem an overly controlling system of spaces of consumption. It shows how spaces can provide a resource for people's own practices, an opportunity to produce their own meanings in consumption. The reception and mediation of the mall by its users therefore suggests not passive 'dupes' or 'suckers', but potentially 'savvy' spatial practices. Instead, there are "individual reversals, destabilizations, and interventions in a continuous play for the freedom of this space made by users who must not be 'written off' as passive consumers", argues Shields, oppositional practices that are "a continuous reassertion of the rights and freedoms of the marketplace, the *communitas* of the carnival" (1989: 161). Nevertheless, we need to think carefully about how actually resistant these practices can be.

CONCLUSION: BEING MALLED

We have given an historical overview of the ways that shopping spaces have transformed the experiences of consumption over time. Through iron and glass, Benjamin had thought that the arcades of the nineteenth century were a dream or anticipation of the following century, and we can see a direct lineage in terms of the actual constructions of these spaces, as well as their uses as spaces of desire, wishing and looking. Running throughout this discussion of the spaces of consumption is the observation that both the flux and the fluidity of identity formations and subjectivity are, at least in part, a function of the spaces in which consumption is performed. We have seen how shopping malls offer different performances of identity, away from the world of work and domestic roles. Secretaries who take their lunch hour to try on different outfits, young mothers who use the heating or air conditioning, or mallrats whose existence depends on their being perceived, signal the fluidity of spaces as different populations inhabit them at various times, and the shifting nature of individual and group subjectivities as they are performed and experienced within such spaces.

With a self-aware nod to the Frankfurt School (see Chapter 1), Max Weber's "iron cage" of bureaucracy (1930: 181, discussed in Chapter 3 in terms of McDonaldization), and Erving Goffman's theory of "total institutions" (1968), Langman plays Devil's advocate about the culture and homogenisation of shopping malls:

> Eating *en masse*, the wearing of uniforms and constant surveillance of personal behaviour ensure the loss of freedom, subjectivity and integrity. The mall generations have now eaten almost 100 billion identical burgers and express their pseudo-individuality in the mass-produced fads and fashions of 'The Gap' or 'Limited' brand clothing. They experience not degradation but celebration. They flock to the malls or other carnival sites to seek the surveillance, scrutiny and recognition by the Others who share their tastes. When they grow up and work for the [...] corporations, they will have been well socialized, malled, to deny any genuine individuality or any kind of critical consciousness.
>
> (1992: 72)

While we may recognise this sentiment, it should now seem overly simplistic given the variety and complexity of historical and contemporary practices within shopping malls, some of which we have covered in the course of this chapter. Rather than agreeing with Langman, we can argue that to be 'malled' is to admit yet another consumer paradox: the imposition of rationalisation, surveillance and control at the same time as the consumer's illusion of subjectivity, individuality and freedom of expression. Being malled is to admit a deep ambivalence, another consumer paradox of freedom, fantasy and control. As either consumer paradox, or as the dialectic of enfeeblement and empowerment in subjectivity, the end result is immersion within the massively proliferating series of spectacles and signs, which produces a form of hegemony to which we grudgingly assent. To enter the non-place of the mall, returning briefly to Augé, is to surrender ourselves to the "passive joys of identity loss", suspend our usual self in order to play with our identities and feelings, and to enjoy the "more active pleasures of role-playing" (1995: 103). We approach such spaces, whether the gleaming iron and glass of the nineteenth-century arcades, or the box-like modernity of the out-of-town mall, with these complex and sometimes contradictory feelings and attitudes.

8

LOGO OR NO LOGO?

THE POETICS AND POLITICS OF BRANDING

> 'The old merchant used to tote about commodities; the new one creates values ... He takes something that isn't worth anything – or something that isn't particularly worth anything, and he makes it worth something.'
>
> (Ewart, in H.G. Wells's *Tono-Bungay* (1997: 169))

Building upon previous discussion of the aestheticisation of commodities, this chapter examines the semiotics of advertising, and more specifically the poetics and politics of brand, brand image and logo. Like the character in H.G. Wells's novel of 1909 we depart from the idea of the 'commodity' as material entity, instead concentrating on immaterial 'values' that become associated with the commodity through judicious marketing. Following the logic of the logo, the history of marketing starts from tangible commodities and ends with intangible values. Nike's infamous 'swoosh' is a dynamic, globalised and instantly recognisable example, a visual icon that involves other associations and connotations (see Barthes (1999) on the difference between 'denotation' and 'connotation'). For some, brands and logos help us articulate a sense of freedom through consumer choice, and express our sense of identity. The main focus here will be the functioning of the logo and the brand within a globalised sign-system. Later, the analysis of logos, brands and advertisements, along with ironic strategies of reading them, will tease out implications concerning representations of ethnicity and gender.

Particular advertisements for branded commodities show contradictory tendencies, for example, the flattening out of difference, as the same commodity becomes marketed across different cultures, and at the same time the counter-tendency, the celebration or fetishisation of racial difference. This is to proceed from Marx's commodity fetishism, discussed in the first chapter, to 'commodity racism', and the performances of authenticity and ethnic identity through the consumption and therefore display of goods.

Bringing things satisfyingly full circle, we return to those definitions of consumption, as *consumere* (to use up, destroy) and *consumare* (to bring to completion, fulfilment). Firstly, consumption as fulfilment or creation is perhaps the flipside of commodity fetishism. There is a *poetics* (the Greek word *poesis* means creation) of the brand and the brand image, seeing how logos have become iconic in status, and how they became part of the fabric of everyday experience. The poetic aspect involves the ability to be creative, to be playful, to establish new imaginative metaphors or signs that work as intermediaries between producers and consumers. Secondly, consumption as destruction, as using up, is very much concerned with the *politics* of the brand. Consumption as an activity of everyday life largely relies on commodity fetishism, thereby masking the more troubling aspects of unequal labour relations. But it also obscures the issue of sustainability, the depletion of the Earth's resources for our own ends in a consumer society.

Structurally the chapter follows this logic, so is split accordingly between poetics and politics. 'Poetics' starts with the history of brands and logos, beginning in the nineteenth century but accelerating after the Second World War. The rise of the brand and its symbolic visual cousin the logo to internationally recognisable prominence is charted in the section 'From material manufacture to immaterial brand'. The formation of a brand or logo necessarily involves a dynamism and creativity, and this is specifically addressed. However, while the created brand is historically part of the arts of persuasion, splitting the seducers (marketing and advertising) and the seduced (consumers), we will see how increasingly sophisticated use of social research techniques in the 1950s onwards involved seducer and seduced in more of a feedback loop. 'Politics' considers brands and logos primarily as the clash of first and third worlds. Brands lie at the interface of first and third worlds in terms of commodity fetishism, which should be familiar at this stage, but also in what McClintock (1995) terms 'commodity racism'. In recent decades, and riding on geographically specific race relations mostly concentrated in western Europe and the USA, brands and brand imaging have relied on white fetishisation of blackness, where inner-city black culture becomes the epitome of cool. But, as Klein (2001) has shown, this relies on a black fetishisation of white wealth and taste, too.

Soap features several times within the chapter, as the first branded commodity in 1884, as a marker of civilisation and the fetishisation of cleanliness as whiteness and therefore the validation of Empire, and in terms of the bonding of advertising and the media in soap operas, where daytime melodramas on radio and television featured advertisements for household soaps and cleaning products. "Soap is civilization" is the slogan of Unilever (in McClintock 1995: 207). Soap also features in the film *Fight Club* (1999), where the character Tyler Durden (who also claims: "Soap – the yardstick of civilization") manufactures soap out of human body fat – a potent symbol of the excesses of consumerism. It would be entirely possible to weave a story concerning everyday consumption of global brands and logos through soap alone. However, the case of Nike's infamous logo and brand image is too interesting a history and too pervasive an influence to ignore completely, and so will be examined as an exemplar of both the poetics and the politics of the brand image and logo.

POETICS

From material manufacture to immaterial brand: a brief history of branding

> Brands migrated from household products to retail to service to corporations themselves, and the media migrated with them so that now brands have become – whether we like it or not – part of the very air we breathe.
>
> (Olins 2004: 62)

Let us start with clarification. Advertising, branding and the logo are distinct but interrelated. Perhaps the difference between *strategy* and *tactics* is useful once again, as raised by de Certeau (1984). For a corporation to deploy a longer-term strategy of building a brand or a brand image, it must utilise various tactics, short-term actions or methods. Those tactics will invariably include advertising specific products, yet the actual product range will alter over time. Or we could follow Klein: "Think of the brand as the core meaning of the modern corporation, and of the advertisement as one vehicle used to convey that meaning to the world" (2001: 5). From this, we could think of the logo as the extension of advertising, a symbol rather than a vehicle, which becomes deployed across a diverse range of media, communicating the bare minimum of information within the fastest time. A great deal of this chapter will consider the role of brands and logos as meaning-generating devices, as pushers of information, as signs and symbols working within a larger sign system. These are not neutral signs. The information is not value-free. The intent of such efforts, of course, is to alter the purchasing behaviour of the consumer, or to build brand awareness and brand loyalty, and this factor should be borne in mind. There are irrational affinities to brands, and any meaning delivery system builds upon such feelings, no longer needing to stress rational choice but attempting to evoke warmth, loyalty, friendliness and even love, as if the brand is a person (Lury 2004: 84). The personification happens literally (Aunt Jemima's pancake mix, Uncle Ben's rice) or in the abstract (Orange having "connotations of hope, fun and freedom", according to Lury (2004: 83)). Extending the analogy, the brand personification persuades, influences, even seduces. Walter Olins, a brand consultant who has worked for BT, Prudential and even the Polish government eager to rebrand its national image, argues that branding, advertising and marketing are all about "persuading, seducing and trying to manipulate people into buying products and services. In companies that seduce, the brand is the focus of corporate life" (in Sutcliffe 2003).

In order to contextualise the rise of branding and the logo, a brief history of advertising and marketing shows the increasing importance of primarily visual and symbolic forms of information delivery within the newly emerging media and its conventions. With newly audio-visual media available, the emphasis shifted from presenting the product to promoting a brand image. Photography and design in magazines, for example, allowed innovations in associations between products and qualities, helping to constitute and consolidate a distinct 'brand image', the perception of the brand by the consumer. An early pioneer of television advertising, David Ogilvy developed a series of techniques for filming advertisements in this newly dynamic visual medium. Were it not for the brand image, he argued, most consumers would simply not be able to discern a difference between products. In his classic 1983 book *Ogilvy on Advertising*, for example, he declared that most consumers cannot tell the difference between their own, supposedly 'favourite' whiskey and the closest two competitors':

> Have they tried all three and compared the taste? Don't make me laugh. The reality is that these three brands have different images which appeal to different kinds of people. It isn't the whiskey they choose, it's the image. The brand image is ninety percent of what the distiller has to sell.
>
> (2003: 14)

To understand the power of the brand, the brand image and the rise of the logo, the history of advertising reflects some of the theoretical concerns of rationality and emotion, the psychological profiling of consumers, over many years. It also mutates from static printed form to more dynamic audio and – increasingly – visual form, adapting its techniques to whatever media works best. Time and again, the history of marketing and advertising since its inception in the 1870s is separated between a 'rational' stage, an 'irrational' stage, and then a synthesis of the two. In the first stage, corresponding roughly from 1870–1910, consumers were thought to be essentially rational and not easily persuaded by gimmickry. Leiss *et al.* term this stage the 'Rationalistic Image of Human Nature' (2000: 246). A product's worth was gauged by such straightforward factors as price, function, craftsmanship and durability. Any advertising of products must speak to those concerns of rational utility, with price being of paramount consideration. This first great surge of branding in the 1870s and 1880s, according to Olins, occurred through the standardisation of products and prices, and commodities began to be advertised in newspapers for the urban working classes. William Hesketh Lever saw the standard of living in England rise to the extent that eggs and butter were regularly bought. But soap was sold as an undifferentiated commodity in inconsistent grey bars. In 1874, Lever launched Lever's Pure Honey soap, and soon Sunlight, as separately packaged, consistent and branded products (Olins 2004: 53). By the 1890s, the Coca-Cola Company had become the biggest single advertiser in the US, and its advertising had changed tack. From being one of many patent medicines that appealed to the public's need for health tonics, Coca-Cola became simply a refreshing drink (Olins 2004: 50). The second phase, from 1910 to 1930, Leiss *et al.* term as the 'Irrational Conception of Human Nature' (2000: 247). Consumers were seen to be more irrational than rational, and so techniques were used to appeal to nonrational impulses rather than rational considerations:

> Advertising operated by suggestion, pictures, attention-gathering stimuli, and playing on human sympathy to persuade the consumer to buy the product. Campaigns were based on 'appeals' and imputed motives, and sales would depend on how well the advertiser could take advantage of peoples' competitiveness, shame, desire for approval or need for reward for achievement.
>
> (2000: 247)

The third stage began with the Great Depression in the 1920s onwards. It corresponds with the rise of the behavioural sciences, including marketing and social research, when Dr Gallup from Northwestern University in Chicago was recruited to use scientific methods to gather information about consumers. This stage is characterised as the synthesis of the previous two stages, the rational and irrational views of human nature, being merged and modified according to the psychology of the time (Leiss *et al.* 2000: 247). As Curti explains, this also involved the recognition of emotional responses to symbols, as advertising learnt from psychologists "that whatever decision we make, however purely rational it may seem, is deeply influenced by emotional forces, conscious, subconscious or unconscious. Of special importance was the increasing recognition of symbols in invoking emotional responses" (1967, in Leiss *et al.* 2000: 247). From 1925–1945 especially, the direct address to the consumer through a rational appeal to the qualities of the object or its uses shifted towards "non-rational or symbolic grounding of consumption based on the notion of appeals or motives" (Leiss *et al.* 2000: 250). As such, products were presented as 'resonating' with qualities desired by consumers such as status, glamour, reduction of anxiety and a happy family unit. Within this symbolic stage, depictions of fictitious families advertising products in newspapers appeared, and radio soap operas commenced with 'The Smith Family' in 1925 (Swasy 1994: 58). These episodic dramas had advertisements targeted to housewives, mostly for soap powders and cleaning products, consolidating associations and building brand image, and referring to a social context for consumption rather than the pure functionality of the product. At the same time, domestic appliance manufacturers were beginning to sell products, and were beginning to adopt the branding techniques that had worked so well for household consumables (or Fast-Moving Consumer Goods, in marketingspeak).

From 1945 to 1965, Leiss *et al.* identify a tendency of 'Personalization' in marketing strategy and advertising styles, revolving "around the idea of a prototypical mass consumer accessible through television, the quintessential mass medium, and characterized by a limited set of traits (interest in convenience, fascination with technology and science, desire for glamour)" (2000: 251). This prototypical mass consumer is little more than an easily recognised stereotype in current advertising, an observation which shows two things. Firstly, how advertising constructs the consumer in recognisable or stereotypical ways, as valid after 1945 as now. The forms of address within advertisements have not changed, since we often recognise appeals to glamour or convenience in current advertising. Secondly, how these forms of address are not continually reinvented according to the medium, but are present in various forms despite the possibilities of new media and the differentiation of the population. Computers are pitched now to those with an interest in new technologies, and detergents are still pitched predominantly to housewives, whether in print, on the radio, on television, or on the internet. New forms of address and innovative uses of media do occur, of course, with the ability to target groups of consumers more selectively (so-called "market segmentation", occurring from 1965–1985 according to Leiss *et al.* (2000: 251)). But the fact that stereotypical constructions of mass consumers are recognisable even now means they still persist throughout different media forms. The traces of the past history of advertising, in other words, are present in contemporary forms.

According to Olins, there was an explosion of branding in the 1970s, and branding moved from mostly household products to become a much larger commercial and cultural phenomenon (2004: 63), and in the 1990s branding was applicable to services as well as tangible commodities, so that Ford are able to make more profit on financing arrangements than on the cars themselves (Lury 2004: 3). But the proliferation of branding and the rise in market research from the 1970s onwards started to have negative consequences. Consumers started to realise that increasing use of scientific consumer research and the broad-based demographic targeting of advertising was too blunt a tool, and marketing companies realised some immunity amongst consumers was developing. From this realisation we can broadly identify another phase, based around much more individually defined affinities and aspirations. For example, Jim Schroer, executive marketing director at Ford, summarises this shift from broad-brush *demographics* to more individually focused *psychographics*: "It's smarter to think about emotions and attitudes, which all go under the term 'psychographics'—those things that can transcend demographic groups" (in Rushkoff 2000: 177). This involves an appeal to consumers' images of themselves. Psychographics are based on more qualitative than quantitative methods of researching consumer behaviour, trying to understand the causal links between feelings, self-image and purchases. Previously broad-brush demographics, racial or gendered stereotypes were ditched, and more personality-based values and aspirations were singled out. Brand image starts to explore more emotional themes, and so we will speak of the 'passionate consumer' later in the chapter. These psychographic tendencies are certainly successful, feeding on the status anxiety that the endless pursuit of distinction and appeals to self-image engender, and will be explored in the following section.

The brand image

With changes in the spaces of consumption and therefore the transformation of the shopping experience (discussed in Chapter 7), traditional shopkeepers were no longer necessary. Measuring out bulk commodities like rice and sugar, kept in vats that were potentially unhygienic and often adulterated in order to eke out their profits, the role of friendly shopkeeper was increasingly replaced by packaging. Rachel Bowlby describes the rise of packaging and elementary marketing as the replacement of the shopkeeper by the "silent salesman" in the 1920s and

1930s. Unlike the human shopkeeper, "No packet ever turned to the potential buyer with a smile of welcome, genuine or otherwise; but at the same time, nothing prevents a buyer from seeing a package as having a nice personality" (2000: 40–41). The transference of personality from human to packaging is an entry point into brands, as the nonhuman interface between producer and consumer:

> Familiar personalities such as Dr. Brown, Uncle Ben, Aunt Jemima, and old Grand-Dad came to replace the shopkeeper, who was traditionally measuring bulk foods for customers and acting as an advocate for products ... a nationwide vocabulary for brand names replaced the small local shopkeeper as the interface between consumer and product.
>
> (Lupton and Abbott Miller, in Klein 2001: 6)

The rise of the global brand connects with what has been discussed in previous chapters: our ideas about identity, taste and lifestyle. Any analysis of consumer *choice* also entails connecting up with the arrival of the 'brand', and the consumer's ability to read the brand image. Mass-produced items such as biscuits, rice or bread needed to have a unique identity, to stand out for the consumer. In England in 1884, soap was sold for the first time as a packaged commodity and marketed as distinctive through the use of signatures or brands such as Pears or Monkey Brand (McClintock 1995: 211). Similarly, a generic product like rice becomes Uncle Ben's Rice in the 1940s. The white president of the company that was to become Uncle Ben's Converted Rice placed the friendly face of a black farmer from Houston, known for the quality of his rice crops, on the packaging (Kern-Foxworth 1994: 49). This helped to communicate a sense of homeliness, friendliness, and non-threatening familiarity to the middle-class shopper. As identified above, the building of brand awareness arose by cultivating associations between the brand (Uncle Ben's, Aunt Jemima) and intangible values (homeliness, friendliness). But racism is never far away, as Kern-Foxworth shows, since the appellation 'Uncle' or 'Aunt' in the southern United States was used for older enslaved peoples, who were denied use of their courtesy titles. Some more implications of commodity racism will be examined in the section on 'Politics', below.

Proceeding from the personalisation of the goods through packaging, marketing techniques soon caught on to the way that particular products could give expression to consumers' self-perception of personality. In much the same way as the narrator in *Fight Club* asks, "What kind of plates define me as a person?" (see Chapter 2), different makes and models of products like cars show a different notion of 'personalisation'. Egocentric and based on one's own perceived qualities, certain brands of commodities are seen as giving voice or expression, helping the consumer to define themselves by their relation to objects:

> The conservative, in choosing and using a car, wishes to convey such ideas as dignity, reserve, maturity, seriousness ... Another definite series of automotive personalities is selected by the people wanting to make known their middle-of-the-road moderation, their being fashionable ... Further along the range of personalities are the innovators and ultramoderns.
>
> (Martinau, in Baudrillard 2000: 235)

Martinau was writing in 1957, and there is something quaint and nostalgic in the construction of the consumer as a result. Yet the picture remains instantly recognisable, since stereotype remains a recurrent form of addressing, and seeking recognition from, the consumer, as noted in the previous section. Compare this with a recent book on brands, where the real competition between brands such as BMW, Audi and Mercedes is "about emotion as much as function", according to Olins:

> All three brands are good, they all perform well, although they have rather different personalities, and model for model cost about the same. In practical terms there isn't that much to choose between them, although they do feel a bit different from each other when you drive them. But it isn't so much how the cars perform, because the differences in performance are marginal although not insignificant; it's what they stand for that increasingly matters ... Even in [macho car magazines] the brand is recognized as an extension of the individual's identity. Which car suits my image best?
>
> (2004: 38)

These comments echo Ogilvy's on three types of whiskey written almost twenty years earlier. In an early essay concerning consumption and signification, Baudrillard's concern was to ask if the "object/advertising system", the system of consumer goods and their marketing, constituted a new 'language' as such. His answer is negative; it is not technically a language but a system of classification, a "gamut of distinguishing criteria more or less arbitrarily indexed on a gamut of stereotyped personalities" (2000: 235). That is, the recognition of certain brands of products helps to reinforce stereotypes, an assurance of one's social position or status based on almost arbitrary criteria. While Mercedes-Benz is more self-assuredly conservative than BMW, for example, in fact these are merely markers or signs that became fixed at some historical juncture, and from thenceforth simply bolster stereotypes and form self-selective status groups that share similar tastes and affinities. Baudrillard's concern in the essay is not with the way each commodity is actually used or appropriated, but is almost structurally determined by the object/advertising system which throws up false needs and satisfactions, and which settles categories of consumers and particular objects into these status groups. The commodity has become so abstract that there only remains a set of signs, and the 'needs' we express through the marketplace are "simply a way of conceptualising our participation in the symbolic system", as Heath and Potter (2005: 107) summarise. Comparable to Bourdieu, therefore, Baudrillard's Marxist influence is evident, and the centrality of a deep structure entails a fairly reductive analysis of consumption. Nevertheless, there are two aspects of his analysis that are worthy of consideration here. Firstly, the emphasis on the sign-system, so that the 'brand' as a sign first raises the possibility of consumption as a potential 'language'. Even if the language analogy is negated in favour of a hierarchical gamut of objects and commodities, the semiotic content of advertising remains considerable, so that

> The concept of 'brand,' the principal concept of advertising, summarizes well the possibilities of a 'language' of consumption. All products (except perishable foods) are offered today as a specific acronym: each product 'worthy of the name' has a brand name (which at times is substituted for the thing itself: Frigidaire or Xerox). The function of the brand name is to signal the product; its secondary function is to mobilize connotations of affect.
>
> (2000: 236)

Secondly, and corresponding to Baudrillard's secondary function of the brand name, the "connotations of affect", the ability to engender feelings, affections and loyalties to particular brands is part of an ongoing relationship with the consumer that one-off transactions cannot have. Brand loyalty is the cultivation of emotional attachments not simply to particular commodities or objects but to a known and familiar brand, so that the product range may regularly alter or be updated, while the affective link remains. A double articulation, of sign (signal, image) and affect (emotional content, reaction), the most valuable brands evoke strong feelings as a coordinated assemblage. For example, the word 'Orange' and its conjunction with the particular shade of orange used for the mobile telephone company is supposedly "warm and friendly as opposed to the cold, blue tones of [other] telecommunication companies and banks", according to a Wolff Olins agency executive (in Lury 2004: 84). If the agency does its job well, it is the service provider, via the interface of the brand, with whom we enter into an affective relationship, and not the particular phone or manufacturer.

The conjunction of signal and affect in this way forms an elementary group of word-objects based on certain psychological factors; it is a "basic lexicon, which covers walls and haunts consciences", according to Baudrillard, familiar to us now through part-words, trademarks, logos sprawling onto billboards, television, magazines, other peoples' apparel and even videogames. A lexicon is a group of words, not a fully formed language. Utterances in brand-lexicon or 'logoese' will be broken, stuttered, incomplete; like children, based on repetition, or the mentally troubled character in Peter Schaffer's play *Equus* (filmed in 1977), compelled to repeat advertising jingles and half-nonsense phrases. Or, as Baudrillard puts it,

> It is an erratic lexicon where one brand devours the other, each living for its own endless repetition. This is undoubtedly the most impoverished of languages: full of signification and empty meaning. It is a language of signals. And the 'loyalty' to a brand name is nothing more than the conditioned reflex of a controlled affect.
>
> (2000: 236)

Here we depart from Baudrillard, as there are overtones of manipulation and the Frankfurt School's admonishing attitude to 'false needs' (see Chapter 1), or the debate (in Chapter 6) concerning consumers as knowing or duped, sucker or savvy. Instead, over the following few sections, the cultivation of a brand image is examined through the focus just raised of 'sign' and 'affect': firstly, through building up associations with the brand (often affective); and secondly, through the design and implementation of a logo (a sign or symbol). We will address these in reverse order.

The logo: icon and iconicity

The icon is a simple sign, logo or visual depiction that represents a whole story, an experience or even a whole way of seeing. We are familiar with icons for computer operating systems, but icons were originally small religious paintings displayed in churches or cathedrals, and within a small pictorial space they represented a larger story from the Bible. Thus, a more complex context of interpretation is necessary for the small visual depiction to make sense. The art historian Erwin Panofsky termed the linking of artistic motifs with themes, concepts or conventional meaning "iconography". But another level of analysis exists, since the conventions or themes must emerge from somewhere. The intrinsic meaning or content of the work was apprehended through "iconology", which looks at the deeper cultural context (Panofsky 1970: 40ff.). So we might think of this when looking at logos that brands employ, for there is an instant recognisability that logos communicate, based on learned contexts, which because of their reduction to reproducible image slip easily through global media networks, proliferating relentlessly. This is complicated by the diverse channels through which the brand is communicated. For example, with Nike there is more than one mark that makes up its logo:

- the graphic marks 'Swoosh' (the familiar tick image) and 'Jumpman' (Michael Jordan silhouette in jumping pose)
- the words 'Nike' and 'Swoosh'
- associated words and acronyms including Just Do It, Total Body Conditioning, Zoom-Air Conditioning, P.L.A.Y., NIKEF.I.T., etc.

THE *LOGOS* OF LOGO

The word 'logo' is derived from the Greek word meaning 'reason' or 'word', and hence 'logic'. So what is the reasoning behind the logo? What explains its power and immediacy? Less about the words as such, it is increasingly about typography (the instantly recognisable fonts that The Gap or Microsoft use, for example) or pure image, pure sign, the mark (Nike's infamous Swoosh). Like Simmel's notion of neurasthenia, the increasing speed of perception within urban modernity (see Chapter 2), the immediacy of the logo's recognition similarly depends on the increasing speed of perception, its ability to be mobilised into different media (billboards, newspapers, television) and hence achieve ubiquity. "Each mark operates in multiple registers, moving in diverse media, and directing the movements of the bodies of both producers and consumers", says Lury (1999: 499–500). Its ability to migrate almost virally across diverse media and to proliferate so successfully is partly due to the speed of perception that the visual, and iconicity, allows. When browsing in a supermarket, picking out Uncle Ben's beaming, friendly face on packets of easy-cook rice is easier than reading captions or explanations. For pure economy of expression, Nike's Swoosh is hard to beat – endlessly reproducible in whatever media, yet instantly recognisable. Interestingly, the history of Nike's logo goes through progressive abstraction, starting with the tick and various combinations of lettering, and ending up purely with the tick. This simplified Swoosh – the chunky tick – was apparently recognisable enough to denote the brand (Goldman and Papson 1998: 17). The immediacy of nonverbal communication is enhanced, and interpretations are nondiscursive, so there is no need for textual explanation. Instead, the economy of expression is admirable, and its effectiveness transpires from immediate visual interpretation and subsequent brand recognition. Lury's interpretations of the Nike logos cut right into this emphasis on visuality:

> This use of the visual is especially important because so much of peoples' use of things is nonverbal, bodily, habitual, unreflective.
>
> (Lury 1999: 500)

Thus, part of the poetics of the logo is this ability to plug into the almost primal components of affective, bodily perception. The Swoosh graphic's ability to connote movement and dynamicism instantly and across cultures, through whichever media, is premised on a person's "bodily, affective memory and the cultural history of the perceptual mechanics of motion" (Lury 1999: 500). This is the other type of brand 'image', where the logo as visual component, especially in the case of the

Swoosh, draws on the notion of "image in general", as "mobile material, as universal variation, the identity of matter with movement and light" (Lury 2004: 75). The Swoosh does not represent anything as much as connotes or implies movement and dynamicism, and because of its brand image, therefore those other Nike values of competitiveness, determination and so on. Similarly, the silhouetted depiction of Michael Jordan in the Jumpman logo, like the Swoosh, connotes the idea of dynamism, competitiveness: "As a symbol, the Jumpman signals not a specific movement but imaginary movement, movement in abstraction" (Lury 1999: 516). These symbolic values also hold for Nike's competitor Reebok, whose logo is known as the 'vector' (Goldman and Papson 1998: 18) – also a movement-image.

LOGOPHILIA: PASSIONATE CONSUMERS

> By 18 months babies can recognise logos [fi] By two they ask for products by their brand name. During their nursery-school years, children will request an average of 25 products a day. By the time they enter primary school, the average child can identify 200 logos and children between the ages of six and twelve spend more time shopping than reading, attending youth groups, playing outdoors or spending time in household conversation.
>
> (Schor, in Bowditch 2005: 21)

Logos and branding illustrate another consumer paradox (see also Miles 1998). We wish to accommodate brands and buy into the system, with anxieties that drive us to show people that we are a smart Lexus person with inscrutable good taste, or a happy, friendly Disney person. But simultaneously we have a longing for the 'real', for the 'authentic', for the expression of individuality, our 'true' selves. The two are sometimes, but not always, reconcilable. In effect, we are sufferers of *logophilia*, defined as the irrational love of logos or brands, and we have difficulty coming to terms with it. *Elle* magazine described logophilia as "I am who I wear" (in Boyle 2004: 19). The viral proliferation of logos and brands into whatever spaces are available, in advertising, media spaces, and increasingly more public spaces like churches, streets and schools, is an attempt to make us all succumb to logophilia.

A worrying aspect of marketing techniques based on emotional appeal and status anxiety designed for adults, who base their brand choices on 'taste' and 'distinction' (Bourdieu's (1984) terms, examined in Chapter 2), is their extension to younger groups of consumers. In her book *Born to Buy*, Juliet Schor argues that 'tweens' and teens are explicitly targeted by advertisers and have emerged as "the most brand-orientated, consumer-involved, and materialistic generation in history" (in Bowditch 2005: 21). Partly this is due to a phenomenon she terms "age compression", where adults, teenagers and tweens can all be marketed various 'youth' products (see Chapter 6). By the end of her sociological study on advertisers' targeting of children she concluded that: "Involvement in consumer culture causes dysfunction in the forms of depression, anxiety, low self-esteem and psychosomatic complaints" (quoted in Bowditch 2005: 21). One component of bullying in schools is the fiercely competitive social groupings based on particular branded clothing, with a sense of rejection and exclusion if those brands are not displayed. This is the flipside of the cosy sense of community cultivated by brand image, since those who cannot display the requisite labels are not admitted into the fold. In a BBC *Panorama* documentary ('Meet the Tweens', 21 November 2004), one tweenager confessed to being uncomfortable wearing non-branded clothing ('Nicky no-names') and feared being made unpopular and even bullied as a result. Asked if she would even be friends with someone who wore non-branded clothing, she said: "I'd still be their friend, but I wouldn't hang around with them as much because you're just going to get bullied with them." Further negative aspects of branding will be examined in the 'Politics' section, below.

ilove iPod The irrational desire for particular brands, and the perceived necessity to display logos that best define us within a social grouping, certainly has alarming implications. But attachment, loyalty and an ongoing relationship to particular brands might also be symptomatic of what Brady *et al.*, in an article ranking the 100 most valued brands for *Business Week*, abstracted into a new phenomenon: the information-savvy "passionate consumer" (2004: 64). In fact, one of the words that recurs throughout this chapter and much of the literature on brands is "irrational" or "nonrational". Saatchi and Saatchi executive Kevin Roberts, whose book *Lovemarks* celebrates this irrationality, argues that successful brands inspire consumers who are "loyal beyond reason" (2004: 123). He thereby stresses the emotional connection that brands may have, and suggests the next stage after trademarks is 'lovemarks'. But brands have often inspired irrational feelings of attachment or loyalty, as we have seen. If logophilia is an irrational love of logos and branded commodities, the feelings can go either way, either love or hate. One example that both Brady *et al.* (2004) and Roberts (2004) identify is the case of Apple, whose computers have offered a real alternative to Microsoft. From a design and usability perspective, Apple computers have long attracted fierce loyalty amongst consumers. The release of the iPod, a masterpiece of design in terms of looks, packaging and simplicity of operation, has boosted Apple's share price and influenced the design of other consumer electronics. But when an avid Apple devotee and iPod owner found that the battery was irreplaceable and lasted only eighteen months, he set up a protest website with his brother and made a short film. Nevertheless, the protest was an "act of love" (Brady *et al.* 2004: 64). This example demonstrates a number of things. Firstly, the ongoing emotional connection that consumers have with brands, clearly identified as inspiring the "passionate consumer" or "loyalty beyond reason". Secondly, that brands are vulnerable and subject to harsh scrutiny by consumers, who can break a previously solid brand, and can flip logophilia into logophobia. Thirdly, access to greater networks of information concerning consumer products entails consumers are not just savvy bargain-hunters but potential whistle-blowers or critics of brands. Consumers become not just media literate but "market literate", able to position their own consumption in terms of marketing practices (Lury 2004: 43). With an ironic twist, both protest website and film were made with Apple computers.

ASSOCIATIONS

Celia Lury elsewhere terms the cultivation of the logo a "specular/speculative device" which magnifies sets of associations, personalising the product and therefore cementing the affective relations between the brand and consumers (2004: 12). Accordingly, it is through the cultivation of associations that brand positioning – the placement of the logo, its management in various media – is effected. This is how brand image arises. The Swoosh logo was initially received poorly by CEO Phil Knight, and was devoid of meaning. But the Swoosh *acquired* meaning purely through repeated associations with Michael Jordan (Goldman and Papson 1998: 17). Like a halo effect, the Swoosh attained its meaning through pure brand positioning, repeated associations with other culturally meaningful symbols and situations. Thus the Nike brand image melds an empty logo with the personality of Michael Jordan, and consequently has the association of sports, determination and competitiveness.

Another example is the growth of Starbucks, whose CEO Howard Schulz built a global brand from a small chain of coffee shops, transforming coffee "from a commodity ('something to be bagged and sent home with the groceries') into a branded offering that consumers associated with (consistent) quality, service and community" (quoted in Lury 2004: 28). What is offered through such associations is, according to a Starbucks annual report, "coffee ... community ... camaraderie ... connection" (in Klein 2001: 135). Of course, what I have earlier described as the Starbucks Effect™ in Chapter 3 is not simply down to the cultivation of associations, but also the result of aggressive business practices and the controversial method of 'clustering' new franchises around already existing independent coffee shops (Klein 2001: 135ff.).

Marx discussed the commodity fetish as the erasure or forgetting of the manufacturing process, the material properties of a commodity and its history, in order to make it appear magically shiny and new. We can make a similar argument about the recognisability of and responses to the brand (e.g. Nike), the brand image and the logo (e.g. Swoosh). These similarly erase the histories of the production and have a magical, almost totemic quality. The *materiality* of production – that is, the actual material and its shaping into commodities like shoes, plus the conditions of production (factories, sweatshops, tax breaks), plus the relations between workers and employers and the state-sponsored, legally empowered institutions that make this possible – are all obscured and become *immaterial* as the brand becomes more prominent. Lury shows that "the brand is now one of the most significant ways in which the objective properties of things are constituted" (1999: 499).

POLITICS

> 'When deep space exploitation ramps up, it will be corpora-
> tions that name everything. The IBM Stellar Sphere. The
> Philip Morris Galaxy. Planet Starbucks.'
>
> (Narrator, *Fight Club*, 1999)

It is important to remember that, just like the fact that consumption is simultaneously a creating or fulfilment *at the same time* that it is destroying or using up, the issues of the poetics and the ethics of consumption are intrinsically related. The bigger the brand, the more it is recognised on a global scale, the more creative it has to be to ride the whims and desires of consumers in capitalist society, plugging into diverse areas of interest and being visible in a number of different media realms. And as the brand diversifies, becomes spread into so many areas, the material value of the commodity – the actual trainers or clothes themselves – becomes decreasingly important, shifted to the back of our consciousness, as the brand and the iconic logo remain at the forefront. But it is the actual material manufacturing performed in sweatshops and Temporary Export Zones that perpetuates the whole structure: without this increased systematic exploitation, the multi-million-dollar fees of Michael Jordan cannot be paid and the ludicrously expensive advertising airtime around the world cannot be bought. This is why the issue of ethics is intrinsic to the discussion in this chapter, not made supplementary or parenthetic. In a rare, ethically reflective moment, brand consultant Wally Olins states the problem:

> Brands are amoral in their lust to outsource at the lowest cost and
> sell at the highest price. They are intent on becoming ubiquitous as
> they move from one country and one continent to another, ignoring
> or overwhelming venerable ethnic, cultural and religious traditions.
> Brands are increasingly disingenuous and duplicitous in their relent-
> less pursuit of our money and they will stop at nothing in their over-
> whelming imperative to manipulate us.
>
> (Olins 2004: 216)

Let us look briefly at some historical and economic reasons for this.

Nike: post-Fordism, lifestyle and the 'brand'

We have charted one reorganisation of capitalism, from Fordism to post-Fordism, in Chapters 1 and 3. In Fordism, because of standardisation and mass production, along with higher wages, the workers could start to afford the commodities they produced. In post-Fordism, the problems of high wages and increasingly global movements of capital, plus the need to make more individually tailored products, meant domestic manufacture and production moved overseas, and the result was a shift in domestic employment to more leisure-based or service industries. As a continuation of this, we see another, more ruthless shift in capitalism that arises because of our love affair with the brand, and capitalism's insatiable need for profit. Along the same logic of post-Fordism, to be able to shift production to wherever the wages are lowest means it no longer makes sense to actually own any factories. If all production is outsourced, the only thing 'owned' is the brand, and the rest is pure profit (and pure exploitation). The actual manufacturing of commodities can be someone else's problem. We go from the logic of the material commodity (the shoe, the shirt) to the logic of the immaterial brand (Nike, The Gap) and then the immaterial logo (the Swoosh).

Naomi Klein's *No Logo* (2001) charts the rise of brands such as Nike, which started off as an importer of cheap Japanese clothing, but which reinvented itself as a 'lifestyle company', selling a lifestyle rather than particular physical or material products. It is a truism now, but the most successful 'lifestyle' companies no longer make anything; brands like Tommy Hilfiger and Nike outsource their manufacturing, meaning the real dirty work of actually stitching, folding, and cutting on the production line is performed by nameless labourers in different countries; as soon as the tax laws change, or the wages become too high, it is simply cheaper to shift the factories and exploit another third-world labour force on the edge of starvation. Klein powerfully argues that global brands have resulted in the exploitation of third-world workers, increased domestic unemployment, reduced domestic wages, and the continual erosion of workers' rights.

This leaves such companies to concentrate on brand ubiquity, using diverse media channels. Encouraging consumers to buy products that work as advertisements for the brand itself, effectively turning ourselves into 'walking billboards', is only the start. There are numerous examples of innovative and invasive forms of advertising, a trend that increasingly occupies public spaces; Levi's repaints an entire street to promote its SilverTab jeans, and music festivals and sporting events are sponsored, co-opted by beer companies. Then there is the phenomenon of the 'logo police', as observed at the 1996 Olympic Games in Atlanta by journalist Bob Baum, writing for the *Chicago Tribune*:

> logo cops prowl the sidelines in the NFL [National Football League], protecting a $3 billion licensing business by making sure everyone is wearing the right cap. A player caught wearing the wrong logo faces a $5,000 fine, $100,000 if he does it in the Super Bowl.
>
> (in Goldman and Papson 1998: 18)

More worryingly, these public spaces include educational institutions, where in the USA and Canada especially, Coke is the 'official soft drink' of some universities, school lesson plans come courtesy of McDonalds, mega-brands have their logos on textbooks and toilet cubicles, and university departments are wholly reliant on corporate sponsorship (Klein 2001; Boyle 2004). Just like the 'logo police' in operation in Atlanta, one student at a high school in Georgia dared to be different, wearing a Pepsi T-shirt to the school's 'Coke Day', and was suspended (Boyle 2004: 31). Even the human body is susceptible to branding, with the Nike Swoosh being the most popular request in tattoo parlours across the US, and the very recent trend for renting headspace: shaving the hair to advertise various products, as Boyle (2004: 29) identifies.

According to Nikebiz.com, which reveals the inside story of the phenomenal success of Nike, the Swoosh design was purchased from a graphic design student in 1971 for $35 (www.Nikebiz.com). Nike is a $10 billion company, with CEO Phil Knight himself worth $4.5 billion in 2003 according to ESPN. To put this into perspective, an article by Sue Collins states that in 1992 Michael Jordan earned $20 million to put his name, 'creativity' and 'final touches' on Nike shoes. "His pay amounted to more than the total wages of the women in South East Asia who actually made the shoes" (Collins 2001). Jordan's name on the product, pure (immaterial) brand image, outweighs the actual (material, physical) labour and manufacture of the commodities themselves. The brand is perhaps the most elevated example of the commodity fetish; an insubstantial graphic mark obscures the whole history of its production, the human labour and exploitative relations involved therein. Remembering Bourdieu's distinction (in Chapter 2) between *economic capital* and *cultural capital*, it is no surprise that a large economic investment is required to build up cultural capital, and this works as much for the individual, for taste and lifestyle, as for a brand. The surprise lies in just how much economic capital is required; how much more than the labour and materials involved.

Summarising the shift from material commodity to immaterial brand, of how highly desirable branded logos no longer signify 'product', but are metaphors for dynamism and movement, the very things that exemplify athletic prowess or positive character traits, Varda Burstyn reminds us that

> no matter how appealing shoes and jackets may appear to be, it is the idea of the athlete the equipment represents, not the equipment itself, that is so passionately emulated and identified with, and so carefully cultivated by the mass media.

(1999: 145)

The clash of first and third worlds

After a series of investigative reports of sweatshop labour practices that peppered the internet and news broadcasts in the mid- to late 1990s, and which looked at such companies as Nike, The Gap, and more recently Kathy Lee Gifford, it is increasingly clear that the two worlds of production and consumption, of third-world sweatshop labour and first-world mass consumption, cannot remain so separate for so long. By keeping the worlds separate and concentrating on everydayness, of shopping as just 'something we do', we are perpetuating commodity fetishism and therefore the inherently exploitative relations of capitalism – but this time, and in a way Marx predicted but was not alive to see, on a massively global scale.

It is not difficult to find an example of the two worlds being brought together. We should not become inoculated to this clash of culture and capital, first world and third world. One example is through Walt Disney-branded T-shirts. In an open letter to Walt Disney, for example, Charles Kernaghan disclosed to the third-world workers making

Pocahontas shirts how much they are sold for in the US, and hence illustrates the alienation of the worker from the work produced. In doing so he shows how separate the worlds actually are:

> it was only when I translated the $10.97 into the local currency – 178.26 gourdes – that, all at once, the workers screamed with shock, disbelief, anger, and a mixture of pain and sadness, as their eyes remained fixed on the Pocahontas shirts [...] In effect, each worker assembles fifty Disney shirts in a day, which at $10.97 each, would sell for a total of $548.50 in the US. For her eight hours of work sewing these shirts, the [factory] employee earns just $2.22!

> (1997: 101)

A straightforward way of showing the clash of first and third worlds through the brand, a slew of commentators on consumerism examine sweatshops and the exploitation of third-world labour, both abroad (e.g. Klein 2001; Hertz 2002) and closer to home through immigrant communities in New York and LA (e.g. Bakan 2004). The following section deals with this clash in terms of production and consumption in colonial history.

Commodity racism

At this stage it might seem unusual to return to colonial history, but the current existence of the brand is inseparable from the clash of first and third worlds. This clash also occurs in the production of commodities from Britain's colonies and dominions for consumption back home, and so is illustrative of the way that race enters into the discussion of commodity fetishism. In this section I wish to look at the role of brands in the fetishisation of whiteness and blackness, both in colonial history and in recent times, to make a final point about the racial politics of brands and brand image.

Buying into whiteness

"The first step toward lightening the white man's burden is through teaching the virtues of cleanliness", ran an 1899 advertisement for Pears' soap. The image depicted is of an old colonial Englishman, labouring to maintain cleanliness in one of the far-flung corners of Empire. This advertisement and others are symptomatic of what Anne McClintock calls 'commodity racism' in her book *Imperial Leather* (1995). "Pears' soap is a potent factor in brightening the dark corners of the earth as civilization advances", goes the advertisement (1995: 32). English soap and its aggressive marketing in the late nineteenth century was a potent symbol of "scientific rationality and spiritual advance ... the lesson of imperial progress and capitalist civilization", she argues (1995: 32). Perhaps the most obvious and uncomfortable example of soap as a signifier of white imperial superiority is another, undated Pears advertisement, in which a white-aproned white boy poises over a black boy sitting in a washtub. In a second frame, only the boy's head and hair remain black, while the parts of his body previously submerged in the water have become 'clean'. McClintock later argues that these advertisements were a visible manifestation of a rewriting of racial history, so that the white man took his place at the apex of civilisation, with female and non-white constituents of the human species fixed in inferior positions. This she calls the "White family of man" (1995: 207ff.). Thus "the magical fetish of soap promises that the commodity can regenerate the Family of Man by washing from the skin the very stigma of racial and class degeneration" (1995: 214). Through consumption the natural order of whiteness can be re-established, and by no means is this limited to soap.

There are numerous other examples of domesticated imperial images, such as biscuit tins featuring "tea time in the jungle". Advertisements such as these found their zenith in the Empire Marketing Board, set up by the British government between 1926 and 1933, encouraging people to buy products from the colonies. In the memorable words of a 1926 advertisement, British people were encouraged to "Buy Empire Every Day". By buying commodities that originated in the British colonies and dominions, they were buying into colonial ideology, and the favourable trade terms and tariffs between coloniser and colonised – a parasitic economics of interdependency – could be maintained. But these spectacles of imperial conquest were commodified not only in consumables such as fruit and golden syrup, but also in boys' own adventure novels such as H. Rider Haggard's *King Solomon's Mines* (1885) and *She* (1887), or English zoos and museums filled with exotic plunder, and elaborate public displays of Britain and her Empire such as the Great Exhibition of 1851, with the Queen as Empress over all. Commodity racism, in other words, arose at the historical juncture of capitalism and colonialism, with the need to forge and maintain mutually beneficial trade networks of commodities, along with an explicit and undisputed assumption of white racial superiority. The colonies found their mediation back home through trade and an association with exoticism and adventure, and such mediations enforced separations between whiteness and blackness, cleanliness and dirtiness, purity and danger, home and away. These separations were rigidly enforced by the fetishisation of the colonies, as they became the blank slate onto which were projected fantasies of adventure and desire. The Pears' and Monkey Brand soaps worked as a double movement, allowing the danger and fetishisation of the dark, savage (and dirty) corners of the earth, while retaining the civilisation (and cleanliness) that a trusted brand affords.

Buying into blackness

We need only revisit the more recent history of the 1990s for an example of how commodity racism persists, but is now complicated by hiphop's aspiration for 'living it large', the seduction of the 'bling bling', and the quite different assumption that young urban black men are the stylistic innovators which other youth, especially suburban white males, must follow. Recollecting the forms of social emulation that Veblen identified at the beginning of the twentieth century, within the twenty-first century these mechanisms are now more often reversed. Instead of the landed aristocracy setting trends that other social groups, from the *nouveaus riches* and downwards, would follow, in recent years it is the disinherited, the disenfranchised that are emulated by other youth groups across a range of ethnic origins. In investigating some of the shocking stories of exploitation and sweatshop labour that lie behind iconic and globally recognised brands, Naomi Klein's *No Logo* (2001) is salutary. Along the way she charts some disturbing methods used by marketing departments that ensure certain brands are hot, that set the trends, even if this means infiltrating the ghetto. This practice is called 'cool hunting', and if the elusive prey is found the rewards are potentially vast.

One example Klein describes is that of clothes brand Tommy Hilfiger, which started off life as "white-preppy wear in the tradition of Ralph Lauren and Lacoste" (2001: 76). In other words, a brand of clothing worn by white youth with expensive tastes, decidedly far from the cutting edge of cool.

What subsequently occurred was a transformation, a synergetic movement that capitalised on social and economic aspirations, yet which validated a brand of clothing across the board. As the poor ghetto kids aspired to an affluent lifestyle far beyond their means in order to obtain respect amongst their peers, including such bastions of white wealth as skiing, golfing, and yachting, they wore the apparel associated with these activities as part of their urban fantasy, their fetishisation of another, more affluent, lifestyle. Noticing this tendency, Hilfiger advertised his clothing line in these leisure settings with their associations of affluence and the good life, while also redesigning the clothes to conform to a more 'hip-hop aesthetic', and furnishing prominent rap artists such as Snoop Dogg with freebies. The seed was sown. No longer limited to the young black urban poor, the association of the Hilfiger brand with the height of inner-city cool virally spread to far larger and more profitable Asian and white markets. Thus we see an alternative commodity racism coming into effect. As Klein says,

> Like so much of cool hunting, Hilfiger's marketing journey feeds off the alienation at the heart of America's race relations: selling white youth on their fetishization of black style, and black youth on their fetishization of white wealth.

> (2001: 76)

Grand theft black stereotype

Commodity racism is also evident in another more recent franchise of videogames, namely *Grand Theft Auto*. While various incarnations have celebrated Italian-American gangster stereotypes, the latest version, *Grand Theft Auto: San Andreas* (2004), one of the biggest-selling videogames so far, has a young, urban, black man as protagonist, freshly released from jail and living in an unambiguously depicted impoverished neighbourhood. With a thumping rap soundtrack, white fetishisation of black urban cool and of violent gangster life has never been so blatant, with the ability to choose the branded trainers or clothes of your character. White suburban males dressing up and playing with virtual black gangsters, carjacking and performing drive-by shootings and wearing fashionable, branded apparel – an interesting, multi-layered take on commodity racism and urban alienation.

Finally, to reconnect videogame brand obsession and logophilia into actual bodies, Lury (1999: 517) says of Jordan and the Jumpman symbol: the brand as slave-owner's mark persists. That other form of branding from an earlier clash of first and third worlds.

9

WHERE DO WE WANT TO GO TODAY?

THE POSTMODERN CONSUMER

'Where do you want to go today?'™
(Microsoft slogan, circa 1995)

Are we all postmodern now? If so, how did it happen, and when? Are you convinced? What does this well-worn word 'postmodernism' mean, for a start? Not to worry. This is neither the time nor the place for a lengthy exposition of postmodernism and consumer culture. This has been done elsewhere (especially by Featherstone 1991a). Instead, I argue that issues raised in previous chapters have already covered the most important issues in modernism and postmodernism, at least as regards consumption and consumer culture. It will be worth briefly recapitulating some of these issues in this light, because you might need convincing still. So the first part of this brief concluding chapter will trace the narrative arc that the book has taken in order to convince you. The remainder of this chapter will address some outstanding issues that need theoretical 'closure', as it were.

Perhaps most importantly, we then draw out some of the ethical implications of consumerism and consumer culture, based on a revision of earlier chapters, and make it explicit here. Throughout each chapter there is a morally ambivalent tone, suggesting that our consumer practices are constant negotiations with our wants, desires or needs and the forces that coerce us. But equally, within these negotiations I assume that there is guilt, not just for selfish personal reasons of over-expenditure or lack of restraint, but concerning our duties to others and to the environment. Is there such a thing as 'ethical consumerism', or is this an oxymoron, like 'huge dwarf' or 'brave coward'? The counterculture has always protested against excessive consumerism, bemoaning the effects of excessive waste and greed on the environment. Riding on this discussion is the final, concluding and contentious observation: that the counterculture has now become consumer culture. Any alternative lifestyle or anti-consumerist ethic has become co-opted, been branded, marketed and sold back to us. This is the thesis of Heath and Potter (2005), and perhaps will leave a slightly nasty taste in the mouth in the last few pages. Although not a novel thesis, it is worth considering here since it revisits the contested 'terrain of culture' that Gramsci (1971) and Hall (1989) describe. Thus the idea of the counterculture itself becomes oxymoronic, for no real countering is being achieved, only more consumption.

CONSUMPTION AND EVERYDAY LIFE: MODERN OR POSTMODERN?

In discussing McDonaldization in Chapter 3, Ritzer had identified some features of postmodernity as "the proliferation of signs, dedifferentiation of institutional spheres, depthlessness, cultivated nostalgia, and the problematization of authenticity and reality" (1998: 43). As a thumbnail sketch, this neatly summarises some of the concerns we have already dealt with throughout the book, although Featherstone's "the aestheticization of everyday life" (1991a) should be added. Most theorists of postmodernity will admit that there is no substantial break with modernity, and that the factors Ritzer and Featherstone describe are simply accelerated continuations of these trends.

For example, the proliferation of signs is nothing new, and when Simmel wrote in 1903 about developing the "blasé outlook" as a way of overcoming the proliferation of neon and imagery, and the sheer speed of urban experience in modernity, he was describing something comparable. More recently, McRobbie compares the "single, richly coded image" to one's experience of busy everyday life where "a slow, even languid" examination is "out of tempo with the times" (1994: 13). The aesthetics of the everyday "deflect attention away from the singular scrutinizing gaze … and asks that this be replaced by a multiplicity of fragmented, and frequently interrupted 'looks'" (1994: 13). Having looked at a range of contemporary sites of consumption including theme parks, shopping malls, stores such as The Nature Company and The Body Shop, and experiences of travel and tourism, we have seen other processes that Ritzer has identified. Not only is there a proliferation of signs, images and symbols through the 'gaze' and its fragmentation (see Chapter 5), but we have also looked at nature as simulation and as virtualised – problematising 'reality' as a result – as a corollary of its commodification. We have seen how arcades, shopping malls and theme parks (Chapters 3, 5 and 7) collapse into each other to form that quintessential recreation space that allows shopping and themed experiences. This process, dedifferentiation, is happening increasingly in museums, too, and allows one student to portray SeaWorld™ as "a mall with fish" (in Davis 1995: 206). We have looked at malls as depthless spaces, as examples of Augé's "non-places" (1995). And we have woven throughout several chapters the anxiety of consumers over authenticity, such that it appears in considerations of choosing the best places to visit, encountering authentic 'others', finding authentic 'nature', the right olive oil (Chapter 2). Less explicitly, the notion of brands and logos (Chapter 8) is premised on the foundation of the authentic logo rather than cheap imitations, and this is how playground and workplace cachet is accrued.

What Featherstone formulates as the aestheticisation of everyday life "refers to the rapid flow of signs and images which saturate the fabric of everyday life in contemporary society" (1991a: 67). Returning to the concept of dedifferentiation, postmodern theory draws attention to the idea that we live in a "culture society" where the once-separate discourses of money-making and aesthetic experience constantly implode as part of our normal daily life (Lash and Urry 1994). Characteristic sites of everyday aesthetics often involve consumption in some form, such as theme parks, shopping malls, city streetscapes with their advertising hoardings and neon signs, and tourist attractions, as well as mass media images, especially on television or in videogames. The aesthetics of the everyday are objects, events, places, and experiences that for most of us, whether adults, children, kidults or adulescents, help to shape our everyday life. Thus they are a central aspect to our culture and inform much of this book's analysis of consumption. A concern for everyday aesthetics arises from the turn towards cultural markers of identity and distinction, still pursued through practices of consumption. And this is in keeping with the history of consumption in modernity, as we have seen in Veblen, Simmel and Bourdieu (Chapters 1 and 2). The same logic operates in the sense of belonging and differentiation, of homology and heterology, through subcultures that define themselves against the 'mainstream' like the Mods (Chapter 7). The need for markers of differentiation has placed increasing emphasis on the visual more than any other modality, and this has been the focus for aspects such as the 'gaze', despite some interspersed attempts to talk of the other sensory modalities, such as the embodied immediacy of touching and smelling commodities (Chapter 6).

Everyday aesthetics involves immediacy, participation, and desire (Lash and Urry 1994). When we approach artworks reverentially we must cultivate a respectful distance, and this has been called the 'aesthetic attitude'. In contrast, everyday aesthetics emphasises involvement, participation, fragmented looks. Where the cultivated aesthetic attitude delays gratification and encourages refinement, everyday aesthetic experience is characterised by immersion in dreamlike states, a revelling in immediate pleasure. Desiring, wishing, or daydreaming often characterises our drifting mode of window-shopping, of mall-going, the fantasies of ownership and of playing with our subjectivity (Chapters 4 and 6).

ETHICAL CONSUMPTION

It is difficult to examine consumption without considering the way that our social and environmental reality has altered so extensively. Some of these effects have been documented in previous chapters, such as the 'Politics' of the brand and the clash of first and third worlds (in Chapter 8), and the class-based limitations on access to consumer goods (Chapters 1 and 7). Space does not permit an entire chapter on ethical consumption, but rather than pursue the illusion of depthlessness and weightlessness that myths of postmodern consumer capitalism might employ, such as Baudrillard's 'System of Objects' (1988), or to argue for a commodified world of perpetual simulation, this section stays relatively grounded in the morality of consumption, what Miller refers to as "the triple-headed Cerberus of materialism, capitalism and planetary exploitation" (2001: 226).

While consumer capitalism allows us freedoms and luxuries that previous generations could only dream of, we are increasingly aware of the negative aspects. Well-documented examples from the media will suffice: out-of-town shopping developments accessible only by car which impoverish whole sections of inner cities, and even city centres; increasing separation within the West between the 'haves' and the 'have-nots'; separation between global 'North' and global 'South'; and so on. And it is difficult not to acknowledge the vast devastation of the natural world through the reproduction and uptake of an addictively Western lifestyle, fed around the world through MTV, Hollywood, and globalised branding and advertising, based on Americanised consumer capitalism (Ritzer's argument about forms of credit (1998)), with the resultant pollution, decimation of rainforests, impoverishment of farmworkers through unfair commodity prices, child sweatshop workers, and so on. Within our everyday acts of consumption, a significant proportion of us are aware of ethical and environmental concerns, hence the rise of The Body Shop and Fair Trade, and the popularity of Klein's *No Logo* (2001).

Yet to continue rehearsing these arguments, to assume consumption must be inherently bad, that we have too many 'things', and that other, pre-industrial societies are less wasteful, is mistaken. For it equates 'consumption' with 'consumerism' and excess, instead of as a rich, symbolic 'material culture'. The anthropologist Miller is adamant that simplistic separations between 'us' and 'them' make this worse. *Us* (as restrained consumers) and *them* (as "a deluded, superficial person who has become the mere mannequin to commodity culture" (2001: 229)) never quite admits the possibility that these people might be rounded subjects with respectable motives, so too easily falls into critique of mass culture like the Frankfurt School. Or *us* (as relatively rich Westerners) and *them* (inhabitants of pre-industrial societies) fails to accommodate the richness of material culture and the necessity of goods for societal cohesion. Recalling his anthropological training, the notion that fewer goods is somehow more 'authentic' is dispelled. The people of Amazonia, Melanesia and Aboriginal Australia, argues Miller, are far from being people of simple or basic needs:

> It is precisely the richness of their symbolism, the interpenetration of social and material relations, the way cosmology and morality is absorbed in and expressed through myth, material culture and other such media that makes up the core of anthropological teaching.
>
> (2001: 230)

So it is not consumption *per se* that requires moral consideration. In fact, Miller has argued that the only way to lift the population of this planet out of poverty and disease is through *more* consumption rather than less – "more pharmaceuticals, more housing, more transport, more books, more computers" (2001: 228). From a humanitarian viewpoint it is hard to disagree, although one would hope that environmental impact would be reduced. Nevertheless, we might concur with Bauman that factors surrounding consumption, rather than consumption itself, have detrimental effects:

> Consumption does not sell us anything; it's the marketing that does sell us 'commodified life' [...] re-presenting the world as a whole, complete with all its fragments and aspects, as a container full of consumer chances; of potential objects of consumer pleasures – objects to be treated as such, handled the way in which objects of consumption are handled and judged by the criteria designed for such objects.
>
> (in Rojek 2004: 305)

Inherent in this critique of marketing is the notion of an attitude towards objects as replaceable, disposable, endlessly upgradeable.

THE WASTE, THE EXCESS

In Italo Calvino's magical and poetic story *Invisible Cities* (1997), Kublai Khan invites the explorer Marco Polo to describe, one by one, the fantastic cities he has visited from his explorations around the world. A series of short and surreal descriptions show vastly different ways of life and types of people. In actuality they are all descriptions of the same city, Venice, but seen from different perspectives. One of these 'invisible cities' is Leonia, a thinly disguised allegory of our consumer society where the residents' passion is "the enjoyment of new and different things", and each morning they "wear brand-new clothing, take from the latest model refrigerator still unopened tins, listening to the last-minute jingles from the most up-to-date radio" (1997: 114). The fixation on novelty has a price, however, for every morning the no-longer new is discarded for the garbage truck. From an outsider's perspective it might seem that the true passion is not just novelty but also "the joy of expelling, discarding, cleansing themselves of a recurrent impurity" (1997: 114). As the Leonians excel in their continual pursuit of novelties, a "fortress of indestructible leftovers" surrounds the city, "dominating it on every side, like a chain of mountains" (1997: 115). There seemed to be no connection in the minds of Leonia's residents between the odious heaps of waste and their pursuit of novelty. "Perhaps the whole world, beyond Leonia's boundaries, is covered by craters of rubbish, each surrounding a metropolis in constant eruption", muses Marco Polo (1997: 115).

I am grateful to Zygmunt Bauman (in Rojek 2004: 307–308) for reminding me of Leonia in this context, and Calvino's allegorical style is less heavy-handed than most critiques of consumption. Yet it still manages to focus on the central dialectic of consumerism, the tendency to excessive consumption: that, for anything to appear shiny, appealing and new – notwithstanding commodity fetishism – our constant *up*grading of consumer goods relies on a corresponding *down*grade. Taking pleasure in our rapacious lust for the new, the disposal and expulsion of the old is shamefully and wilfully ignored.

CODA

Arriving full circle, let us briefly remind ourselves of the figure of the cannibal, suggested in the introduction to this book, and the subject of textual analysis by Probyn (2000: 40ff.). Albeit without the anthropological insight of Miller, the cannibal figure was invoked as exhibiting restraint in excess; savagely hungry but, unlike their savagely greedy colonial counterparts, able to exercise control. I will end on this note: on numerous occasions throughout this book, the excessive features as a mode of engagement with consumption – through bodily behaviour and the carnivalesque, through daydreaming and fantasy, through the felt desires of the everyday. Rather than equating excess with wastefulness, thereby spawning an ethical problem, from Bataille's perspective excess is a characteristic of joy, of exuberance, of the functioning of an organism within its rich symbolic and material culture. After all, shopping is both painful *and* pleasurable.

BIBLIOGRAPHY

TEXTS

Adorno, Theodor W. (1974) *Minima Moralia: Reflections from a Damaged Life*, trans. E.F.N. Jephcott, London: Verso.

—— (2001) *The Culture Industry: Selected Essays on Mass Culture*, ed. J.M. Bernstein, London: Routledge.

Adorno, Theodor W. and Horkheimer, Max (1973) *Dialectic of Enlightenment*, trans. J. Cumming, London: Allen Lane.

Ahmed, Sara (2000) *Strange Encounters: Embodied Others in Post-Coloniality*, London: Routledge.

Appadurai, Arjun (1993) 'Consumption, duration and history', *Stanford Leisure Review* 10: 11–33.

Arthurs, Jane (2004) *Television and Sexuality: Regulation and the Politics of Taste*, Milton Keynes: Open University Press.

Arthurs, Jane and Grimshaw, Jean (eds) (1999) *Women's Bodies: Discipline and Transgression*, London: Cassell.

Ashley, David and Orenstein, David M. (1990) *Sociological Theory: Classical Statements*, 2nd edn, Boston: Allyn & Bacon.

Augé, Marc (1995) *Non-Places: Introduction to an Anthropology of Supermodernity*, trans. J. Howe, London: Verso.

Bachelard, Gaston (1994) *The Poetics of Space*, trans. M. Jolas, Boston: Beacon Press.

Bakan, Joel (2004) *The Corporation: The Pathological Pursuit of Profit and Power*, London: Constable.

Bakhtin, Mikhail M. (1984) *Rabelais and His World*, Indianapolis: Indiana University Press.

Ballinger, Lucy (2003) 'Life coaches', *The Observer* (London), Cash, 12 January.

Barber, Benjamin R. (2003) *Jihad Vs. McWorld: Terrorism's Challenge to Democracy*, London: Corgi Books.

Barker, Martin (2000) *Cultural Studies: Theory and Practice*, London: Sage.

Barnett, Clive (1998) 'The cultural turn: fashion or progress in human geography?', *Antipode* 30(4): 379–394.

Barrow, Becky (2002) 'Man United accused of replica kit price-fixing', *The Daily Telegraph* (London), 17 May, p. 15.

Barthes, Roland (1973) *Mythologies*, trans. A. Lavers, London: HarperCollins.

—— (1975) *The Pleasure of the Text*, New York: Hill & Wang.

—— (1999) 'Rhetoric of the image', in J. Evans and S. Hall (eds) *Visual Culture: The Reader*, London: Sage.

Bataille, Georges (1991) *The Accursed Share: An Essay on General Economy*, vol. 1, *Consumption*, trans. R. Hurley, New York: Zone Books.

Baudrillard, Jean (1988) *Selected Writings*, ed. M. Poster, Cambridge: Polity.

—— (1994a) *In the Shadow of the Silent Majorities or, The End of the Social and Other Essays*, trans. Paul Foss, John Johnston and Paul Patton, New York: Semiotext(e).

—— (1994b) *Simulacra and Simulation*, trans. Sheila F. Glaser, Ann Arbour: University of Michigan Press.

—— (2000) 'A new language?', in M.J. Lee (ed.) *The Consumer Society Reader*, Oxford: Blackwell, pp. 233–240.

Bauman, Zygmunt (1998) *Globalization: The Human Consequences*, Cambridge: Polity Press.

Beardsworth, Alan and Bryman, Alan (2001) 'The wild animal in late modernity: the case of the Disneyization of zoos', *Tourist Studies* 1(1): 83–104.

Beilharz, Peter (1999) 'McFascism? Reading Ritzer, Bauman and the Holocaust', in B. Smart (ed.) *Resisting McDonaldization*, London: Sage, pp. 222–233.

Bell, Annie (2001) 'Olive oil – it's a slippery issue: do we really need to keep five different types in the cupboard?', *The Independent* (London), Features, 28 April, p. 17.

Bell, David (2002) 'Fragments for a new urban culinary geography', *Journal for the Study of Food and Society* 6(1): 10–21.

Bell, David and Valentine, Gill (1997) *Consuming Geographies: We Are What We Eat*, London: Routledge.

Benjamin, Walter (1999) *The Arcades Project*, trans. H. Eiland and K. McLaughlin, Cambridge, MA: Belknap Press.

Benson, Susan P. (1986) *Counter Cultures: Saleswomen, Managers and Customers in American Department Stores, 1890–1940*, Chicago: University of Chicago Press.

Bermingham, Ann (1995) 'Introduction', in A. Bermingham and J. Brewer (eds.) *The Consumption of Culture, 1600–1800: Image, Object, Text*, London: Routledge, pp. 1–22.

Bernays, Edward L. (2004 [1928]) *Propaganda*, Brooklyn, NY: Ig Publishing.

Bernstein, J.M. (2001) 'Introduction', in J.M. Bernstein (ed.) *The Culture Industry: Selected Essays on Mass Culture*, London: Routledge, pp. 1–28.

Bocock, Robert (1993) *Consumption, Key Ideas*, London: Routledge.

Bordo, Susan (1993) *Unbearable Weight: Feminism, Western Culture and the Body*, Berkeley: University of California Press.

Bourdieu, Pierre (1986a) *Distinction: A Social Critique of the Judgement of Taste*, trans. R. Nice, London: Routledge.

—— (1986b) 'The forms of capital', in J. Richardson (ed.) *Handbook of Theory and Research for the Sociology of Education*, New York: Greenwood Press, pp. 241–258.

Bowditch, Gillian (2005) 'Your child in their sights', *The Scotsman*, 28 March, p. 21.

Bowlby, Rachel (1985) *Just Looking: Consumer Culture in Dreiser, Gissing and Zola*, London: Methuen.

—— (1993) *Shopping with Freud*, London: Routledge.

—— (2000) *Carried Away: The Invention of Modern Shopping* London: Faber & Faber.

Boyle, David (2004) *Authenticity: Brands, Fakes, Spin and the Lust for Real Life*, London: Harper Perennial.

Brady, Diane, Hof, Robert D., Reinhardt, Andy, Ihlwan, Moon, Holmes, Stanley and Capell, Kerry (2004) 'Cult brands', *Business Week*, 9 August, pp. 64–68.

Bryman, Alan (1995) *Disney and His Worlds*, London: Routledge.

—— (1999a) 'The Disneyization of society', *Sociological Review* 47(1): 25–47.

—— (1999b) 'Theme parks and McDonaldization', in B. Smart (ed.) *Resisting McDonaldization*, London: Sage, pp. 101–115.

—— (2004) *The Disneyization of Society*, London: Sage.

Burstyn, Varda (1999) *The Rites of Men: Manhood, Politics and the Culture of Sport*, Toronto: University of Toronto Press.

Calvino, Italo (1997) *Invisible Cities*, trans. W. Weaver, London: Vintage.

Campbell, Colin (1987) *The Romantic Ethic and the Spirit of Modern Consumerism*, Oxford: Blackwell.

Clarke, David B., Doel, Marcus A. and Housinaux, Kate M.L. (eds) (2003) *The Consumption Reader*, London: Routledge.

Clarke, John (2000) 'Dupes and guerrillas: the dialectics of cultural consumption', in M.J. Lee (ed.) *The Consumer Society Reader*, Oxford: Blackwell, pp. 288–293.

Cohen, Stanley (1972) *Folk Devils and Moral Panics*, London: MacGibbon & Kee.

Collins, Sue (2001) '"E" ticket to Nike Town', *Counterblast: e-journal of Culture & Communication* 1(1), online at www.nyu.edu/pubs/counterblast.

Conrad, Joseph (1995) *Youth, Heart of Darkness, The End of the Tether*, ed. John Lyon, London: Penguin.

Conrad, Peter (1997) 'I see no chimps ...', *The Observer* (London), Review, 19 October, p. 8.

Conway, W. (1996) 'From zoos to conservation parks', in M. Nichols and J.C. Coe (eds) *Keepers of the Kingdom: The New American Zoo*, New York: Thomasson-Grant & Lickle, pp. 27–34.

Corrigan, Peter (1998) *The Sociology of Consumption: An Introduction*, London: Sage.

Cowie, Elizabeth (1999) 'Fantasia', in J. Evans and S. Hall (eds) *Visual Culture: The Reader*, London: Sage, pp. 356–369.

Crang, Mike (1998) *Cultural Geography*, London: Routledge.

Crawshaw, Carol and Urry, John (1997) 'Tourism and the photographic eye', in C. Rojek and J. Urry (eds) *Touring Cultures: Transformations of Travel and Theory*, London: Routledge, pp. 176–195.

Crossick, Geoffrey and Jaumain, Serge (eds) (1999) *Cathedrals of Consumption: The European Department Store, 1850–1939*, Aldershot: Ashgate.

Culler, Jonathan (1981) *The Pursuit of Signs: Semiotics, Literature, Deconstruction*, London: Routledge & Kegan Paul.

Daily Mail (2004) 'Shoppers pick olives', 2 August, p. 11.

Daily Post (Liverpool) (2004) 'Driving seat: spray-on smell that can clinch a sale', Features, 27 August, p. 34.

Datamonitor (2002) 'Tweenagers', Report DMCM0131, 31 December 2002, summary online at:
www.datamonitor.com/~43ef8535fcd04e7d9c1b1ba69cc1dddc~/industries/research/?pid=DMCM0131&=Report (last accessed 15 January 2005).

—— (2003) 'Teenage consumers', Report DMFS1600, 6 October 2002, summary online at: www.datamonitor.com/~43ef8535fcd04e7d9c1b1ba69cc1dddc~/industries/research/?pid=DMFS1600&type=Report (last accessed 15 January 2005).

Davis, Susan G. (1995) 'Touch the magic', in W. Cronon (ed.) *Uncommon Ground: Toward Reinventing Nature*, London: W.W. Norton & Co., pp. 204–232.

—— (1997) *Spectacular Nature: Corporate Culture and the SeaWorld Experience*, Berkeley: University of California Press.

de Certeau, Michel (1984) *The Practice of Everyday Life*, trans. S. Rendall, Berkeley: University of California Press.

de Certeau, Michel, Giard, Luce and Mayol, Pierre (1998) *The Practice of Everyday Life*, Volume II, trans. Timothy J. Tomasik, Minneapolis: Minnesota University Press.

Debord, Guy (1995) *The Society of the Spectacle*, New York: Zone Books.

Dittmar, Helga (1992) *The Social Psychology of Material Possessions*, Hemel Hempstead: Harvester Wheatsheaf.

Doig, Liz (1999) 'There's something in the air ...', BBC News Online, 26 March, http://news.bbc.co.uk/1/hi/uk/303810.stm (last accessed 20 January 2005).

Douglas, Mary (2003) 'The consumer's revolt', in D.B. Clarke, M.A. Doel and K.M.L. Housiaux (eds) *The Consumption Reader*, London: Routledge, pp. 144–149.

Douglas, Mary and Isherwood, Baron (1979) *The World of Goods*, London: Allen Lane.

Dunne, Pete (1989) 'In the natural state', *New York Times*, New Jersey Sunday section, 7 May, p. 000.

Dyer, Christopher (1994) *Everyday Life in Medieval England*, London: Hambledon & London.

Eagleton, Terry (1981) *Walter Benjamin: Towards a Revolutionary Criticism*, London: Verso.

Edensor, Tim (1998) *Tourists at the Taj: Performance and Meaning at a Symbolic Site*, London: Routledge.

Evernden, Neil (1992) *The Social Creation of Nature*, Baltimore: Johns Hopkins University Press.

Ewen, Stuart (2001 [1976]) *Captains of Consciousness: Advertising and the Social Roots of the Consumer Culture*, New York: McGraw-Hill.

Falk, Pasi (1994) *The Consuming Body*, London: Sage.

Farganis, James (ed.) (1993) *Readings in Social Theory: The Classic Tradition to Post-Modernism*, New York: McGraw-Hill.

Featherstone, Mike (1990) 'Perspectives on consumer culture', *Sociology* 24(1): 5–22.

—— (1991a) *Consumer Culture and Postmodernism*, London: Sage.

—— (1991b) *The Body in Consumer Culture*, London: Sage.

—— (2003) 'The body in consumer culture', in D.B. Clarke, M.A. Doel and K.M.L. Housiaux (eds) *The Consumption Reader*, London: Routledge, pp. 163–167.

Feifer, Maxine (1985) *Going Places. Tourism in History: From Imperial Rome to the Present*, New York: Stein & Day.

Ferguson, Harvie (1992) 'Watching the world go round: atrium culture and the psychology of shopping', in R. Shields (ed.) *Lifestyle Shopping: The Subject of Consumption*, London: Routledge, pp. 21–39.

Fine, Ben (1993) 'From political economy to consumption', in D. Miller (ed.) *Acknowledging Consumption: A Review of New Studies*, London: Routledge, pp. 127–163.

Fine, Gary A. (1992) 'Wild life: authenticity and the human experience of "natural" places', in C. Ellis and M.G. Flaherty (eds) *Investigating Subjectivity: Research on Lived Experience*, London: Sage, pp. 156–175.

Fischler, Claude (1988) 'Food, self and identity', *Social Science Information* 27: 275–292.

Fiske, John (1989a) *Understanding Popular Culture*, London: Routledge.

—— (1989b) *Reading the Popular*, London: Unwin Hyman.

Foucault, Michel (1973) *The Birth of the Clinic: An Archaeology of Medical Perception*, London: Tavistock.

—— (1977) *Discipline and Punish: The Birth of the Prison*, trans. A. Sheridan, London: Allen Lane.

—— (1990) *The History of Sexuality*, vol. 1, *An Introduction*, trans. R. Hurley, New York: Vintage.

Franklin, Adrian (1999) *Animals and Modern Culture: A Sociology of Human-Animal Relations in Modernity*, London: Sage.

Franklin, Sarah, Lury, Celia and Stacey, Jackie (2000) *Global Nature, Global Culture*, London: Sage.

Freud, Sigmund (1991) 'Beyond the Pleasure Principle', in *The Penguin Freud Library*, vol. 11, *On Metapsychology*, trans. J. Strachey, London: Penguin.

Friedan, Betty (1965) *The Feminine Mystique*, Harmondsworth: Penguin.

Friedberg, Anne (1993) *Window Shopping: Cinema and the Postmodern*, Berkeley: University of California Press.

Fullagar, Simone (2000) 'Desiring nature: identity and becoming in narratives of travel', *Cultural Values* 4: 58–76.

Furedi, Frank (2003) 'The children who won't grow up', *Spiked*, posted 29 July, online at:
www.spiked-online.com/Articles/00000006DE8D.htm (last accessed 7 May 2005).

Galbraith, John K. (2000) 'The dependence effect', in M.J. Lee (ed.) *The Consumer Society Reader*, Oxford: Blackwell, pp. 217–222.

Garcia, Bonito (2003) *Where'd You Get Those? New York City's Sneaker Culture 1960–1987*, New York: Powerhouse.

Gardiner, Michael E. (2000) *Critiques of Everyday Life*, London: Routledge.

Gibson, James J. (1966) *The Senses Considered as Perceptual Systems*, Boston: Houghton Mifflin.

Glennie, P. and Thrift, N.J. (1996) 'Consumers, identities, and consumption spaces in early-modern England', *Environment and Planning A* 28(1): 25–45.

Goffman, Erving (1968) *Asylums: Essays on the Social Situation of Mental Patients and Other Inmates*, Harmondsworth: Penguin.

Goldman, Robert and Papson, Stephen (1998) *Nike Culture*, London: Sage.

Gramsci, Antonio (1971) *Selections from the Prison Notebooks of Antonio Gramsci*, ed. and trans. Q. Hoare and G.N. Smith, London: Lawrence & Wishart.

Green, Nicholas (1990) *The Spectacle of Nature: Landscape and Bourgeois Culture in Nineteenth-Century France*, Manchester: Manchester University Press.

Hall, Stuart (1981) 'Notes on deconstructing "the popular"', in R. Samuel (ed.) *People's History and Socialist Theory*, London: Routledge, pp. 227–240.

—— (1989) 'The meaning of New Times', in S. Hall and M. Jacques (eds) *New Times*, London: Lawrence & Wishart.

—— (1992) 'The question of cultural identity', in S. Hall, D. Held and T. McGrew (eds) *Modernity and Its Futures*, Oxford: Polity Press, pp. 274–316.

Hamblett, Charles and Deverson, Jane (1964) *Generation X*, London: Tandem.

Hammersley, Ben (2005) 'Generation Text', *The Guardian*, G2 Online section, 13 January, pp. 23–24.

Haraway, Donna J. (1991) *Simians, Cyborgs, and Women: The Reinvention of Nature*, London: Routledge.

—— (1997) *Modest_Witness@Second_Millennium: FemaleMan© Meets_Onco_Mouse™*, London: Routledge.

Harvey, David (1989) *The Condition of Postmodernity: An Enquiry into the Origins of Cultural Change*, Oxford: Blackwell.

Hayles, N. Katherine (1995) 'Simulated nature and natural simulations: rethinking the relation between the beholder and the world', in W. Cronon (ed.) *Uncommon Ground: Toward Reinventing Nature*, London: W.W. Norton & Co., pp. 409–425.

Heard, Nick (2003) *Trainers*, London: Carlton Books.

Heath, Joseph and Potter, Andrew (2005) *The Rebel Sell: How the Counter Culture Became Consumer Culture*, Chichester: Capstone Publishing.

Hebdige, Dick (1979) *Subculture: The Meaning of Style*, London: Routledge.

—— (1988) *Hiding in the Light: On Images and Things*, London: Routledge.

—— (2000) 'The object as image: the Italian scooter cycle', in Martyn J. Lee (ed.) *The Consumer Society Reader*, Oxford: Blackwell, pp. 125–161.

Hertz, Noreena (2002) *The Silent Takeover: Global Capitalism and the Death of Democracy*, London: Arrow Books.

Hirsch, Fred (1977) *The Social Limits of Growth*, London: Routledge.

Hobsbawm, Eric J. (1980) *Industry and Empire*, The Pelican Economic History of Britain, Volume 3: From 1750 to the Present Day, Harmondsworth: Penguin.

hooks, bell (1992) 'Eating the other: desire and resistance', in *Black Looks: Race and Representation*, Boston: South End Press.

Husserl, Edmund (1999) *The Essential Husserl: Basic Writings in Transcendental Phenomenology*, trans. D. Welton, Bloomington: Indiana University Press.

Ingold, Tim (2000) *The Perception of the Environment: Essays on Livelihood, Dwelling and Skill*, London: Routledge.

Jameson, Fredric (1995) *Postmodernism, or The Cultural Logic of Late Capitalism*, London: Verso.

Kahn, Stephen (2003) 'Bombay calling', *The Observer* (London), News, 7 December, p. 19.

Kellner, Douglas (2000) 'Hollywood film and U.S. society: some theoretical perspectives', in J. Hill and P.C. Gibson (eds) *American Cinema and Hollywood: Critical Approaches*, Oxford: Oxford University Press, pp. 128–137.

Kenna, Rudolph (1996) *Old Glasgow Shops*, Glasgow: Glasgow City Libraries.

Kernaghan, Charles (1997) 'An appeal to Walt Disney', in Andrew Ross (ed.) *No Sweat*, New York: Verso.

Kern-Foxworth, Marilyn (1994) *Aunt Jemima, Uncle Ben, and Rastus:*

Blacks in Advertising Yesterday, Today, and Tomorrow, New York: Praeger.

Klein, Naomi (2001) *No Logo*, London: Flamingo.

Kowinski, William S. (1985) *The Malling of America: An Inside Look at the Great Consumer Paradise*, New York: William Morrow & Co.

Laermans, Rudi (1993) 'Learning to consume: early department stores and the shaping of modern consumer culture (1860–1914)', *Theory, Culture & Society* 10(4): 79–102.

Langman, Lauren (1992) 'Neon cages: shopping for subjectivity', in R. Shields (ed.) *Lifestyle Shopping: The Subject of Consumption*, London: Routledge, pp. 40–82.

Laplanche, Jean and Pontalis, Jean-Bertrand (1968) 'Fantasy and the origins of sexuality', *International Journal of Psychoanalysis* 49(1): 1–18.

Lash, Scott and Urry, John (1994) *Economies of Signs and Space*, London: Sage.

Latham, Rob (2002) *Consuming Youth: Vampires, Cyborgs and the Culture of Consumption*, London: University of Chicago Press.

Latour, Bruno (1993) *We Have Never Been Modern*, trans. Catherine Porter, London: Harvester Wheatsheaf.

Lee, Martyn J. (1993) *Consumer Culture Reborn: The Cultural Politics of Consumption*, London: Routledge.

Leiss, William, Kline, Stephen and Jhally, Sut (2000) 'The bonding of media and advertising', in M.J. Lee (ed.) *The Consumer Society Reader*, Oxford: Blackwell, pp. 243–252.

Lindahl-Elliot, Nils (2001) 'Signs of anthropomorphism: the case of natural history documentaries', *Social Semiotics* 11(3): 289–305.

Lunt, Peter K. and Livingstone, Sonia M. (1992) *Mass Consumption and Personal Identity: Everyday Economic Experience*, London: Open University Press.

Lupton, Deborah (1996) *Food, the Body and the Self*, London: Sage.

Lury, Celia (1996) *Consumer Culture*, Cambridge: Polity Press.

—— (1999) 'Marking time with Nike: the illusion of the durable', *Public Culture* 29(11.3): 499–526.

—— (2004) *Brands: The Logos of the Global Economy*, London: Routledge.

MacCannell, Dean (1976) *The Tourist: A New Theory of the Leisure Class*, New York: Schocken Books.

—— (1999) *The Tourist: A New Theory of the Leisure Class*, rev. edn, Berkeley: University of California Press.

MacInnes, Colin (1961) *Absolute Beginners*, 2nd edn, Harmondsworth: Penguin.

Mackay, Hugh (1997) 'Introduction', in H. Mackay (ed.) *Consumption and Everyday Life*, London: Sage, pp. 1–14.

Maffesoli, Michel (1996) *The Time of the Tribes: The Decline of Individualism in Mass Society*, trans. D. Smith, London: Sage.

Marcuse, Herbert (1968) *One Dimensional Man*, London: Sphere.

Markwell, Kevin (2001) 'An intimate rendezvous with nature?', *Tourist Studies* 1(1): 39–57.

Martin, Luther H., Gutman, Huck and Hutton, Patrick H. (eds) (1988) *Technologies of the Self: A Seminar with Michel Foucault*, London: Tavistock Press.

Marx, Karl (1959) *Economic and Philosophical Manuscripts of 1844*, London: Lawrence & Wishart.

—— (1973) *Grundrisse: Foundations of the Critique of Political Economy*, trans. M. Nicolaus, London: Pelican.

—— (1990) *Capital: A Critique of Political Economy*, vol. 1, trans. Ben Fowkes, London: Penguin.

Marx, Karl and Engels, Friedrich (1985) *The Communist Manifesto*, trans. S. Moore, Harmondsworth: Penguin.

Massey, Doreen (1984) *Spatial Divisions of Labour: Social Structures and the Geography of Production*, London: Macmillan.

McClintock, Anne (1995) *Imperial Leather: Race, Gender, and Sexuality in the Colonial Contest*, London: Routledge.

McCracken, Grant (1988) *Culture and Consumption: New Approaches to the Symbolic Character of Consumer Goods and Activities*, Bloomington: Indiana University Press.

McDougal, Doug (2002) 'Silver service safari', *The Scotsman*, 8 June, p. 14.

McGuigan, Jim (2000) 'Sovereign consumption', in M.J. Lee (ed.) *The Consumer Society Reader*, Oxford: Blackwell, pp. 294–299.

McKibben, Bill (1989) *The End of Nature*, Harmondsworth: Penguin.

McKie, Rob (2004) 'Super size me', *The Guardian*, Review, 31 December, p. 13.

McRobbie, Angela (1994) *Postmodernism and Popular Culture*, London: Routledge.

Miles, Steven (1998) *Consumerism – As a Way of Life*, London: Sage.

Miller, Daniel (1987) *Material Culture and Mass Consumption*, Oxford: Blackwell.

—— (1993) 'Consumption as the vanguard of history: a polemic by way of an introduction', in D. Miller (ed.) *Acknowledging Consumption: A Review of New Studies*, London: Routledge, pp. 1–57.

—— (1997a) 'Consumption and its consequences', in H. Mackay (ed.) *Consumption and Everyday Life*, London: Sage, pp. 14–50.

—— (1997b) 'Coca-Cola: a black sweet drink from Trinidad', in D. Miller (ed.) *Material Cultures*, London: University College London Press, pp. 168–187.

—— (2001) 'The poverty of morality', *Journal of Consumer Culture* 1(2): 225–243.

Mintz, Stanley (1986) *Sweetness and Power: The Place of Sugar in Modern History*, Harmondsworth: Penguin.

Morris, Meagan (1999) 'Things to do with shopping centres', in S. During (ed.) *The Cultural Studies Reader*, 2nd edn, London: Routledge, pp. 391–409.

Muggleton, David (2000) *Inside Subculture: The Postmodern Meaning of Style*, Oxford: Berg.

—— (ed.) (2003) *The Post-Subcultures Reader*, Oxford: Berg.

Mullan, Bob and Marvin, Garry (1999) *Zoo Culture*, 2nd edn, Urbana: University of Illinois Press.

Mulvey, Laura (1981) 'Visual pleasure and narrative cinema', in T. Bennett, S. Boyd-Bowmann, C. Mercer and J. Woollacott (eds) *Popular Television and Film*, London: British Film Institute.

Mumford, Lewis (1961) *The City in History: Its Origins, Its Transformations, and Its Prospects*, New York: Secker & Warburg.

Münch, Richard (1999) 'McDonaldized culture: the end of communication?', trans. S.C. Madiedo, in B. Smart (ed.) *Resisting McDonaldization*, London: Sage, pp. 135–147.

Nava, Mica (1997) 'Modernity's disavowal: women, the city and the department store', in Pasi Falk and Colin Campbell (eds) *The Shopping Experience*, London: Sage, pp. 56–91.

—— (1998) 'The cosmopolitanism of commerce and the allure of difference: Selfridges, the Russian Ballet and the tango 1911–14', *International Journal of Cultural Studies* 1(2): 163–196.

Nikebiz.com 'Origin of the Swoosh', online at www.nike.com/nikebiz/nikebiz.jhtml?page=5&item=origin (last accessed 6 December 2004).

Nuttall, Mark (1997) 'Packaging the wild: tourism development in Alaska', in S. Abram, J. Waldren and D.V.L. Macleod (eds) *Tourists and Tourism: Identifying with People and Places*, Oxford: Berg, pp. 223–239.

Ogilvy, David (2003) *Ogilvy on Advertising*, London: Prion Press.

Olins, Wally (2004) *On Brand*, London: Thames & Hudson.

O'Neill, John (1999) 'Have you had your theory today?', in B. Smart (ed.) *Resisting McDonaldization*, London: Sage, pp. 41–56.

Osgerby, Bill (1998) *Youth in Britain Since 1945*, Oxford: Blackwell.

Palahniuk, Chuck (1997) *Fight Club*, London: Vintage.

Panofsky, Erwin (1970) *Meaning in the Visual Arts*, Harmondsworth: Penguin.

Paterson, M. (2004) 'Merleau-Ponty', in J. Baggini and J. Stangroom (eds) *The Great Thinkers A–Z*, London: Continuum, pp. 158–160.

Penaloza, Lisa (1998) 'Just doing it: a visual ethnographic study of spectacular consumption behavior at Nike Town', *Consumption, Markets and Culture* 2(4): 337–465.

Pile, Steven and Thrift, Nigel (eds) (1995) *Mapping the Subject: Geographies of Cultural Transformation*, London: Routledge.

Pine, B. Joseph and Gilmore, James H. (1999) *The Experience Economy: Work is Theatre and Every Business a Stage*, Harvard: Harvard Business School Press.

Plant, Sadie (1992) *The Most Radical Gesture: Situationist International in a Postmodern Age*, London: Routledge.

—— (2002) 'On the mobile', *receiver #06: The Mobile Self*, online at www.receiver.vodafone.com (last accessed 15 January 2005).

Plato (1981) *The Republic*, trans. D. Lee, 2nd edn (rev.), Harmondsworth: Penguin.158–160

Pollock, Griselda (1988) *Vision and Difference: Femininity, Feminism and Histories of Art*, London: Routledge.

Prendergrast, Mark (1993) *For God, Country and Coca-Cola: The Unauthorized History of the World's Most Popular Soft Drink*, London: Wiedenfeld & Nicolson.

Price, Jennifer (1995) 'Looking for nature at the mall: a field guide to The Nature Company', in W. Cronon (ed) *Uncommon Ground: Rethinking the Human Place in Nature*, London: W.W. Norton & Co., pp. 186–203.

Probyn, Elspeth (2000) *Carnal Appetites: FoodSexIdentities*, London: Routledge.

Radner, Hilary (1995) *Shopping Around: Feminine Culture and the Pursuit of Pleasure*, London: Routledge.

Rappaport, Nigel (1997) 'Edifying anthropology: culture as conversation; representation as conversation', in A. James, J. Hockey and A. Dawson (eds) *After Writing Culture: Epistemology and Praxis in Contemporary Anthropology*, London: Routledge.

Ritzer, George (1993) *The McDonaldization of Society: An Investigation into the Changing Character of Contemporary Social Life*, New York: Pine Forge Press.

—— (1994) *Sociological Beginnings: On the Origins of Key Ideas in Sociology*, New York: McGraw-Hill.

—— (1996) *The McDonaldization of Society: An Investigation into the*

Changing Character of Contemporary Social Life, rev. edn, Thousand Oaks, CA: Pine Forge Press.

—— (1998) *The McDonaldization Thesis: Explorations and Extensions*, London: Sage.

Ritzer, George and Liska, Allan (1997) '"McDisneyization" and "post-tourism": complementary perspectives on travel and tourism', in C. Rojek and J. Urry (eds) *Touring Cultures: Transformations of Travel and Theory*, London: Routledge, pp. 52–74.

Roberts, Kevin (2004) *Lovemarks: The Future Beyond Brands*, New York: Powerhouse Books.

Robertson, Roland (1995) 'Glocalization: time-space and homogeneity-heterogeneity', in M. Featherstone, S. Lash and R. Robertson (eds) *Global Modernities*, London: Sage, pp. 25–44.

—— (1997) 'Comments on the "global triad" and "glocalization"', paper presented at *Globalization and Indigenous Culture* Conference, Kokugakuin University, Japan, online at:

www2.kokugakuin.ac.jp/ijcc/wp/global (last accessed 9 April 2005).

Rojek, Chris (1993) *Ways of Escape: Modern Transformations in Leisure and Travel*, London: Macmillan.

—— (2004) 'The consumerist syndrome in contemporary society: an interview with Zygmunt Bauman', *Journal of Consumer Culture* 4(3): 291–312.

Rushkoff, Douglas (2000) *Coercion: Why We Listen to What 'They' Say*, New York: Riverhead Books.

Russo, Mary (1994) *The Female Grotesque: Risk, Excess and Modernity*, London: Routledge.

Schickel, Richard (1986) *The Disney Version: The Life, Times, Art and Commerce of Walt Disney*, rev. edn, London: Pavillion.

Schivelbusch, Wolfgang (1986) *The Railway Journey: Trains and Travel in the Nineteenth Century*, Oxford: Blackwell.

Schor, Juliet B. (2004) *Born to Buy: The Commercialised Child and the New Consumer Culture*, New York: Scribner.

Selwyn, Tom (1996) 'Introduction', in T. Selwyn (ed.) *The Tourist Image: Myths and Myth Making in Tourism*, London: Wiley.

Shields, Rob (1989) 'Social spatialisation and the built environment: the West Edmonton Mall', *Environment and Planning D: Society and Space* 7: 147–164.

—— (1991) *Places on the Margin: Alternative Geographies of Modernity*, London: Routledge.

—— (1992) 'Spaces for the subject of consumption', in R. Shields (ed.)

Lifestyle Shopping: The Subject of Consumption, London: Routledge, pp. 1–20.

Shilling, Chris (1993) *The Body and Social Theory*, London: Sage.

Simmel, Georg (1957) 'Fashion', *American Journal of Sociology* 62(6): 541–558.

—— (1997) 'The metropolis and mental life', trans. E. Shils, in N. Leach (ed.) *Rethinking Architecture: A Reader in Cultural Theory*, London: Routledge, pp. 69–79.

Slater, Don (1997) *Consumer Culture and Modernity*, Cambridge: Polity Press.

Smith, Neil (1984) *Uneven Development: Nature, Capital and the Production of Space*, Oxford: Blackwell:

Spangenberg, Eric R., Crowley, Ayn E. and Henderson, Pamela W. (1996) 'Improving the store environment: do olfactory cues affect evaluations and behaviors?', *Journal of Marketing* 60(April): 67–80.

Stallybrass, Peter and White, Allon (1986) *The Politics and Poetics of Transgression*, Ithaca: Cornell University Press.

Stead, William T. (1901) *The Americanization of the World: or, The Trend of the Twentieth Century*, London: H. Marckley.

Storey, John (1999) *Cultural Consumption and Everyday Life*, London: Hodder Arnold.

Strinati, Dominic (1995) *An Introduction to Theories of Popular Culture*, London: Routledge.

Sutcliffe, Thomas (2003) 'A life in full: welcome to a brand new future', *The Independent on Sunday* (London), 12 October, pp. 28–29.

Swasy, Alecia (1994) *Soap Opera: The Inside Story of Procter & Gamble*, New York: Simon & Schuster.

Taylor, Arthur J. (ed.) (1975) *The Standard of Living in the Industrial Revolution*, London: Methuen.

The Pier (2005) 'Spring is here', online at www.pier.co.uk (last accessed 2 March 2005).

Thornton, Phillip (2003) *Casuals*, Lytham: Milo Books.

Thrift, Nigel J. (2005) *Knowing Capitalism*, London: Sage.

Tournier, Michel (1988) *The Golden Droplet*, trans. B. Wright, London: Collins.

Townsend, Mark (2000) 'Olive oils fail the taste test', *Daily Express* (London), 6 July, p. 27.

Trevor-Roper, Hugh (1983) 'The invention of tradition: the highland tradition of Scotland', in E.J. Hobsbawm and T. Ranger (eds) *The Invention of Tradition*, Cambridge: Cambridge University Press, pp. 15–42.

Turner, Bryan S. (1992) *Regulating Bodies: Essays on Medical Sociology*, London: Routledge.

Turner, Victor (1974) *Dramas, Fields, and Metaphors: Symbolic Action in Human Society*, Ithaca: Cornell University Press.

Underhill, Paco (2003) *Why We Buy: The Science of Shopping*, New York: Texere.

Urry, John (2000) *Consuming Places*, 2nd edn, London: Routledge.

—— (2002) *The Tourist Gaze: Leisure and Travel in Contemporary Societies*, 2nd edn, London: Sage.

—— (2003) 'The "consumption" of tourism', in D.B. Clarke, M.A. Doel and K.M.L. Housiaux (eds) *The Consumption Reader*, London: Routledge, pp. 117–121.

Veblen, Thorstein (1994) *The Theory of the Leisure Class*, Harmondsworth: Penguin.

Vidal, John (1997) *McLibel: Burger Culture on Trial*, London: Pan Books.

Wasko, Janet (1996) 'Understanding the Disney universe', in J. Curran and M. Gurevitch (eds) *Mass Media and Society*, 2nd edn, London: Arnold, pp. 348–368.

Weber, Max (1930) *The Protestant Ethic and the Spirit of Capitalism*, trans. T. Parsons, New York: Charles Scribner's Sons.

—— (1970) *From Max Weber: Essays in Sociology*, ed. H.H. Gerth and C. Wright Mills, London: Routledge & Kegan Paul.

—— (1971) *The Protestant Ethic and the Spirit of Capitalism*, trans. T. Parsons, London: Allen & Unwin.

Wells, Herbert G. (1997) *Tono-Bungay*, Oxford: Oxford University Press.

Wiener, Norbert (1948) *Cybernetics: or Control and Communication in the Animal and the Machine*, Cambridge, MA: MIT Press.

—— (1950) *The Human Use of Human Beings: Cybernetics and Society*, Boston: Houghton Mifflin.

Williams, Raymond (1980) *Problems in Material History and Culture*, Verso: London.

Willis, Susan (1991) *A Primer for Daily Life: Is there More to Life than Shopping?*, London: Routledge.

Wills, John (2002) 'Digital dinosaurs and artificial life: exploring the culture of nature in computer and video games', *Cultural Values* 6(4): 395–417.

Wilson, Alex (1992) *The Culture of Nature: North American Landscape from Disney to the Valdez*, Oxford: Blackwell.

Wolff, Janet (1990) *Feminine Sentences: Essays on Women and Culture*, Berkeley: University of California Press.

Zola, Emile (1998 [1883]) *The Ladies' Paradise*, trans. B. Nelson, Oxford: Oxford University Press.

TELEVISION PROGRAMMES

Panorama, 'Meet the tweens', broadcast 21 November 2004, BBC One.

The Simpsons, episode 3G04, 'The Simpson tide', broadcast 29 March 1998, written by Joshua Sternin and Jeffrey Ventimila, directed by Milton Gray.

FILMOGRAPHY

Dawn of the Dead (1978) dir. George Romero, Italy/USA, colour, 126 mins.

Equus (1977) dir. Sydney Lumet, USA/UK, colour, 137 mins.

eXistenZ (1999) dir. David Cronenberg, Canada/UK/France, colour, 97 mins.

Fight Club (1999) dir. David Fincher, USA, colour, 139 mins.

Shaun of the Dead (2004) dir. Edgar Wright, UK, colour, 99 mins.

Super Size Me (2004) dir. Morgan Spurlock, USA, colour, 100 mins.

The Matrix (1999) dir. Andy and Larry Wachowsky, USA, colour, 136 mins.

INDEX